Foundations of Insurance Production

Principles of Insurance
Segment A

Daniel P. Hussey, Jr., CPCU, AAI, ARM
Director, Western Region
American Institute for CPCU/Insurance Institute of America

Peter R. Kensicki, D.B.A., CPCU, CLU, FLMI
Professor/Chairholder
Eastern Kentucky University

Coordinating Editor
Christine O. Quay, AAI
Associate Director
American Institute for CPCU/Insurance Institute of America

Second Edition

American Institute for Chartered Property Casualty Underwriters/
Insurance Institute of America
720 Providence Road, Malvern, Pennsylvania 19355-0716

© 2002

American Institute for Chartered Property Casualty Underwriters/
Insurance Institute of America

All rights reserved. This book or any part thereof may not be reproduced without the written permission of the publisher.

Second Edition • Fourth Printing • March 2005

Library of Congress Control Number: 2001098672
ISBN 0-89462-157-2

Printed in Canada.

Foreword

The American Institute for Chartered Property Casualty Underwriters and the Insurance Institute of America are independent, nonprofit organizations serving the educational needs of the risk management, property-casualty, and financial services businesses. The Institutes develop a wide range of curricula, study materials, and examinations in response to the educational needs of various elements of these businesses. The American Institute confers the Chartered Property Casualty Underwriter (CPCU®) professional designation on people who meet its examination, ethics, and experience requirements. The Insurance Institute of America offers associate designations and certificate programs in the following areas:

- Accounting and Finance
- Agent Studies
- Claims
- Information Technology
- Insurance Fundamentals
- Management
- Marine Insurance
- Performance Improvement
- Personal Insurance
- Premium Auditing
- Regulation and Compliance
- Reinsurance
- Risk Management
- Surety Bonds and Crime Insurance
- Surplus Lines
- Underwriting

The American Institute was founded in 1942 through a cooperative effort between property-casualty insurance company executives and insurance professors. Faculty members at The Wharton School of the University of Pennsylvania in Philadelphia led this effort. The CPCU designation arose from the same type of business and academic partnership at Wharton as the Chartered Life Underwriter (CLU) designation did in 1927.

The Insurance Institute of America was founded in 1909 by five educational organizations across the United States. It is the oldest continuously functioning national organization offering educational programs for the property-casualty insurance business. It merged with the American Institute in 1953.

The Insurance Research Council (IRC), founded in 1977, is a division of the Institutes. It is a not-for-profit research organization that examines public policy issues that affect property-casualty insurers and their customers. IRC research reports are distributed widely to insurance-related organizations, public policy authorities, and the media.

The broad knowledge base in property-casualty insurance and financial services created by the Institutes over the years is contained mainly in our textbooks. Although we use electronic technology to enhance our educational materials, communicate with our students, and deliver our examinations, our textbooks are at the heart of our educational activities. They contain the information that you as a student must read, understand, integrate into your existing knowledge, and apply to the tasks you perform as part of your job.

Despite the vast range of subjects and purposes of the more than eighty individual textbook volumes we publish, they all have much in common. First, each book is specifically designed to increase knowledge and develop skills that can improve job performance and help students achieve the educational objectives of the course for which it is assigned. Second, all of the manuscripts for our texts are reviewed widely before publication, by both insurance business practitioners and members of the risk management and insurance academic community. In addition, the revisions of our texts often incorporate improvements that students and course leaders have suggested. We welcome constructive comments that help us to improve the quality of our study materials. Please direct any comments you may have on this text to my personal attention.

We hope what you learn from your study of this text will expand your knowledge, increase your confidence in your skills, and support your career growth. If so, then you and the Institutes will truly be *succeeding together*.

Terrie E. Troxel, PhD, CPCU, CLU
President and CEO
American Institute for CPCU
Insurance Institute of America

Preface

The Accredited Adviser in Insurance (AAI) program is designed to meet the educational needs of insurance producers, customer service representatives, and other agency personnel. In that regard, the courses in the AAI program focus on three primary areas: (1) the technical aspects of the insurance business, including coverage and pricing; (2) the marketing of insurance products, including producer relationships with both clients and underwriters; and (3) the operation and management of insurance agencies and brokerages.

AAI 81, Foundations of Insurance Production, is the first of the three AAI courses. It contains three segments that group topics of a similar nature. This text, *Principles of Insurance*, is the first segment of AAI 81. It begins this course by discussing the basic principles on which the insurance business and our legal system are based. This segment concludes with discussions of risk management and account development, two topics crucial to professional insurance production.

Although this text is identified as the first edition, it is based on the former *Principles of Insurance Production* and *Multiple-Lines Insurance Production* texts. Those four volumes were first published in 1981 and were most recently in their third editions. Many people contributed to those texts as authors and reviewers during the three editions. The American Institute for CPCU and the Insurance Institute of America recognize their efforts, especially Seeman Waranch, CPCU, and Stephen Horn II. Their work continues to be included in this edition of the text.

The former director of the AAI program, Daniel P. Hussey, Jr., CPCU, AAI, ARM, is the principal author of this edition of the text. He is also the coordinating author of the remainder of the AAI 81 texts. Several reviewers from both outside and inside the Institutes also contributed to this edition of the text to ensure that the material was correct and complete. The primary outside reviewer was Cheryl L. Koch, CPCU, AAI, ARM. Cheryl is an insurance and risk management consultant and an active course leader for many CPCU and IIA courses. She is also a member of the AAI Advisory Committee.

The authors accept full responsibility for all errors and omissions. Readers detecting errors or wishing to add to the content of future editions are encouraged to send their contributions and criticisms to the Institutes.

Chuck Hussey

Contents

1 The Insurance Business: An Overview — 1-1
Principles of Insurance — 1-3
The Nature and Contributions of the Insurance Business — 1-20
The Organization of the Insurance Business — 1-25
Summary — 1-41

2 Insurance and the Legal System — 2-1
Tort Law — 2-4
Agency — 2-17
Law of Contracts — 2-30
Insurance Policy Construction and Analysis — 2-44
Summary — 2-51

3 Risk Management and the Producer — 3-1
Selling and the Shift to Risk Management — 3-3
The Risk Management Process — 3-10
The Wilson Family Case — 3-45
Summary — 3-49

4 Insurance Sales and Account Development — 4-1
Sales Management — 4-3
Selling — 4-6
The Sources of Business in an Agency — 4-19
The Account Review Process — 4-28
Agency Procedures for Complete Account Development — 4-34
The Benefits of Account Development — 4-39
Summary — 4-51
Appendix A
  1: A Checklist of Personal Insurance Needs — 4-53
  2: A Checklist of Commercial Insurance Needs — 4-55
  3: Insured's Data Sheet — 4-58
  4: Customer Profile Sheet — 4-59
  5: Commercial Lines Policy Review — 4-60
Appendix B
  Client General Information — 4-62
Appendix C
  New/Renewal Information Checklist — 4-64

Answers to Review and Application Questions — 1

Bibliography — 19

Index — 21

The Insurance Business: An Overview
Assignment 1

Assignment Objectives

After completing this assignment, you should be able to:

1. Explain the parts of the "sales trilogy."
2. Given an insurance agency case, explain how the principles of insurance play a key role in the sales and management processes of the agency.

   In support of the assignment objective listed above, you should be able to do the following:

   a. Explain the principles of insurance.
   b. Explain how those principles are interrelated.

3. Define the various categories of risks and hazards and explain their relationship to insurability.
4. Given a case involving an insured, explain why certain exposures may be either uninsurable or insurable only with limitations.

   In support of the assignment objective listed above, you should be able to describe the requisites of an ideally insurable exposure.

5. Explain the benefits and costs of insurance to society and provide an illustration of each.
6. Determine whether the insurance producer works in a more competitive or less competitive environment than that found in noninsurance businesses and defend this point of view.
7. Explain how insurance is
   a. different from other businesses.
   b. similar to other businesses.
8. Compare insurer organizational forms.
9. Compare the various insurance distribution systems.
10. Define or describe each of the Key Words and Phrases for this assignment.

Assignment Outline

I. Principles of Insurance
   A. Producer
   B. Insurers and Insurance Markets
   C. Loss
   D. Risk and Related Terms
   E. Loss Frequency and Loss Severity
   F. The Law of Large Numbers
   G. Perils and Hazards
   H. Indemnity, the Heart of Insurance
   I. Insurable Interest
   J. Requisites of an Ideally Insurable Exposure
   K. Insurability
   L. Risk Management and Insurance
II. The Nature and Contributions of the Insurance Business
   A. Insurers as Financial Intermediaries
   B. The Insurance Business Is Different
III. The Organization of the Insurance Business
   A. Types of Insurance Providers
   B. Types of Distribution Systems
IV. Summary

Assignment 1

The Insurance Business: An Overview

> **Orient** yourself to this assignment by reading the following introduction.

In most businesses, "nothing happens until something is sold." That statement is as true for the insurance business as it is for any business.

The Accredited Adviser in Insurance (AAI) program is primarily about marketing insurance. Selling (one component of marketing insurance) coupled with identifying the insurance needs of individuals and organizations makes agents and brokers marketers of insurance.

Modern marketing techniques frequently include what is sometimes called the **sales trilogy**. The sales trilogy represents the fundamental elements necessary to the sale of any product: (1) product knowledge (understanding the technical details of the product being sold), (2) market knowledge (knowing where to find customers and how to identify and satisfy their needs), and (3) selling skills (how to bring the sale to a successful close).

The AAI program is primarily an educational tool that can help producers increase their product knowledge and marketing knowledge and improve their selling skills. This assignment concentrates on basic insurance principles, the place of the insurance business in our economy, the benefits society derives from the insurance business, and insurance organizations and insurance marketing systems.

> **Read** the definitions of the *Key Words and Phrases* that follow. Being familiar with these important words will help you better understand the first part of this assignment. *Key Words and Phrases* appear in bold in the text when they are defined.

Sales trilogy	The elements necessary to the sale of any product: (1) product knowledge, (2) market knowledge, and (3) selling skills
Producer	One who markets insurance and related services
Agent	The authorized representative of an insurance company

1-2 / Foundations of Insurance Production: Principles of Insurance

Broker	The authorized representative of an insured
Marketing	Finding, identifying the needs of, selling to, and providing service to insureds
Markets	Homogeneous groups of insureds or potential insureds (people with money to buy products and services from the producer)
Direct loss	The reduction in the value of an asset
Indirect loss	The financial consequences of a reduction in the value of an asset
Risk	The chance of financial loss
Fundamental risk	A risk of loss to which all members of a society, or at least a large number of people, are exposed in a single occurrence
Particular risk	A risk of loss to which relatively few members of a society are exposed in a single occurrence
Pure risk	A chance of financial loss that does not also offer a chance of financial gain
Speculative risk	Offers the chance of financial loss and also the opportunity for gain
Loss frequency	The number of times loss occurs over a specific period of time
Loss severity	The amount or size of a single loss
Law of large numbers	The larger the number of similar units exposed to similar loss, the more accurate the loss predictions based on that data will be
Peril	A cause of loss
Hazard	Anything that increases the frequency or severity of a loss
Physical hazard	One that can be seen, felt, or touched
Moral hazard	A trait of the insured's character that tends to increase the probability or severity of loss
Morale hazard	Stems from the insured's attitude of "Who cares? It's insured."
Legal hazard	A hazard that can increase the severity of loss because of the involvement of the legal system and its associated costs and can increase the frequency of loss because of the escalating number of suits filed
Indemnity	Restoring the insured to the same financial position held immediately before a loss
Insurable interest	The financial interest an entity has in the continued existence of the subject of insurance
Independent exposures	Group of many persons purchasing insurance independently and not affected by the losses of others
Similar exposures	Exposures that are homogenous
Definite	A loss must be defined by what caused it, where and when it happened, and what its value is

Calculable	The loss must be able to be calculated
Accidental	A random event, neither intended nor expected by the insured
Risk management	A process to manage the pure risks of an individual or an organization

Study the first part of this assignment, which includes the following sections:

I. Principles of Insurance

Principles of Insurance

Insurance is misunderstood by many consumers. The producer is, however, ideally situated to explain insurance to the consumer because the producer is the front-line educator. To be successful as an educator, the producer must thoroughly understand insurance principles.

Mastering the principles of insurance can also help producers learn the business faster and become productive more quickly. A knowledge of insurance principles can eliminate the frustration of learning through trial and error, provide the know-how to best meet consumer needs, and consequently, help earn commissions faster. If a producer also learns the principles of risk management, the long learning time "in the trenches" or in on-the-job training can be decreased. Understanding insurance and risk management principles also improves communication among insurance professionals.

Producer

A **producer** markets insurance and related services. The producer can be an **agent**—the authorized representative of an insurance company—or a **broker**—the authorized representative of an insured. For the sake of simplicity, the producer's employer or office is called the "agency" throughout the AAI program. In this sense, the independent agent in Pierre, South Dakota; the sales representative of Liberty Mutual in Chicago; the Nationwide agent in Belpre, Ohio; and the broker in New York City all work out of an agency.

Insurers and Insurance Markets

Using the terms "insurers" and "insurance markets" interchangeably is common. For producers, "marketing" frequently means placing business with an insurer. In the AAI program, however, **marketing** means finding, identifying the needs of, selling to, and providing service to insureds. **Markets** are homogeneous groups of insureds or potential insureds (people with money to buy products or services from the producer). One important part of marketing is an insurer's acceptance of an account submission. When placing business with an insurer is discussed, this text clearly identifies any reference to insurers as markets. In all other cases, "markets" refers to those groups of potential buyers or actual insureds, not insurance companies.

Marketing Tip

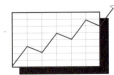

Knowing the principles of insurance and risk management does more than help meet client needs and increase sales—it also helps decrease the possibility of errors and omissions (E&O) claims. E&O claims hurt the producer and the agency in several ways. First, the financial cost of a large deductible typically used in an agency's errors and omissions insurance policy decreases the agency's profitability. Second, although establishing the cost of the time spent in claim investigation and defense is difficult, this time certainly affects the profitability and productivity of both the producer and agency. Finally, the reputations of the producer and agency will probably suffer, even if the alleged error or omission proves to be incorrect. The possibility of lost new sales or loss of existing clients could have a devastating effect. A sound foundation in the principles discussed in AAI provides the producer with the tools necessary to reduce the possibility of errors that might lead to E&O claims.

Loss

"Loss" means a reduction in the value of an asset (**direct loss**) and the financial consequences of a reduction in the value of an asset (**indirect loss**). Loss, therefore, has two meanings. An example of a direct loss is the burning of a home. Because of the fire, a valuable asset becomes relatively worthless. If the family who lived in the house destroyed by fire incurred the expense of temporarily living in a motel while the house were being repaired, that expense would be an indirect loss.

Risk and Related Terms

The word "risk" has a variety of meanings in the insurance business. "Risk" has been used to mean "insured," "exposure," "relative probability of the outcome of an event," and other things. For the AAI program, **risk** means the chance of financial loss. People face a series of risks daily—the risk that an investment will decrease in value, that food will be contaminated, that furnaces will explode, and so on. Insurance protects against the chance of financial loss accidentally brought about by a specific cause or causes. Risks are classified according to two factors: (1) by the number of people affected (fundamental or particular risk) and (2) by the type of financial loss involved (pure or speculative risk).

Fundamental or Particular Risk

A **fundamental risk** is a risk of loss to which all members of a society, or at least a large number of people, are exposed in a single occurrence. A **particular risk** is a risk of loss to which relatively few members of a society are exposed in a single occurrence. For instance, the threat of recession and subsequent unemployment can be said to be a fundamental risk. Everyone working for a living or deriving a living from some working person is subject to financial loss. On the other hand, if a group of investors contributes to a project to develop a commercial process to convert wood chips into fuel oil and the project fails because of poor management, only that particular group of investors is hurt. The risk to those investors is called a "particular risk."

Producers have an interest in the distinction between fundamental and particular risks because particular risks lend themselves more readily to treatment by insurance. No producer has the opportunity to sell a Social Security plan, but producers *do* have the opportunity to sell individual life and disability insurance policies.

Pure and Speculative Risk

Pure risk is a chance of financial loss that does not also offer a chance of financial gain. A **speculative risk** offers not only the chance of financial loss but also the opportunity for gain.

Pure risks are generally insurable and therefore important to the producer. If an individual owns a new car, he or she is going to suffer a loss if the car is involved in an accident. The same individual's financial position is not changed, however, if no accident occurs. Pure risks have sometimes been described as "loss or no-loss situations."

Gambling is the classic example of a speculative risk. If an individual decides to place a $100 bet on a horse with a payoff of two to one, that person could lose $100 or win $200. Two elements are important with speculative risks: first, the chance of gain exists; and second, individuals usually intentionally *create* a speculative risk. Pure risks, on the other hand, are normally accidental and present no opportunity for financial gain.

Loss Frequency and Loss Severity

Loss frequency is the number of times loss occurs over a specific period of time. **Loss severity** is the amount or size of a single loss. Loss frequency is usually stated in terms of a fraction, a decimal, or a percentage, while loss severity is expressed in dollars. Those terms can be illustrated by a coin toss. Assume that John bets George $500 on the coin toss—if the coin lands heads up, John wins; if the coin lands tails up, George wins. If the coin is "fair," that is, has two sides, a head and a tail, each with an equal probability of occurrence, the chance of loss for both John and George is 1/2 or 0.50, or 50 percent. Theoretically, if a coin is flipped an infinite number of times, it will come up heads half the time and tails half the time. The frequency of heads or tails will be, in this case, 0.50 times the number of flips. The severity, or amount of the loss, in this case, is $500. (This is also an example of speculative risk.)

Analyzing loss frequency and severity can help producers identify additional services for clients. If, for example, a producer is selling insurance to a bakery prospect with a fleet of 500 trucks, the producer should consider that potential losses with a high frequency and a low severity (such as collision) might be best treated by the insured retaining the risk or using a very high deductible. If collision damage to the delivery trucks historically involves fifty trucks a year (plus or minus five trucks) with an

I. Principles of Insurance
D. Risk and Related Terms
E. Loss Frequency and Loss Severity
F. The Law of Large Numbers
G. Perils and Hazards
H. Indemnity, the Heart of Insurance

average loss of $1,000 loss per accident ($45,000–$55,000 per year), it might be best for the bakery to pay those losses out of current income rather than to pay collision premiums of $500 per truck ($250,000 per year) to an insurer. On the other hand, the exposure from a tornado that could wipe out the entire fleet of trucks in a few minutes (a low frequency, high severity condition) could be treated with insurance. In that case, the producer might recommend the purchase of comprehensive coverage, without collision, or collision with a high deductible, as a way of saving the bakery money.

Generally, the exposures best suited for insurance treatment are those with a low frequency and high severity.

Marketing Tip

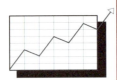

Most producers are paid by either commission or a salary plus bonuses for production. In the previous example, it appears that the producer would earn less in commission or bonus dollars by recommending that this prospect *not* purchase collision insurance. In reality, the producer might actually earn *more* money because of the long-range importance of this recommendation. First, the producer would likely offer this bakery a lower premium than that of competitors suggesting collision coverage. That lower premium would probably help this producer to close the sale with this prospect and result in immediate income. This new client would be impressed that the producer suggested an option that saved money. The client's positive attitude usually leads to two good, long-term results for the producer: the client remains loyal to the producer (renewal commissions) and might also refer new clients to the producer (additional new business income).

E&O Alert!

When making recommendations to clients or prospects about saving premium by retaining all or part of a risk, a producer must be sure to clearly identify the extent of the retention. A client might hear "saving premium" but not hear "retaining all or part of a risk." Asking the client to sign the proposal that suggests this retention is a good way to ensure that the client understands and accepts this uninsured risk. This written acceptance can help to prevent or defend against potential errors and omissions claims when the client has losses that fall within the retention level.

The Law of Large Numbers

The **law of large numbers** basically states that the greater the number of similar units exposed to a similar loss, the more accurate the loss predictions based on that data will be.

For example, in life insurance, statistics on the probability of death of individuals of a certain age are readily available. If women aged seventy-four have a probability of death of 0.056, and one woman aged seventy-four is insured, it is ridiculous to say that 0.056 of this woman will die in her seventy-fourth year. Either the insured woman dies or does not die. The actual death rate will be 1.00 (death) or 0.00. But if an insurance company insured 100,000 women aged seventy-four, then they could be reasonably sure that about 5,600 of those women would be likely to die within one year.

Exactly 5,600 women dying at age seventy-four would not likely happen, but the range would be relatively close, say between 5,000 and 6,000. Suppose another life insurance company insures 1,000,000 women aged seventy-four. That company expects 56,000 deaths from the group, but the range turns out to be between 55,000 and 57,000. Even though the range for the second group is 2,000 deaths (57,000 minus 55,000), the range is a smaller *percentage* of the expected number of deaths than in the first case. Two thousand is 3.57 percent of the 56,000 expected deaths, whereas 1,000 deaths, in the first example, is 17.9 percent of the 5,600 expected deaths.

Perils and Hazards

An insurance policy includes an important section that describes or lists the causes of loss for which the insurer will pay if losses occur. A **peril** is a cause of loss. In the property insurance Causes of Loss—Basic Form, for example, the perils or causes of loss for which coverage applies include fire, lightning, and loss by removal. In other policies, perils may not be listed by name. For instance, some inland marine policies read, "We insure against risks of direct physical loss of or damage to the property covered except. . . ." A policy that identifies what events are covered in this language is often called an "all-risks" form. The Causes of Loss—Basic Form is an example of a named or limited perils form.

A **hazard** is anything that increases the frequency or severity of a loss. An example of a hazard in life insurance would be becoming a race car driver. The probability of an early death increases with that occupation. The severity remains the same. The severity of some illnesses increases without periodic medical examinations, but the probability (frequency) of contracting a particular disease does not increase. Storing 500 gallons of gasoline in a home basement increases both the frequency and severity of loss. Four types of hazards are as follows:

1. Physical
2. Moral
3. Morale
4. Legal

Physical Hazard

A **physical hazard** is one that can be seen, felt, or touched. It is a tangible characteristic of property, persons, or operations. Building a home in a flood plain, storing excessive amounts of combustibles, and keeping oily rags near a furnace are all physical hazards. Insurance coverage can be suspended if hazards controlled by the insured change, with the

I. Principles of Insurance
  F. The Law of Large Numbers
  G. Perils and Hazards
  H. Indemnity, the Heart of Insurance
  I. Insurable Interest

insured's knowledge, in a way that could increase the frequency or severity of loss.

Producers should take the time to inspect and become familiar with their clients' property and operations to spot physical hazards and suggest corrective action. Insurers might be requested by either the prospect or producer to have their loss control representatives or engineers inspect a prospect's operations. A building or activity that has been "engineered" could become an acceptable risk. For instance, a properly protected restaurant might be accepted by an insurance company even though the general class of restaurants might be considered undesirable. If corrective action is not taken, insurance coverage might be unavailable or severely restricted.

Marketing Tip

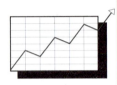

When a producer submits an insurance application, pictures of the prospect's facility and a concise description of operations help the underwriter make a decision. The more information the producer can relay to the underwriter about the physical hazards and action taken to correct them, the more likely the application will be accepted and priced competitively.

Moral Hazard

Moral hazards are traits of the insured's character that tend to increase the probability or severity of loss. Moral hazards are more difficult to detect than physical hazards.

The insurance contract is one of utmost good faith in which the insurer and insured must rely on the honesty of the other party. The insured has certain responsibilities within the insurance contract. If those responsibilities are not met, payment might be reduced or refused at the time of loss. Certain requirements help protect the insurer from the moral hazard—in forms in which the insured must periodically report insured values, provisions are included for timely and accurate reports. If timely and accurate reports are not made, loss payments are adjusted downward. Pre-underwriting on the part of the producer will help eliminate most of these problems.

If a prospect has a reputation for less-than-honest dealings, has gone bankrupt repeatedly, has had a series of questionable fires, has associates who are known felons, or has engaged in any activities that cast doubt on his or her integrity, the producer should not solicit the account. The insurance business must exist in a climate of honesty. Moral hazards make this impossible.

Morale Hazard

A **morale hazard** stems from the insured's attitude. Insureds who have the attitude "Who cares? It's insured." are insureds with a morale hazard. Morale hazards can be easy to detect if they are physically manifested, such as poor housekeeping, or they may be more difficult to detect if the insured's attitude is not reflected in his or her surroundings or practices.

If a producer spots an obvious housekeeping physical hazard (such as oil on a concrete factory floor) and brings the hazard to the attention of the insured, the insured's reaction can give a clue to the insured's attitude. If no action is taken, the morale hazard as well as the physical hazard might be present. Insureds with a morale hazard tend to have more losses, severely affecting the producer's profitability, relationships with underwriters and companies, and the producer's own pocketbook.

Legal Hazard

A **legal hazard** can increase both the severity and frequency of loss. The severity of a loss increases because of the involvement of the legal system and its associated costs—both the cost of dealing with the loss and the ultimate settlement amount are affected. Frequency of loss increases with the escalating number of lawsuits filed.

> **Marketing Tip**
>
> To be successful, a producer must learn to identify all of a client's hazards. New clients are obtained and existing clients retained by producers who eliminate or decrease hazards *before* the insurer inspects and finds those hazards present. Clients will see the producer's efforts as value-added service that reduces not only the frequency and severity of losses but also the ultimate cost of insurance. Saving premium dollars for a client now can mean many more commission dollars for the producer later through client retention and referrals.

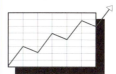

Indemnity, the Heart of Insurance

Indemnity has many meanings. The definition of **indemnity** for the AAI program, as well as the intent of insurance, is to place the insured in the same financial position held immediately before a loss: no better and no worse. Although indemnity seems to be a simple concept, the reality of indemnifying an insured can be a complicated and difficult process. This is true, in part, because there are different ways to determine the value of a loss and different interpretations of the terms of valuation such as actual cash value, depreciation, and replacement cost. Consequently, it might be impossible to absolutely and accurately determine the insured's true financial loss. Even when courts make the final decision, results vary widely. Insureds often add to this problem by allowing premium considerations to affect their willingness to purchase the best available coverages. Despite those difficulties, the risk management and selling processes used by a producer should be designed to provide actual indemnity for the insured.

Several policy provisions control loss payment, so the insured is not overpaid—that is, does not gain from the loss. In many cases, producers can explain why certain provisions are in insurance contracts by referring to the principle of indemnity. In property insurance, for instance, finding a loss payable clause or a mortgage clause is common. These clauses are used when a mortgage or other lien exists on property. One function

I. Principles of Insurance
   G. Perils and Hazards
   H. Indemnity, the Heart of Insurance
   I. Insurable Interest
   J. Requisites of an Ideally Insurable Exposure
   K. Insurability

of these clauses is to allocate a loss payment among those with an insurable interest in the property. If a fully insured building suffers a total loss from an insured cause of loss, payment would be made in the names of both the insured and the mortgagee (or lienholder). Mortgagees want to be sure the insured owner rebuilds. If an insured owner does not rebuild, the mortgagee can declare the balance of the mortgage due immediately.

Insurable Interest

Insurable interest is the financial interest an entity has in the continued existence of the subject of insurance. Although the courts are often called on to decide an issue, some generally accepted definitions of insurable interest exist.

Insurable Interest in Life Insurance

People have an unlimited insurable interest in their own lives. Spouses, children, parents, grandchildren, grandparents, and other family members have an insurable interest in the lives of each other. A business relationship may also create an insurable interest. A corporation has an insurable interest in its executives and other key personnel, and a creditor has an insurable interest in the life of a debtor.

The nature and extent of insurable interest are issues that the life insurance underwriter will want to establish before issuing a policy. The general rule is that an insurable interest in the life of the insured must exist *at the time the policy is issued*. There is no requirement for an insurable interest to exist at the time of death. Thus, two people in a partnership may insure each other's life while the partnership exists. If the partnership is dissolved, no further insurance may be purchased by either partner on the life of the other partner, assuming there is no relationship other than the business that established the insurable interest. However, the contracts purchased while the partnership existed remain valid at the time of death even though the partnership may have been dissolved. As a result, if the policy remains in force, the death benefit will be paid.

Insurable Interest in Property-Liability Insurance

The general rule in property-liability insurance is that an insurable interest *must exist at the time of loss*. A homeowner has an insurable interest in his or her home and its contents. A corporation has an insurable interest in its plant and equipment. A lessor (equipment owner) and the lessee (person leasing the equipment) have insurable interests in leased equipment. A lessor might require the lessee to be responsible for damage to a rented building. In this case, the lessee has an insurable interest in the building.

Anyone with an insurable interest in something or someone can insure that entity to the extent of that insurable interest. The nature and extent of an insurable interest must be determined separately for every situation. When an insurable interest exists, some attempt should be made by the producer to treat that interest using insurance or another appropriate risk management technique.

Requisites of an Ideally Insurable Exposure

If there is an insurable interest in a particular and pure risk, the exposure is usually insurable. In theory, five requirements must be met for an exposure to be commercially insurable:

1. Many persons must be independently exposed to the loss.
2. The exposures should be similar.
3. The losses should be definite in cause, time, place, and amount.
4. The expected loss for each insured during the policy period should be calculable.
5. The loss should be accidental from the insured's viewpoint.

Independent Exposures

For an exposure to be commercially insurable, many persons must independently purchase insurance. Further, the chance of loss for one insured should not affect the chance of loss for another insured. By combining **independent exposures** in large numbers, insurers allow the law of large numbers to work. With more insureds, the data will be more accurate and losses will be more predictable, which enables insurers to reduce risk for insureds.

Similar Exposures

Another way to state **similar exposures** is "exposures should be homogenous." A large number of insureds independent of each other is not enough. By definition, the exposures must be somewhat similar if the law of large numbers is to work.

Definite

For statistics to be accurate, losses must be **definite**. That is, a loss must be defined in terms of what caused it, when it occurred, where it occurred, and what its value is. A large portion of each property-liability policy is devoted to loss adjustment procedures. To make those procedures work, definiteness is important.

Calculable

Expected loss amounts must be of a frequency and in an amount that is **calculable** to determine equitable rates. During the Chernobyl nuclear accident, the losses were definite as to cause, time, and place. But how can the cost of such a catastrophe be calculated? Because the long-term effects of radiation are unknown, and because many effects will not even emerge until well into the future, the financial consequences of a nuclear accident are not always known at the time of the accident and thus almost defy calculation.

Accidental

Accidental means that the loss must be a random event so that the law of large numbers can operate. Accidental also means that losses are neither *intended* from the activities of the insured nor *expected* by the insured from forces outside of the insured's control. For instance, a

I. Principles of Insurance
   I. Insurable Interest
   J. Requisites of an Ideally Insurable Exposure
   K. Insurability
   L. Risk Management and Insurance

II. The Nature and Contributions of the Insurance Business

producer was called early one morning and asked to add a location to an existing insurance package. The location was beachfront property, and a strong hurricane was due to hit the coast at 6 P.M. on that date. Allowing the insured to purchase property coverage at that time would be "selecting against the insurer." The fact that the hurricane happens to hit the insured's beachfront property and causes damage is an accident because it is beyond his control. However, if the insured is allowed to purchase insurance to cover such a loss after the insured becomes aware of the expected loss, the loss would not be considered accidental.

Insurability

By understanding the five requirements for an insurable exposure, a producer can see why certain exposures are not commercially insurable. Certain exposures are considered too few in number to combine (the lives of the president and vice president flying on the same plane); or they are not similar (foreign credit exposures); not definite in time, place, or amount (wear and tear); catastrophic (war, nuclear accidents); or not accidental from the insured's viewpoint (flood coverage on a building in a flood plain) for insurers to handle commercially. In contrast, it is also easier to understand why certain exposures or perils are commercially insurable. Fire is a commonly insured peril because it meets all of the requirements. Nearly everyone is exposed to the possibility of loss from fire. Construction classifications and protection classes assist in grouping similar risks. Decades of statistics from insurers and fire departments add definiteness and calculability, and policy provisions restrict coverage to accidental fires.

Some of the above examples *are* commercially insurable but only with certain restrictions. For example, flood insurance is available for the building in the flood plain if certain community eligibility, construction, and elevation requirements are met.

Marketing Tip

If a client's exposure is commercially uninsurable, it is good public relations to explain why in terms of the requisites of an insurable exposure rather than just to say the coverage is not available. A properly phrased explanation builds confidence and respect for the producer in the mind of a client or prospective insured.

Risk Management and Insurance

Risk management is a process designed to manage systematically the pure risks of an individual or organization. It can also be defined as a series of five steps encompassing what risk managers do:

1. Identifying and analyzing the loss exposures faced by a business or family
2. Evaluating techniques for dealing with loss exposures

3. Selecting the best technique or combination of techniques to treat the exposures
4. Implementing the technique or combination of techniques for treating exposures
5. Monitoring the effectiveness of those techniques

Insurance is only one important risk management technique that a risk manager should consider while performing step two of the risk management process. A risk manager can—in addition to or in lieu of insurance—avoid, control, make a noninsurance transfer of, or retain a risk.

"Avoidance" means the risk to the insured has been eliminated. A way to avoid the risks of skydiving is not to skydive. Controlling the risk means to take some action to reduce hazards or loss exposures. Adding an alarm system to a jewelry store is an example of controlling burglary and robbery losses. A lease requiring the lessee of a building to be responsible for building damage is an example of a noninsurance risk transfer. Finally, the bakery that pays for physical damage to its trucks out of current income is one example of risk retention. The risk management process will be treated in depth in Assignment 3 of this segment.

There are numerous definitions of insurance. A risk manager would define "insurance" as a *technique* that makes it possible to transfer the financial consequences of potential accidental losses from the insured firm, family, or individual to an insurer. States have their own legislated definitions of insurance.

What is important in any definition of insurance is that it includes the following four elements:

1. At least two, and almost universally more than two, people contribute to a fund or pool.
2. The insurer administers the pool as a financial intermediary and invests it, reducing overall premium charges to insureds.
3. Accidental losses are paid from this pool to those who helped form the pool.
4. The relationship between the contributors and the pool is contractual.

Check your understanding of the *Key Words and Phrases* found in the first part of this assignment.

Sales trilogy (p. 1)

Producer (p. 3)

1-14 / Foundations of Insurance Production: Principles of Insurance

Agent (p. 3)

Broker (p. 3)

Marketing (p. 3)

Markets (p. 3)

Direct loss (p. 4)

Indirect loss (p. 4)

Risk (p. 4)

Fundamental risk (p. 4)

Particular risk (p. 4)

Pure risk (p. 5)

Speculative risk (p. 5)

Loss frequency (p. 5)

Loss severity (p. 5)

Assignment 1—The Insurance Business: An Overview

Law of large numbers (p. 6)

Peril (p. 7)

Hazard (p. 7)

Physical hazard (p. 7)

Moral hazard (p. 8)

Morale hazard (p. 8)

Legal hazard (p. 9)

Indemnity (p. 9)

Insurable interest (p. 10)

Independent exposures (p. 11)

Similar exposures (p. 11)

Definite (p. 11)

Calculable (p. 11)

Accidental (p. 11)

Risk management (p. 12)

> **Review** the concepts presented in the first part of this assignment by answering the following questions. **Note: Acceptable answers to all questions appear at the end of this segment.**

1. Why is the sales trilogy important in insurance sales? (p. 1)

2. How does an insurance agent differ from an insurance broker? (p. 3)

3. In what ways do fundamental risk and particular risk differ? (pp. 4-5)

4. How are pure risk and speculative risk different from each other? (p. 5)

5. Of the four classes of risk mentioned in Questions 3 and 4, which classes are most likely to be insurable? Justify your answer. (pp. 4-5)

6. How do loss frequency and loss severity affect a business firm's choice between the purchase of insurance and retention of an exposure? (pp. 5-6)

7. Contrast peril and hazard. (p. 7)

8. What are four types of hazards? Which one(s) may not be insurable? (pp. 7-9)

9. How is the requirement of insurable interest related to the concept of indemnity? (pp. 9-10)

10. When must an insurable interest exist in
    (a) life insurance? (p. 10)

    (b) property insurance? (p. 10)

11. What are the requisites of an ideally insurable exposure? (p. 11)

12. What are three exposures for which commercial insurance is available even though they do not meet all of the requisites of an ideally insurable exposure? (p. 12)

13. What are the five steps in the risk management process? (pp. 12-13)

> **Apply** the concepts presented in the first part of this assignment by answering the following questions.

1. You have been approached by one of your clients, a termite exterminating company, with a request to provide termite damage coverage on all of the homes and buildings serviced by the firm. The requested coverage would protect against *direct property loss* and *indirect loss*.

   (a) Define the two italicized terms.

   (b) To what extent does the termite damage peril (1) meet or (2) fail to meet each of the requisites of an ideally insurable exposure?

   (c) How might the existence of such coverage cause an increase in the morale hazard of the insured's operations? Your answer should include a definition of "morale hazard."

2. Tom and Samantha Fredericks have turned in a property loss claim under their homeowners insurance. "Before I approve any claim payment," the company adjuster tells Tom, "we have to verify the existence of insurable interest."

   (a) Do you agree or disagree with the adjuster's statement? Justify your answer, using the definition of "insurable interest" as it applies to property losses.

(b) Would your answer in (a) be different if the claim had been under a life insurance policy? Explain.

(c) How does the concept of indemnity relate to this claim?

3. A customer comments to you, "Insurance companies make their policies entirely too complicated. Why can't an insurance policy be written that simply covers any loss an insured suffers?" How would you respond to this statement? Include in your answer the concepts of fundamental risk, speculative risk, and morale hazard.

Read the definitions of the *Key Words and Phrases* that follow. Being familiar with these important words will help you better understand the second part of this assignment.

Financial intermediary	An entity that obtains money from one source and redirects it to another
Stock insurance company	A company owned by stockholders, who have invested their money, formed a corporation, and seek an investment return
Mutual insurers	Formally controlled by the policyholders; each policyholder gets one vote
Reciprocal exchange	Each member is an insurer of every other member
Governmental insurers	Help to cover losses considered commercially uninsurable or not feasible to insure
Independent agency system	Agents who can have contracts with more than one insurer are independent contractors and own the business they produce
Exclusive agency system	Agents who represent only one company group
Direct writing system	Agents who are employees of their companies and do not own the business they write
Mail order system	Companies who pre-underwrite and do not use producers
Mixed systems	Companies using two or more distribution systems

Study the second part of this assignment, which includes the following sections:

II. The Nature and Contributions of the Insurance Business
III. The Organization of the Insurance Business

The Nature and Contributions of the Insurance Business

Many businesses manufacture and sell products that are tangible, such as automobiles, soap, furniture, and so on. In contrast, the insurance business provides a service. Insurance is a financial transaction, and consequently the insurance business is in some ways significantly different from other businesses.

Insurers as Financial Intermediaries

The primary role of insurers is to provide protection against financial losses. In the process of providing this protection, insurers operate as financial intermediaries—they collect sums of money from large numbers of people and use this pool of capital by means of investments and loans.

Economic Benefits of Insurance

The insurance business provides society with six measurable benefits that together exceed the cost of producing those benefits:

1. Indemnification for losses
2. Reduction of uncertainty for society
3. An equitable assessment of the cost of uncertainty
4. A source of long-term funds
5. A reduction of losses
6. Promotion of business competition

Indemnification directly helps those who suffer financial losses by restoring them to the financial position they held before the loss. Others also benefit, including employees who keep jobs that would otherwise be lost, the community whose tax base remains stable and perhaps grows with reconstruction, and suppliers and purchasers who retain their customers.

Reducing uncertainty for society is not the same as loss reduction. Whether one is insured might not alter loss frequency and severity, but knowing that if a loss does occur the financial consequences of the loss will be minimized reduces uncertainty. From an insurer's standpoint, the more entities insured, the more predictable losses become, decreasing the uncertainty of insurers. Insurance also provides a degree of social stability and a better price structure for products and services and increases competition, which helps to hold down prices in business generally.

Because businesses know the cost of insurance protection, they can plan premium payments and spread premiums throughout their price structures. Businesses can treat insurance as a cost of doing business. This is more equitable to the consumer who bears the ultimate costs than if businesses tried to rely on the price of their products to cover all potential losses. Insureds and their customers, therefore, also have uncertainty reduced.

Insurers make long-term funds available to businesses and governments. Insurance activities also make it easier to obtain long-term funds from others. Credit can be extended over a longer period of time because of the financial guarantees made available through insurance. For instance, home mortgages and auto loans are more readily made because of the availability of insurance to repay the loans in the event of loss. Sureties are more apt to write bonds for contractors that not only have a strong balance sheet but also have substantial amounts of life insurance on themselves and their key personnel. Similarly, banks are more likely to lend money to organizations if their key personnel are insured.

Loss control activities help to prevent losses or to reduce the effect of losses on property and persons. Arson programs sponsored by insurers have helped reduce "for profit" losses in many cities, defensive driving courses have reduced collision losses, and construction and engineering techniques have reduced accident frequency and severity. These benefits directly accrue to society and individuals.

All of these benefits help to promote competition in business. The job of people in business is to make their assets profitable. Knowing that those assets will be replaced if destroyed makes them more willing to engage in business. Generally, the greater the number of people who provide goods or services, the lower the price of goods or services to the ultimate consumer.

Economic Costs of Insurance

The benefits to society produced by the insurance business outweigh their costs. But the costs *are* considerable. First, many human and material resources are expended to operate the insurance business. If those resources were not used in the insurance business, they could be used in other businesses (perhaps at a reduced cost because of reduced demand). Second, moral hazard losses are true costs of the insurance business. Those losses occur *because* of insurance. Arson for profit is one example of a moral hazard loss. Morale hazard losses are also true costs of insurance to society. The manufacturer who increases the possibility of a loss by storing flammable materials carelessly is an example of a morale hazard. Although it is true that this manufacturer *might* suffer a loss without insurance, it is at least possible that insurance increased the manufacturer's carelessness.

Insurers are aware of these costs to society and take direct action to reduce them. Package policies (discussed in a subsequent assignment) reduce the amount of time, paperwork, and human effort used to conduct the insurance business. Careful underwriting attempts to discover moral and morale hazards. Policy design and loss adjustment in conjunction

- I. Principles of Insurance
- II. The Nature and Contributions of the Insurance Business
  - A. Insurers as Financial Intermediaries
  - B. The Insurance Business Is Different
- III. The Organization of the Insurance Business

with underwriting also attempt to minimize the effects of moral, morale, and legal hazards. The insurance business has extensive educational efforts aimed at the consumer. These efforts include attempts to show consumers how their attitudes toward losses affect premiums. Programs like National Fire Prevention Week, Lock-Your-Car campaigns, and so on help reduce losses. Many insurers and trade associations now direct educational advertisements to the general public to show how large court judgments affect their premiums.

The Insurance Business and the Economy

Insurers are a vital segment of the economy. Not only do insurers provide protection for property and income, but insurers are also financial intermediaries.[1] A **financial intermediary** is an entity that obtains money from one source and redirects it to another. Banks, savings and loan associations, and insurance companies collect sums of money from their clients, pool the money, and lend large sums to or invest large sums in other entities. Not all financial intermediaries operate this way. Consumer and sales finance companies typically obtain large sums of money in the commercial paper market and lend it in smaller sums to individuals and businesses. Investment bankers, who exclusively supply funds to entities by selling large blocks of securities, obtain both small and large sums of money for corporations and governmental bodies that need those funds.

Understanding the role of insurers as financial intermediaries is important. Many consumers believe that overvaluing a claim is justifiable because they have the attitude of "Insurance companies have all the money. I'm just getting my share." A major failure of the insurance business is not better educating consumers about how money is used. Indeed, if insurers, banks, savings and loans, and pension funds did not pool money for use by other segments of the business community, the economy would slow down significantly. Insurers provide a service to society when they are efficient collectors and distributors of capital.

The need for efficient collectors and distributors of capital implies that capital to be used in business pursuits is in demand and that capital is scarce. Both implications are accurate. Studying economics would be unnecessary without scarcity. Money would be unnecessary without scarcity. The insurance business would have little justification without scarcity. The scarcity of products and services determines the price of products and services. The desirability of products and services is expressed in terms of money. For example, gold is scarce compared to sand. Therefore, gold commands a higher price than sand.

The Insurance Business Is Different

Some knowledgeable people in the insurance business believe that the idea that the insurance business is different provides a universal excuse for the business to ignore business practices of other, noninsurance businesses and to avoid explaining the insurance business to the public. Traditionally, they say, the business has taken a "We are different; we are too technical for you (the consumer) to understand, so trust us" stance. Consequently, when major problems arise—rate classification controversy for automobiles or excessive losses and rapidly rising premiums in lines like professional or products liability—the business receives a relatively poor reception from the public. This attitude frequently places the burden of educating the public on producers. Sales presentations and the actions taken jointly by producers and insurers at the time of a loss can go a long way toward improving the public image of the insurance business.

In reality, however, the insurance business *is* different from other, noninsurance businesses. (There are also major differences between the life and the property-liability insurance businesses.) These differences, however, should not be an excuse for the producer or the business as a whole not to explain the nature and purpose of the business to consumers. The following example illustrates these differences.

A business, Crowley Manufacturing, Inc., needs a company car for its president and is also renewing its commercial insurance. The price of the car is $25,000, and the account's insurance premiums total $25,000. An order for the car is placed through Crowley's fleet department. At the time of the order, the auto manufacturer knows its cost of manufacturing the car and can determine its profit on the sale immediately.

The insurance transaction is different. The insurer receives the application from the producer and begins processing the account. When the insurer accepts the business from Crowley Manufacturing, Inc., it establishes the following accounts: written premium for $25,000, a commission payable account (dependent on the level of commissions to be paid), and an "unearned premium" liability for the entire $25,000. The unearned premium reserve (liability) is reduced daily throughout the policy period by a proportionate amount reflecting the cost of each day's protection. Only at the end of the policy year does the unearned premium reserve reach zero and all of the premium become "sales" or earned premium.

At this point, we can see a difference between the insurance company and the manufacturing firm. At the time of the sale the manufacturer knows its profit, but the insurer does not. The following discussion illustrates why.

To slightly but realistically complicate the example, assume that three things happen to Crowley Manufacturing two weeks before the policy year ends. First, one of the company's trucks is in a minor collision (covered by the policy) to the extent of $2,000. Second, an employee is injured on the job to the extent that he will be off the job for two months. Third, a visitor to Crowley's plant trips over a tool negligently left on the sidewalk by an employee. The visitor is injured to the extent that he too will be off the job for two months. The visitor, however, does not immediately report the accident to Crowley Manufacturing.

At the end of the policy period, the insurer has three additional expenses (or, actually, liabilities if all losses are not paid by the end of the year). The first liability is for the physical damage to the truck. The loss was

I. Principles of Insurance
II. **The Nature and Contributions of the Insurance Business**
    A. Insurers as Financial Intermediaries
    B. **The Insurance Business Is Different**
III. **The Organization of the Insurance Business**
    A. Types of Insurance Providers
    B. Types of Distribution Systems

reported, adjusted, but not yet paid in cash because Crowley has not yet received the bill from the body shop. The second liability is for the workers compensation loss to the employee. This liability has been reported to the insurer, but the adjuster has not yet had a chance to evaluate the loss. The third liability is for the injury to the visitor. Not only has the insurer not had a chance for its adjuster to evaluate the loss, the loss has not yet even been reported to the company; however, it is a valid loss that must eventually be paid and charged to Crowley Manufacturing's account.

At the end of the year, the auto manufacturer knows how much profit has been made. The insurer, on the other hand, has fully earned its premium, but still does not know its profit. Estimations are necessary. A liability account called "reported, adjusted, not paid" is established for the collision loss and directly charged to losses paid. A reasonable estimate of the amount to be paid under the workers compensation coverage can be established because of accurate historical statistics available from workers compensation losses. This liability is called "reported, but not adjusted." It is an estimate, but it is reasonably accurate. Finally, the insurer knows that some losses have occurred but have not been reported. It does not know which of its policyholders is affected, but it does recognize that something has occurred to someone. A final liability account, the IBNR (incurred but not reported), is established for these losses. This is the least accurate estimate of liability. From these accounts, the insurer produces its balance sheet and income statement indicating its *estimate* of its profit and financial position. Nevertheless, because of the potential for a lawsuit and a longtime span between the actual accident and payment to the injured visitor, it may be years before the insurer has a true profit or loss picture for the year.

Differences between insurers and noninsurers are real. The product-accounting cycle for the property-liability company might appear to be one year (or the length of the policy) but can actually be much longer because of incurred-but-not-reported losses and consequent liabilities. The cycle for the manufacturer is significantly shorter.

There are also nonaccounting differences. From an operations standpoint, a manufacturer can gain what economists call "economies of scale," which means that as production levels increase, the cost per unit of output decreases. Insurers and producers are not subject to such economies, within certain limits. The insurance business is labor intensive, that is, people play a vital role in the business—people sell, underwrite, adjust, and administer. Equipment plays a relatively minor part—computers, cars, and office equipment—when compared to the vast plants and assembly line equipment used by the manufacturer. To generate more business, the manufacturer must add large sums to its plant and equipment before hiring production employees. To write more business, insurers and producers need to either make employees more productive or efficient, or to add personnel.

The final major difference is that the insurance business, particularly from the producer's standpoint, is truly entrepreneurial. Capital requirements for entry into the business are relatively small compared to manufacturing or other service businesses. Certainly, it takes less capital to become an insurance producer than to enter the oil or automobile industries. Insurance sales is also one of the relatively few occupations in which the limit on income is substantially determined by the desire and effectiveness of the individual. Many producers actually earn more than insurance company presidents. It is hard to imagine employees or associates of General Motors, Exxon, or Proctor and Gamble earning more than the presidents of those companies.

Despite these differences, people in the insurance business should recognize its similarities to other businesses. Businesses operate to make a profit (an excess of revenue over expenses). Profit enables businesses to grow and prosper—to devote resources to product development, to improve working conditions, and to sell more products, thus minimizing price increases. Profit also enables businesses to pay taxes—taxes that governments at various levels use to improve the quality of life for all of their citizens, especially those who are unable to work and generate their own profit, surplus, or savings. Without profit, business and government cease to function.

Like other businesses, the insurance organization must be efficient to make a profit. Any organization that has expenses in excess of revenue eventually goes out of business.

Insurance organizations are as competitive as other businesses. Not only must all businesses compete for the market share within their own business, but they must also compete with other businesses for the consumer's dollar. Insurance producers, for example, compete not only with other producers but also with auto dealers, department stores, and so on for consumer's disposable income. Like the sales representatives of other businesses and industries, producers must educate consumers on wise spending—not only inform clients of the best use of their insurance dollars, but also, in some cases, convince them to give up other consumer items to adequately protect their accumulated assets.

Among the many other similarities between the insurance business and other businesses is that its product must be sold. In this context, producers play a vital role in the insurance business and are in a position that requires integrity, professionalism, and efficiency.

The Organization of the Insurance Business

The insurance business includes many entities. Both the providing of insurance and its distribution can be organized in several ways.

Types of Insurance Providers

The organizational forms of insurance companies vary. Individuals and all types of corporations operate as insurers, though no partnerships do.

II. The Nature and Contributions of the Insurance Business

III. The Organization of the Insurance Business
   A. Types of Insurance Providers
   B. Types of Distribution Systems

Insurers can be proprietary, nonproprietary, or governmental. They can also be profit or nonprofit. The profit status of an organization relates solely to its relationship with the Internal Revenue Service; nonprofit means a nontax-paying entity. Nonprofit organizations still seek an excess of revenue over expenses. This excess, profit, permanent contribution to surplus, residue, or whatever it is called is needed in order for the organization to grow. Ownership and control of the organization represent the major difference between proprietary and nonproprietary insurers. Exhibit 1-1 shows a diagram of the types of insurers.

Exhibit 1-1
Types of Insurers

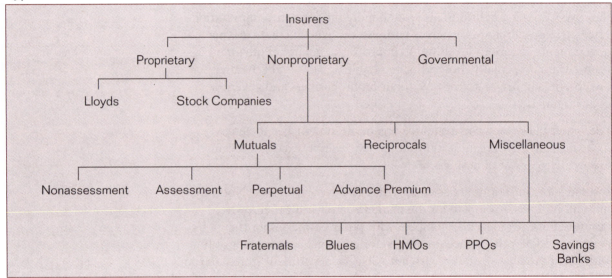

Proprietary Insurers

Proprietary insurers aim to make a profit for their owners. Proprietary insurers are either unincorporated or incorporated.

Unincorporated Proprietary Insurers

Perhaps the most famous insurance name in the world is an unincorporated proprietary insurer, Lloyd's of London. Most people incorrectly view Lloyd's of London as an insurance company. To more completely understand Lloyd's of London, a comparison can be made with stock brokers and their relationship to the New York Stock Exchange (NYSE). Lloyd's is divided into two organizations: the Lloyd's Corporation (similar to the NYSE) and the underwriters at Lloyd's (comparable to brokerage houses). Insuring actually occurs through the underwriters at Lloyd's, comparable to the buying and selling of securities. The service work associated with insurance written—policy typing, claims statistical work, collections, and disbursements—is handled by the Lloyd's Corporation.

In the United States, Lloyd's is considered an excess and surplus lines insurer. That is, it writes business that is hard to place with a producer's normal insurers. Two states, Illinois and Kentucky, have "admitted" Lloyd's of London. In those states, Lloyd's can write insurance directly through brokers. Even though it is an insurer from a foreign country,

Lloyd's is accepted throughout the United States. This is because of its long history and the trust funds established here for claim payments. Those funds exceed $10 billion.

The insurance coverage provided by the underwriters at Lloyd's is underwritten by a syndicate manager, called an "attorney-in-fact." When the manager decides to accept a submission, it is accepted on behalf of all members (underwriters) who belong to the manager's syndicate. Each underwriter actually accepts some small percentage of the syndicate's exposure. This share is based on the capital pledged at the beginning of each year. In return, the underwriter receives a proportionate share of premium and investment income. An underwriter may belong to any number of syndicates. Most underwriters at Lloyd's limit their participation to those lines of insurance with which they feel secure. Syndicates are organized by particular lines of insurance, such as ocean marine hull, aviation hull, war risk, motor (automobile liability), and so on. In almost all lines, multiple syndicates compete for business.

To become an underwriter at Lloyd's requires considerable financial security deposits, character references, and nomination by other underwriters. Until the 1970s, only British subjects were eligible to become underwriters.

An application for insurance must be submitted to Lloyd's through an approved broker. The broker lists all pertinent details on the submission and circulates a "slip" containing the information. The slip goes to those syndicate managers who write the line. The slip indicates the amount of coverage desired and the premium to be paid. The managers determine whether the rate is acceptable and, if so, accept all or a portion of the submission at the indicated rate. Acceptance is noted on the slip by the stamp and signature of the individual syndicate. If a policy is not fully subscribed at the stated rate, the broker might have to go back to the managers with a new proposal. It is not unusual to have more than one syndicate participating on any given submission. Like insurance companies, syndicates have "line limits" or maximum amounts of insurance they will write on any given submission.

Incorporated Proprietary Insurers

The most significant type of proprietary insurer in the United States is the **stock insurance company**. This type of company is owned by stockholders who have invested their money, formed a corporation, and seek an investment return. Technically, these stockholders control the corporation by electing the board of directors. As with any corporation, the board then appoints or elects the officers who run the corporation. Usually, key officers determine who will be nominated for the board and submit their nominations to the stockholders. Frequently, officers not only manage the business but also control its operations, since stockholders are often only interested in the dividends they receive and the appreciation of the stock price. In the property-liability business, almost two-thirds of the total premium is handled by stock insurers. Stock insurers write about 60 percent of the life insurance in force.

II. The Nature and Contributions of the Insurance Business

III. The Organization of the Insurance Business
   A. Types of Insurance Providers
   B. Types of Distribution Systems

Nonproprietary Insurers

Nonproprietary insurers are owned and controlled by their policyholders. These insurers include mutuals, reciprocal exchanges, and miscellaneous cooperatives.

Mutuals

Although formal control of **mutual insurers** rests with their policyholders, they are, in effect, controlled by their officers. Typically, all policyholders are entitled to vote for the company's board of directors, but few policyholders exercise this right. Voting is egalitarian; that is, most mutuals allow a policyholder only one vote no matter how many policies the policyholder has or how much premium is paid. In life insurance, a $1 million policyholder paying $50,000 in premiums a year would have the same vote as a $5,000-term policyholder paying $100 per year. As with stock insurers, executive officers are usually on the board of directors of a mutual. There are four types of mutuals: (1) advance premium mutuals, (2) pure assessment mutuals, (3) assessment mutuals, and (4) perpetual mutuals.

Advance Premium Mutuals The most common, largest, and most significant form of mutual is the advance premium mutual. Like their stock counterparts, advance premium mutuals issue nonassessable policies. Companies in this category pay dividends to their policyholders if more money is earned (the excess of revenue over expenses) than is needed to add to surplus. Some of these mutuals, mostly life insurers, regularly pay dividends. In life insurance, it is not unusual for a mutual to pay, in addition to annual dividends, a termination dividend when the insured dies or cashes in the policy. Other mutuals of this type pay dividends only in years of unusually high profit. In many cases, these dividends are to be applied only against future premiums and cannot be taken in cash.

One major type of property insurance organization that falls into this category is the factory mutual. Factory mutuals were founded by factory owners who were concerned about safety. Relatively little of the factory mutual's premium goes to pay losses. Most of it goes for engineering services to make the property as "fireproof" as possible. Factory mutuals have extensive laboratory facilities in which full-scale buildings can be constructed for testing purposes. This allows for experimentation with construction materials and safety equipment to determine the best combination. It is not unusual for the field representative of a factory mutual to be an engineer. The factory mutuals primarily insure only very large businesses that are expected to adopt their building engineering specifications.

Pure Assessment Mutuals Pure assessment mutuals wait until the end of the year to determine or estimate what losses and expenses were incurred. Losses and expenses are divided among the policyholders, and each pays his or her share by an assessment billing. Pure assessment mutuals limit the geography of their business and the causes of loss they insure. Although in the middle and late 1800s this type of mutual was very common, few exist today.

Assessment Mutuals   Assessment mutuals charge their policyholders a premium in advance that management feels is sufficient to cover expenses and losses for a normal year of operations. If catastrophes or other events cause the initial premium to be insufficient, these mutual companies may assess their policyholders for the difference. Some charge a low initial premium and tend to write only limited lines in small geographic areas. Others charge higher premiums, write more complicated policies, and rarely assess policyholders. As with pure assessment mutuals, few of this type of mutual are operating today.

Perpetual Mutuals   Perpetual mutuals were an important part of the early insurance business in the eighteenth and nineteenth centuries. A few still exist, including the one founded by Benjamin Franklin. Their importance today has diminished because of their inflexibility with regard to the perils covered and policies written. A perpetual mutual charges an advance premium of perhaps twenty times an annual rate. The premium is invested, and investment income from the deposits covers all losses and expenses. When a policyholder sells his or her property, the deposit is refunded. Although charter provisions of the perpetuals do permit assessments, usually none take place.

Reciprocal Exchanges

A **reciprocal exchange** is a hybrid of proprietary and nonproprietary insurers. A reciprocal has two distinct parts: (1) an unincorporated association made up of its members (insureds) and (2) an attorney-in-fact, usually a corporation, that manages the insurance and business affairs of the association. Each member of the association is actually an insurer of every other member. Unlike Lloyd's, members only insure fellow members. The attorney-in-fact sets and collects premiums, invests the money, pays losses, and manages other operations. The attorney-in-fact usually has a contract with the association that allows the attorney-in-fact to retain a portion of the premiums, usually 20 to 30 percent, for expenses. Under the purest form of a reciprocal exchange, separate accounts are kept for each member of the association. They are credited with their premium contributions, assessments, if any, and their share of investment income. They are charged their share of the management fee and losses. When a member is no longer an insured, the member is entitled to the balance of the account. Some reciprocals operate with "undivided surplus," and separate accounts do not exist. Under this system, no withdrawal rights are available. Like large financially secure mutuals, some reciprocals can issue nonassessable policies. Some are associated with other noninsurance organizations and write insurance only for their members. Most write only a few types of insurance. In some parts of the country—for example, Farmers Insurance Group of Companies in California—and for some occupations—for example, United Services Automobile Association (USAA) for commissioned and noncommissioned officers of the military, reciprocals are a major factor in the insurance business. In aggregate numbers and premiums, however, reciprocals are a small factor.

Miscellaneous Cooperatives

The forms of insurers seem to be unlimited. Many early life insurers were lodges or fraternal benefit societies. These organizations were formed to

1-30 / Foundations of Insurance Production: Principles of Insurance

II. The Nature and Contributions of the Insurance Business

III. **The Organization of the Insurance Business**
    A. **Types of Insurance Providers**
    B. Types of Distribution Systems

provide for the welfare of their members. Many of these welfare operations became fraternal insurance operations. The insurance organizations of fraternal societies are a special class and are treated as such as a result of insurance legislation around the country. Because there is an other-than-insurance relationship, the contract given the insured member does not contain all of the coverage provisions. Charters and bylaws of the fraternal society are incorporated into the contract by reference. Just as reciprocals are the exclusive creation of the property-liability side of the business, fraternals are exclusively part of life and health insurers. They all began as assessment operations. With a tendency for the average age of the members of a fraternal to increase because of a lack of new members, most fraternals either changed to a level premium basis or went out of the insurance business altogether. A few assessment types still exist.

Some savings banks established on the East Coast in the 1800s still offer life insurance in addition to savings plans. The amounts of insurance are usually small, and the total volume in force is small, primarily because no agents are employed to sell the policies. Life policies are usually purchased by an individual who requests such coverage from the bank. The small percentage of life insurance in force under this system, less than 1 percent of all the life insurance in force nationally, attests to the need for life insurance to be sold rather than just bought.

The final forms of nonproprietary insurers are the producer or consumer cooperative health expense plans. The two most widely known plans are "the Blues" and HMOs. The Blues, constituted of Blue Cross and Blue Shield, are known as producer cooperatives because they were formed by hospitals (Blue Cross) and physicians (Blue Shield) with excess capacity. They are creations of special insurance laws that give them tax-favored status in many states. Customers are not billed a premium based on characteristics of individual insureds or personal loss histories but rather on relative health care costs and health care facility utilization in a given community. This rating method is called "community rating." These organizations were traditionally run by boards made up of the providers of the service. Today, insurance regulators are encouraging or requiring that public participation be allowed on these boards.

Proprietary health insurers typically provide an "indemnity benefit." That is, the insured incurs health-related costs, and the insurer pays all or a portion of the costs to the insured (or, with a proper release, to the health care provider). The Blues provide service benefits. Those benefits are not stated in dollars but in terms of service to be expected, such as "a semiprivate room for sixty days after an accident or illness." Further, the Blues have contracts with the providers of the service to pay the providers directly based on a prearranged price. The Blues compete with commercial insurers and are a major factor in health care. Proprietary insurers believe the Blues are given two great advantages: tax-favored status and special legislation. The Blues, because of the growing political importance of health insurance, are subject to extreme regulatory examination in rates, forms, and service. Some Blue Cross and Blue Shield organizations have formed life and property-liability insurance subsidiaries and use independent agents as the marketing arm for their operations.

HMOs, or health maintenance organizations, are quickly replacing indemnity and fee-for-service plans. The first HMO, formed by Kaiser Industries while constructing the Hoover Dam, set the basic structure for this type of organization. The subscriber's total health care program is handled by the HMO. Preventive medicine is practiced: members are encouraged to receive annual physicals as part of the benefit package. Even prescriptions may be covered in plans, with a small payment for each prescription. Many HMOs operate large hospitals, extended care facilities, clinics, and diagnostic imaging facilities for their subscribers. The HMO usually contracts with a group of physicians to provide necessary services. If a physician with the necessary expertise to perform open-heart surgery, for instance, is not on the staff, the HMO can go outside for an expert. Physicians are paid a salary and, in some cases, a bonus based on reduction in budgeted expenses. Hospital utilization rates show greater efficiency in HMO operations than in regular hospitals. A major defect of HMOs is that the patient does not have unlimited choice in selection of a physician.

Preferred provider organizations (PPOs) attempt to partially solve this problem while retaining the cost controls of the HMO. These groups negotiate discounted rates from service providers by promising increased volumes of business from PPO members. Patients visit their family physicians or community hospital as they normally would, and if these providers have contracts with the PPO, then the services are paid for by the PPO at the contracted rates. For emergencies, the PPO will usually pay for the treatment even if the provider is not on the approved list.

Marketing Tip

A new trend has emerged as this text was being written. Known generally as "twenty-four-hour coverage," this hybrid is a combination of workers compensation and group health insurance. Based on the concept of managed care, "twenty-four-hour coverage" allows insured employees to use the same doctors and hospitals for all health needs, whether related to an on-the-job injury or a common cold. Producers should be alert to new marketing opportunities presented by this and other new insurance products and services.

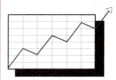

Governmental Insurers

Governmental insurers are active in both the life-health and property-liability insurance businesses. Governmental insurers have come into existence when there have been causes of loss that were considered commercially uninsurable. If there is a good reason from a public policy point of view for providing some kind of insurance protection, the government can become the insurer of last resort and spread the risk of these isolated exposures over the entire population of the United States by using the general revenues of the tax structure to pay losses.

Even if an exposure is commercially insurable and the insurance business does not provide coverage or provides it at a price deemed excessive, the government may become the insurer.

II. The Nature and Contributions of the Insurance Business

III. The Organization of the Insurance Business
   A. Types of Insurance Providers
   B. Types of Distribution Systems

Federal or state governments can offer insurance depending on the impact of the particular problem being addressed. Competition from public insurers may exist, or the government may hold a monopoly. Finally, the government may or may not use the distributive or administrative capacity of private insurers.

The failures of banks and savings and loans are considered fundamental, catastrophic risks not calculable by commercial insurers. Consequently, the federal government offers such coverage under the Federal Deposit Insurance Corporation. This body insures depositors' savings, subject to maximum limits, thus offering protection if a bank fails.

Federal crop insurance is available to farmers for large hail or windstorm losses. Although crop exposures are commercially insurable if underwriters watch their book of business and geographically spread such risks, the market for private crop insurance is relatively small.

Government programs for riot and flood insurance are examples of the insurer of last resort and cooperation with the existing private insurance mechanism. In some of these cases, insurers pool premiums to cover losses, but if losses become excessive, the government is a reinsurer for catastrophic losses. In others, like flood insurance, the federal government is the primary insurer, using agents, brokers, and private insurers ("write-your-own" program) to distribute or sell the coverage. An in-depth discussion of the coverages provided by governmental insurers appears in another assignment of the AAI program.

Types of Distribution Systems

There are many different types of insurance distribution systems. They are classified in this text according to the contractual and ownership relationships between the producer, the client, and the company. This classification system divides all distribution systems into four categories: independent agency system (American agency system); exclusive agency system; direct writers; and mail order. The student should recognize that some distribution systems mix the elements of two or more of these categories.

Independent Agency System

Agencies that participate in the **independent agency system** are independent in the sense that they are not employees of insurers. Instead, they have contracts with insurers to generate new business and to renew and service existing accounts. Their compensation is based on what they sell and is determined by various commission arrangements. If an independent agency principally represents the insured, it is called a brokerage firm. For the AAI program, brokers are considered members of the independent agency system. Independent agents set their own time schedules, pay their own expenses, and operate their own businesses. They "own" the business they produce in the sense that the agent has the right to change the client's insurer. The insurer has no right to try to keep the insured—the renewal business belongs to the agent. In fact, the renewal customer is the most valuable asset of an agency. The independent agency system is a development unique to the United States.

The independent or American agency system developed from the need to spread geographic exposures and to increase sales for insurers. Many foreign-based insurers established branches in the United States. With an office in New York, it was almost impossible to develop business "in the West," as Pittsburgh, Cincinnati, Cleveland, and St. Louis were known in the early 1800s. Domestic insurers also needed to spread their business over large geographic areas to avoid the catastrophic bankruptcies that plagued the business during the 1800s.

Most of those bankruptcies came after great conflagrations such as the New York fire of 1835, the Chicago fire of 1872, and the Boston fire of 1873. American and foreign-based companies alike needed to expand to the West. However, communication was a problem. Canals, railroads, the telegraph, and, eventually, the telephone improved communication, but there was still no way a New York office could sell insurance in Cincinnati. Three alternatives existed: (1) ignore the West and concentrate on local growth, (2) open a western office, or (3) appoint an agent. Many companies did ignore the West, and their growth suffered. Others opened western offices. Others appointed agents who would represent them in the West. Those early agents had to be independent. A company could not afford to pay salaries to untested producers without controlling their sales efforts. The solution was to compensate based on the business generated and to require each producer to be responsible for his or her own expenses. The independent agent grew and became the prototype for the American agency system.[2]

The size of independent agencies is shown in Exhibit 1-2. The smaller agency, under $500,000 in premium, is becoming a less important factor in metropolitan areas but remains important in rural areas. Merger and growth can be seen in the comparisons of agencies by premium volume from 1983 to 1992. Commission income as a percentage of premiums has been falling over the same period, giving further impetus to larger, more efficient agencies.

Exhibit 1-2
Distribution of Agencies by Annual Premium Volume—
The Independent Insurance Agents of America, Inc.

	Percentages of Agencies		
Premium Volume	1987	1992	1995
Under $1 million	46%	41%	28%
$1 million—$5 million	41	44	54
$5 million—$15 million	10	11	13
Over $15 million	3	5	5
Total	100%	100%	100%
Average	$2.7 million	$3.2 million	$4.5 million

1-34 / Foundations of Insurance Production: Principles of Insurance

II. The Nature and Contributions of the Insurance Business

III. The Organization of the Insurance Business

   A. Types of Insurance Providers

   B. Types of Distribution Systems

There are functions other than production that independent agents assume. Some have draft authority from their companies to settle small losses. Usually the draft authority is only for first party losses (losses that involve only the insured). Larger agencies provide risk management, claims, and other services on a fee basis.

Probably no such thing as a "typical" independent agent or agency exists. Because they are independent, they operate in the way the principals or owners of the business desire, not in the way the companies they represent would necessarily prefer. Independence is a valued status of these agencies. Normally, they represent more than one company, although there is a trend to represent fewer companies. Commercial Union, Fireman's Fund, and Ohio Casualty are three examples of companies that use the independent agency system.

Marketing Tip

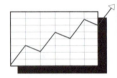

Independent agents have great freedom in selecting insurers with whom they will place business. The ability to search the marketplace of available insurers might make the difference in successfully selling a difficult-to-insure client. But...

E&O Alert!

...with this freedom comes the responsibility to use only those insurers that have the financial stability and legal status necessary to assure that all of their clients' claims will be paid. Many errors and omissions claims have resulted after insurers have gone bankrupt or avoided paying claims because of their unlicensed status within a state.

Exclusive Agency System

Agencies that participate in the **exclusive agency system** sell and service insurance policies that are limited to one insurer. This insurer holds the ownership, use, and control of policy records and expiration dates. Exclusive agents differ from independent agents in two major ways. First, during their initial training, exclusive agents are usually employees of the company they represent. Second, after the initial training phase, agents in this group are "independent" (i.e., they are paid by commissions and must pay their own expenses), but they represent only one company group. Some companies do not even allow their agents to "broker" business, that is, place business with another insurer. If the exclusive agent's company cannot or does not provide a market for a prospect, the agent must pass the business up. Other companies operating under this system do allow brokerage for those lines of insurance not written by the company. (If this is the case, these producers should also be alert to the E&O issue discussed in the E&O Alert above.) In the case of residual programs, such as automobile insurance assigned risk plans or FAIR plans, all exclusive agency companies must allow all agents to participate.

There are advantages and disadvantages to the nonbrokerage rules some companies impose on their agents. On one hand, it can be argued that without access to brokerage markets, some good personal and commercial lines accounts are lost. Many insureds prefer to deal with only one agent or agency. If a company does not write a line of insurance and does not allow brokerage, the client may take the business to another agency. On the other hand, some companies maintain that concentration of the producer's efforts in those lines actively written by the insurer gives the agent significant marketing strengths. Agents can concentrate on those lines written and become experts in those lines, providing better client service.

Commission rates often vary between first and subsequent years in an exclusive agency. First-year business may bring a commission of 15 percent; renewal business may bring an 8 percent commission. By comparison, independent agents generally receive the same percentage on new and renewal business. If exclusive agents were allowed to represent more than one company, shifting the business at renewal would generate greater commission income. Restricting agents to one company not only eliminates moving business but also accounts for the rapid growth of this type of distribution system. Producers are encouraged by the commission structure to constantly seek new business.

Finally, the ownership of renewals for exclusive agents is different from that for independent agents. In many cases, producers in the exclusive system have no renewal ownership rights. In others, there is a limited ownership that usually expires when the contract between the company and the producer expires. The exclusive agent may be compensated for the files in this case, but not to the extent that an independent agent would be if he or she sold the agency. State Farm is an example of a company using the exclusive agency system.

Direct Writing System

In the early 1800s, an insurance company did not typically appoint agents locally. Instead, companies would spring up around the heart of the transportation business. At key points along canals, navigable rivers, and junctions in railroads, companies would establish their home or branch offices. Rates were published in local newspapers (rates were significantly higher in late summer and early fall to coincide with increased demand for insurance on goods shipped). It was not unusual to find insurance operations tied to a shipping company or, in fact, to find individuals willing to write insurance for their personal account, much like Lloyd's without all of the financial and technical backup. Today, direct writers do not operate in this manner—they have recognized the value of people selling insurance rather than waiting for drop-in business.

In the **direct writing system**, producers are generally employees of their companies, not independent entrepreneurs. These producers do not own the business they write—renewals belong to the insurer, even during the period of employment. Compensation arrangements range from salary only to commission only, with many insurers paying both salary and production-based bonuses. Commission rates, if involved, follow the

II. The Nature and Contributions of the Insurance Business

III. The Organization of the Insurance Business

    A. Types of Insurance Providers

    B. Types of Distribution Systems

exclusive agency pattern in that they are higher in the first policy period and lower thereafter, encouraging the producer to concentrate on developing new business. Liberty Mutual is one example of a company that uses the direct writing system.

One important factor for both exclusive agency and direct writing producers is that they are usually relieved of many administrative functions, such as policy issuance, premium collections, and claim functions. In some cases, companies allow the producer to settle small first party claims or to provide minor premium auditing or loss control services. One key ingredient in company relationships with their producers is to actively encourage the development of new business. Relieving the producer of nonselling activities and compensating at a lower renewal rate help accomplish this goal.

Mail Order Systems

In the **mail order system**, the producer is not a factor. Insurance companies using this system claim not only that the expense portion of their business is lower (through the elimination of producer commissions or salaries) but also that through pre-underwriting, the loss portion is also reduced. By concentrating on a group of potential insureds who are considered above average, an insurer can offer a lower premium. Many companies have been successful in this method. United Services Automobile Association (USAA), which concentrates on commissioned and noncommissioned officers in the military, and Government Employees Insurance Company (GEICO) are two examples. Mail order companies operate almost exclusively in personal lines.

Production expenses are low because no commissions are paid to producers. And because of the pre-selection of insureds with certain characteristics through mailing lists, rating methods are simplified, allowing more efficient use of personnel and equipment. These cost-saving elements make the mail order system very price-competitive.

Mixed Systems

When using two or more distribution systems, insurers market through **mixed systems**. For example, Allstate, a direct writing company in metropolitan areas, is appointing independent agents in those locations in which their direct writing system cannot work. One independent agency company, ITT Hartford, also uses direct mail solicitation for the personal insurance needs of members of The American Association of Retired Persons (AARP).

Distribution Systems and the Producer

For producers, there are advantages and disadvantages to all of the distribution systems and to combinations of them. Exhibit 1-3 compares the key elements for producers under these systems: compensation, status with insurer, ownership of expirations, and service performed by the producer. In the end, the best system is the one that works best in a given situation.

Exhibit 1-3
Agent-Based Insurance Distribution Systems

Distribution System	Compensation		Status With Insurer	Expiration— Ownership by Producer	Producer Services
	Commission	On Renewal			
Independent Agent	Yes	Usually same	Independent contractor	Yes	Claims, loss control, others
Exclusive Agent	Yes	Lower	Independent contractor— Salary during training	Possible	Limited claims
Direct Writing Agent	Possible or salary plus bonus based on production	Lower (if any)	Employee	No	None

Consumers, representatives of the federal government, and others too often judge insurance distribution systems on one criterion—price. This approach ignores other important factors such as service and product innovation.

No one distribution system has an overall advantage to the consumer with regard to a combination of price, service, and product. From the point of view of the producer, the mail order system must be the least attractive—it does not use producers. Any judgment about the other three systems must be based on the producer's goals, desires, and personality. The advantage one producer sees in his or her system may be a strong disadvantage to another producer. For instance, the regular salary of the direct writer may be attractive to some, whereas others would rather have relative freedom in their activities and accept a commission for the business they generate.

> **Check** your understanding of the *Key Words and Phrases* found in the second part of this assignment.

Financial intermediary (p. 22)

Stock insurance company (p. 27)

Mutual insurers (p. 28)

1-38 / Foundations of Insurance Production: Principles of Insurance

Reciprocal exchange (p. 29)

Governmental insurers (p. 31)

Independent agency system (p. 32)

Exclusive agency system (p. 34)

Direct writing system (p. 35)

Mail order system (p. 36)

Mixed systems (p. 36)

> **Review** the concepts presented in the first part of this assignment by answering the following questions.

14. What are the economic benefits of insurance? (p. 20)

15. What are the economic costs of insurance? (pp. 21-22)

16. What are the differences between a stock insurer and a mutual insurer? (pp. 27-28)

Assignment 1—The Insurance Business: An Overview / 1-39

17. How does a Lloyd's organization differ from a reciprocal exchange? (p. 29)

18. What are the reasons for the development of governmental insurers? (p. 31)

19. How does the independent agency system differ from (pp. 32-33)
    (a) the exclusive agency system?

    (b) the direct writing system?

20. What functions, other than production, might be performed by independent agents? (p. 34)

21. What is (a) one advantage and (b) one disadvantage of the nonbrokerage rule contained in some exclusive agency contracts? (p. 35)

Apply the concepts presented in the first part of this assignment by answering the following questions.

4. A recent college graduate has expressed an interest in becoming an insurance producer but is uncertain as to the relative advantages of the independent agency system, the exclusive agency system, and the direct writing system. What are the advantages and disadvantages of the three systems from the standpoint of (a) a new producer with limited financial resources and (b) an experienced producer with a substantial amount of renewal business?

5. One of your clients has asked you to explain the differences between stock and mutual insurers and to suggest which might be better for this client's needs.
   (a) How do stock and mutual insurers compare or differ relative to:

   (1) ownership

   (2) management

   (3) ability to raise capital

   (b) Under what circumstances might you recommend the following to this client?
   (1) Lloyd's of London

   (2) a factory mutual

Summary

This assignment began with a survey of basic insurance definitions and principles, followed by an overview of the insurance business's nature, contributions, and organization. The two primary functions of insurers—providing protection against financial loss and acting as financial intermediaries—are the sources of the economic and other contributions of insurance to society.

The insurance business operates differently than other types of businesses, and insurers seldom know what their profits are until years after policies have expired.

There are three basic types of insurers: proprietary, nonproprietary or cooperative, and governmental or public. Proprietary insurers are owned and operated to make a profit. Nonproprietary insurers are owned and controlled by their policyholders. Governmental insurers have primarily developed to provide insurance coverage against losses caused by commercially uninsurable perils.

Insurance distribution systems vary. Independent agents are not employees of insurers but are independent contractors. They are paid commissions for their sales, own the business they produce, and usually represent more than one insurer. Exclusive agents are also independent contractors and paid on commission, but they usually do not own the business they produce.

Direct writing agents are employees of their insurers, often receive a salary, and do not own the business they produce

Generally, insurers will use only one distribution system, but some use more than one. This is called a "mixed system."

No one distribution system is always the best for insureds. Price, service, and products will vary. Likewise, the producer should choose the distribution system that best fits his or her goals, preferences, and personality.

Chapter Notes

1. George Leland Bach, *Economics*, 9th ed. (Englewood Cliffs, NJ: Prentice-Hall, 1977), p. 210.
2. The first trade association of independent agents occurred on April 18, 1838, in Cincinnati. The organization was known as the General Board of Fire Underwriters of Cincinnati. Today, it is known as the Cincinnati Insurance Board.

Insurance and the Legal System

Assignment 2

Assignment Objectives

After completing this assignment, you should be able to:
1. Distinguish between civil wrongs and criminal wrongs and explain the legal remedies for each.
2. Explain the elements of a tort.
3. Explain the various kinds of torts and the various rules of law applicable to each.
4. Explain the four essential requirements for a right of action for negligence to exist.
5. Explain the obligations of an owner or occupant of land to the various categories of persons who might go on the land.
6. Contrast the doctrines of negligence, contributory negligence, and comparative negligence.
7. Given an insurance agency case, explain how an agent's authority might be created.
   In support of the assignment objective listed above, you should be able to do the following:
   a. Illustrate
      (i) express authority,
      (ii) implied authority, and
      (iii) apparent authority.
   b. Explain the duties that agents owe their principals.
   c. Explain the five ways in which an agency can be terminated.
8. Given an insurance policy, explain how the elements of a contract apply to that policy.
   In support of the assignment objective listed above, you should be able to do the following:
   a. Describe the elements of a contract.
   b. Explain the unique aspects of insurance contracts.
9. Given a case involving a client's exposures, apply the policy analysis process to determine whether losses are covered by specified insurance policies.
   In support of the assignment objective listed above, you should be able to do the following:
   a. Describe the purpose of each of the five parts of an insurance policy.
   b. Explain the process used to analyze property and liability policies.
10. Define or describe each of the Key Words and Phrases for this assignment.

Assignment Outline

I. Tort Law
   A. Common Law and Statutes
   B. Essential Elements of a Tort
   C. Legal Rights and Remedies
   D. Invasions of Rights Protected by Tort Law
   E. Breach of Duty Equals Invasion of a Right
   F. Sources of Liability
   G. Statutes Affecting Determination of Negligence
II. Agency
   A. Scope of Agency
   B. Agency in Property-Liability Insurance
   C. Duties of Insurance Agents
   D. Insurance Professionals
III. Law of Contracts
   A. Elements of a Contract
   B. Unique Aspects of Insurance Contracts
IV. Insurance Policy Construction and Analysis
   A. Policy Construction
   B. Policy Analysis
V. Summary

Assignment 2
Insurance and the Legal System

Orient yourself to this assignment by reading the following introduction.

A knowledge of legal concepts is vital to producers. They must be aware of tort liability concepts for two reasons. First, knowledge of tort laws is essential in order to properly advise clients about their liability exposures and the liability insurance coverages needed to protect against these exposures. This text includes Marketing Tips where appropriate to help producers identify sales opportunities presented by many of these exposures. Second, producers are also subject to tort liability laws and must avoid liability whenever possible. The text also provides E&O Alerts in these situations to warn producers of potential errors and omissions exposures and to provide recommendations for avoiding E&O problems.

Other legal concepts are also important in the day-to-day business of an insurance agency and producer. Common law—derived from court cases—and statutory laws—passed by governmental bodies—affect many aspects of insurance policy language and how a policy responds when a claim occurs. The concepts discussed and defined in this assignment are the foundation of insurance policies and agency activities, and these concepts are used throughout the AAI program. Becoming familiar with these concepts now will make future assignments more meaningful.

Insurance is closely tied to the legal system. The concept of negligence, the major issue in liability insurance, involves a court's determination of whether an action is reasonable and prudent. Agency and contract law form the basis for the relationship between the producer and the insurer and its representatives. Ownership, legal title, and possession form the basis for insurable interest, a primary issue in property insurance. A producer must reasonably understand certain legal topics to function effectively because the producer could be asked to give advice and make a judgment for the client in areas that involve the law. Assignment 2 will provide the background needed to handle those situations.

2-2 / Foundations of Insurance Production: Principles of Insurance

> **Read** the definitions of the *Key Words and Phrases* that follow. Being familiar with these important words will help you better understand the first part of this assignment. *Key Words and Phrases* appear in bold in the text when they are defined.

Legal wrong	An unjustified invasion of a legal right, for which the law provides a legal remedy
Criminal wrong	A wrong against society, for which remedies include fines and imprisonment
Civil wrong	A wrong against a person or persons, for which remedies include damages awarded to the victim and court-ordered injunctions to prevent further injury
Common law	Upholds the concept that current court decisions should be based on previous decisions when circumstances of each are similar
Statutory law	Law passed by a legislative body, becoming the precedent for future common-law decisions
Tort	Civil wrong, other than a breach of contract, for which the law provides a legal remedy
Compensatory damages	Monetary awards reasonably related to the extent of injury
Nominal damages	Awards that are symbolic or nominal in amount
Punitive damages	Awards that are far in excess of the actual monetary harm involved when the court views tortious behavior as being particularly repugnant; sometimes awarded in addition to compensatory damages
Injunction	Court order requiring an activity to be stopped or forbidding that a contemplated activity be undertaken
Restitution	The return of specific property by court order
Battery	Intentionally touching another person without that person's permission or taking some other privilege in a manner offensive to the person touched
Assault	The threat of battery; putting someone in fear of physical harm
False imprisonment	Wrongful interference with someone's freedom of movement
Trespass	Unlawful, intentional entry onto land by a person or an object
Defamation	An unprivileged false communication to third parties, by word or deed, which tends to expose an entity to hatred, contempt, or ridicule, or to cause it to be shunned
Invasion of privacy	A tort that involves interference with a person's right to be left alone
Strict liability/absolute liability	The liability of a person responsible for certain hazardous activities involving the possibility of harm to another person regardless of negligence or intent to harm

Negligence	A careless invasion of another's rights
Proximate cause	An unbroken chain of events leading up to an occurrence
Trespassers	People on another's property for their own purposes without the owner's permission
Attractive nuisance	Something that the landowner knows will attract children to his or her property
Licensees	People on another's property for their own benefit and who can be assumed to have implied permission to be on the property
Invitee	Someone on a property for his or her own benefit and for the benefit of the property owner
Contributory negligence	When each party is to some degree negligent, then each is responsible for its own injury
Comparative negligence	Responsibility for damages is allocated based on the degree of fault of each party
Vicarious liability	When the negligence of one party is imputed to another
Agency	When one party represents or acts for another as directed
Principal	The party that delegates responsibilities to another
Agent	The party that acts under the direct orders of the principal
Dual agency	When an agent acts for both parties in a transaction in which each has all the facts, and the agent's representation does not conflict with the interests of either party
Agency by appointment	One party appoints another party to act on its behalf, usually with a written agreement outlining the scope of representation
Agency by estoppel	Creates agency to protect third parties from harm when a principal creates the appearance of an agency relationship
Agency by ratification	The principal affirms that agency has existed and accepts the previous acts as the acts of an agent on the principal's behalf
Express authority	Whatever is agreed to by the agent and principal
Implied authority	Authority that arises from actions that are in accord with accepted custom and are considered to be within the scope of authority granted by the principal
Apparent authority	Authority arising when one party gives the appearance of authority to another party who then relies on that appearance of authority
General agent	An agent with broad powers to represent the insurance company in a given area and for a specific line or lines of insurance
Solicitors	Those with authority only to solicit applications for insurance from the insurance-buying public

Study the first part of this assignment, which includes the following sections:

I. Tort Law
II. Agency

Tort Law

A **legal wrong** is an unjustified invasion of a legal right, for which the law provides a legal remedy. There are two broad classes of legal wrongs: criminal and civil.

A **criminal wrong** is a wrong against society, and remedies include fines and imprisonment. A **civil wrong** is a wrong against a person or persons, and remedies include damages awarded to the victim and court-ordered injunctions to prevent further injury. Some actions are considered both civil and criminal wrongs. A speeding driver who causes an accident, for example, could be involved both in a criminal action for vehicular homicide and in a civil action for recovery of the victim's medical expenses and other damages. Insurance generally addresses only civil wrongs.

There are two broad classes of civil wrongs: torts and breach of contract. Exhibit 2-1 shows the relationships between the types of wrongs.

Exhibit 2-1
Types of Wrongs

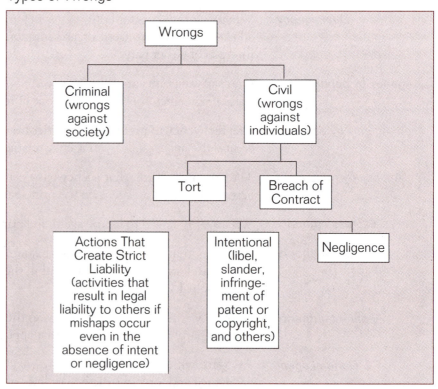

The ideas that form the foundation of tort law are based in English common law, which is a body of legal principles deriving its authority from court decisions. Most English-speaking countries have legal systems based on common law. The basic concept of **common law** is that current court decisions should be based on previous decisions whenever the circumstances of the cases are similar. The idea is not to develop a comprehensive body of written laws covering nearly every subject, as do Napoleonic civil codes, but to develop a logical body of general principles through successive judicial decisions against which cases are compared and future cases are decided. This is not to say that the legal precedent established in some previous case will forever be observed. Often, the courts' ruling on two similar cases seems to have reached opposite conclusions. Circumstances change, and a precedent might no longer be considered legally, socially, or equitably valid.

Common Law and Statutes

Court decisions based on common law are often superseded by **statutory law**—laws passed by a legislative body. Federal and state statutes are created by Congress and state legislatures, respectively. Local ordinances are passed by municipalities in town meetings and council halls. The various statutes then become the precedent for future common-law decisions and alter and adapt the legal system to the emerging societal needs.

The extent of these statutes depends on the body passing them. For example, one state may pass a law altering the concept of negligence in automobile operations through a no-fault law that will not affect drivers living and operating their motor vehicles in other states.

Marketing Tip

A producer must be thoroughly familiar with both statutory and common laws that affect insurance in the producer's marketing territory. This familiarity will have a twofold benefit. First, more business will be produced because the producer will sell the proper coverages, thereby gaining client confidence. Second, and perhaps even more important, . . .

E&O Alert!

Errors and omissions claims can be prevented through proper and adequate coverage recommendations. Use the insurance laws in your marketing area to build your production and avoid E&O claims.

Essential Elements of a Tort

A **tort** is a civil wrong, other than a breach of contract, for which the law provides a legal remedy. There are various torts, each with their own set of elements that must be proven for a successful legal action. For example, to support an action for the tort of negligence, four elements must be present. If any element is lacking, no tort has occurred. The essential elements are listed as follows:

I. Tort Law
A. Common Law and Statutes
B. Essential Elements of a Tort
C. Legal Rights and Remedies
D. Invasions of Rights Protected by Tort Law
E. Breach of Duty Equals Invasion of a Right

1. Legal right or duty—One party (the victim) has the right not to be harmed, and the other party (the tortfeasor) has a duty to refrain from causing harm. This must be a noncontractual right; otherwise, the situation falls under contract law. Also, there must be no justification or valid excuse for not complying with the duty ordinarily owed to the holder of the right.
2. Breach of duty—The right to be free from harm must be violated, or the legal duty not to harm must be breached.
3. Harm—The victim must incur harm (damage or injury) that causes financial loss.
4. Proximate cause—A close causal connection must exist between the damage or injury to the victim and the breach of a duty ordinarily owed to the victim by the tortfeasor.

Legal Rights and Remedies

The presence of the elements of a tort creates a situation in which someone has a legal right, someone violates that right (commits a tort), and a legal remedy exists to redress that violation. The following are types of damages for which tort law provides a remedy:

1. Bodily injury
2. Loss of personal freedom
3. Loss of property
4. Undue interference with an economic right or advantage
5. Damage to public esteem
6. Interference with intrafamily relationships
7. Undue psychological trauma

For the legal rights that tort law protects, the law provides two remedies: direct action on the part of the victim and judicial remedy.

Direct Action

Direct action by the victim must be reasonable in view of the harm. An example of reasonable direct action might be the right to defend oneself against physical attack. The reasonableness of the defense is determined by comparing the amount of force of the defense to the amount of force of the attack. Shooting someone to prevent a slap in the face is an example of unreasonable force. A storekeeper who has an illegally parked auto removed from his or her lot is an example of the use of legal, reasonable direct action. A person who pursues a thief to recover stolen property is also taking reasonable direct action.

Direct action must be reasonably prompt. Failure to pursue direct action as soon as possible compromises that right, and the victim must then seek a judicial remedy.

Judicial Remedies

If direct action did not or will not result in a remedy, judicial action is required. Three legal remedies are available and may be provided by the court:

1. Awarding monetary damages
2. Granting an injunction
3. Requiring restitution

Monetary damages are **compensatory damages**, that is, reasonably related to the extent of injury. Damages can also be symbolic or nominal in amount. **Nominal damages** can be awarded in situations such as simple trespass when no damage to the land is involved. Awards can also be considered **punitive damages** or far in excess of the actual monetary harm involved when the court views tortious behavior as being particularly repugnant. Punitive damages are sometimes awarded in addition to compensatory damages and are labeled as such.

An **injunction** is a court order requiring an activity to be stopped or forbidding that a contemplated activity be undertaken. An injunction is used when monetary damages are not adequate to redress the wrong, and it is often a temporary measure used until an issue is resolved by the court. For example, in a boundary dispute, injunctive relief may be granted to prohibit cutting trees near the property line until that boundary has been precisely established.

For an injunction to be granted, the victim must usually prove that monetary damages would be an inadequate remedy. In the boundary dispute illustration, monetary damages, if the boundary dispute is ultimately decided in favor of the plaintiff, might not be an adequate remedy for the loss of the beauty and shade of mature trees wrongfully cut. An injunction must therefore be used before the trees are cut.

Restitution is the return of specific property by court order. Although this term has the general meaning of compensating for a wrong, in terms of tort law its meaning is precise: return of the property. For instance, no amount of money could remedy the loss of an antique that has sentimental value. The return of this heirloom is the only possible remedy.

Invasions of Rights Protected by Tort Law

People are entitled to reasonable assurances by our system of law that they will be reasonably safe and secure from harm. The harms for which tort law provides protection are discussed below.

Battery and Assault

Battery is intentionally touching another person without that person's permission or taking some other privilege in a manner offensive to the person touched. The word "battery" is often used in conjunction with the term "assault." **Assault** means the threat of battery; that is, putting someone in fear that he or she will be physically harmed. Assault is the threat; battery is actual physical contact.

False Imprisonment

False imprisonment is the wrongful interference with someone's freedom of movement. One need not be put in jail to have suffered false imprisonment. Preventing a person wrongfully suspected of shoplifting from leaving the store is an example of false imprisonment.

I. Tort Law
- C. Legal Rights and Remedies
- D. Invasions of Rights Protected by Tort Law
- E. Breach of Duty Equals Invasion of a Right
- F. Sources of Liability

Both battery and false imprisonment are tortious only when the act occurs without the victim's consent. Also, the rights of a person to freedom from bodily injury and to freedom of movement carry with them the right to use reasonable force in self-defense.

Loss of Property

People are entitled to the quiet enjoyment and exclusive use of their property. This includes both peaceful possession of that property and rights to any profits arising from its use. The torts of trespass and nuisance are invasions of the rights connected with property ownership.

Trespass is defined as unlawful, intentional entry onto land by a person (walking on the land) or by an object (dumping trash on someone's property). A private nuisance is something that unreasonably interferes with one's use of his or her real estate. It can be an intangible interference, such as loud noise.

Personal property is subject to the torts of conversion and trespass to chattels. Conversion is an intentional interference with the owner's legal title to personal property. An example of conversion is attempting to sell something belonging to another. Trespass to chattel is an intentional act that interferes with the owner's right to have physical control over an object. Theft of property is an example of trespass to chattel.

Undue Interference With an Economic Right or Advantage

Economic activity, honestly done, is protected by tort law. Just as the enjoyment of property is protected, so also are honest efforts to acquire property. Deceit, inducing breach of contract, and disparagement are examples of undue interference with an economic right.

"Deceit" is consciously misrepresenting a material fact intended to induce another to rely on the misrepresentation, which, when the victim does so, causes him or her harm.

Parties to a contract have a right to have contractual promises enforced. Under tort law, one who acts intentionally to induce another to breach a contract has committed a tort. A football player's agent who encourages the player not to honor his contract, for example, commits a tort.

"Disparagement" is any unprivileged communication (such as that occurring outside of a court of law) to the public that does the following or has the following characteristics:

1. Is known by the maker to be false
2. Is derogatory to the victim's title to its property, to the quality of its goods or services, or to its business activities generally
3. Is intended to discourage the public from dealing with the victim
4. Causes direct economic harm to the victim

Damage to Public Esteem

Damage to one's reputation does not always result in direct economic loss, yet one's reputation has inherent value and is worthy of protection.

Two rights established under tort law must be protected: (1) the right to be protected from the spread of falsehoods that would be injurious, and (2) the right to be protected from the spread of confidential information that, even though accurate, would subject the entity to derision.

Defamation is an unprivileged false communication to third parties, by word or deed, that tends to expose an entity to hatred, contempt, or ridicule or to cause it to be shunned by those whom the communication foreseeably reaches.

Invasion of privacy is a tort that involves interference with a person's right to be left alone. Invasion of privacy occurs if any of the following four rights are violated:

1. To be physically secluded
2. To prohibit one's name or identity from being used to promote products or causes without permission
3. To prohibit *private* information about oneself from being publicized
4. To prohibit *public* information about oneself from being publicized in a misleading manner

Interference With Intrafamily Relationships

A family has a right, protected by tort law, to the enjoyment of the family's service, affection, and companionship. Spouses have the right to sexual relations with each other. Parent-child relationships are based on the rights of parents to the services, company, and affection of their children who are still dependent members of the household and are not legally considered adults. Interference with these marital or family relationships can be the basis of tort action.

Undue Psychological Trauma

Pain and suffering resulting from an accident are compensable. Nervous breakdown suffered as a result of false imprisonment or defamation of character is also compensable. Psychological trauma not associated with another tort is less widely accepted by the courts and is usually not compensable.

Breach of Duty Equals Invasion of a Right

The second essential element of a tort is an invasion of a right or a breach of a duty. Three actions create the invasion of a right or the breach of a duty:

1. Intentional torts
2. Actions that impose strict liability
3. Negligence

Intentional Torts

An intentional tort requires actual intent to invade the rights of the victim or to take action that would reasonably be expected to result in injury. In such cases, a high degree of moral blame is assessed against the

I. Tort Law
   D. Invasions of Rights Protected by Tort Law
   E. Breach of Duty Equals Invasion of a Right
   F. Sources of Liability

perpetrator because of the intentional nature of the act or the deliberateness of the injury. Battery is an intentional tort against a person's freedom from bodily injury. Conversion is an intentional tort against the freedom to enjoy one's private property. Insurance usually does not provide coverage for intentional torts.

Strict and Absolute Liability

Some activities have been determined by legislation or common law to create liability without regard to fault. Workers compensation is the classic example of no-fault liability created by legislation. Liability for products may be imposed by courts regardless of whether the seller was negligent or intended harm. Even though proof of negligence is not required, it is still necessary for the plaintiff in a products liability claim to show that a defect in the product caused the injury. Although there are important legal distinctions between **strict liability** and **absolute liability**, for purposes of this course those distinctions are set aside and both types of liability are treated as one. The important criterion needed in determining liability is that the "standard of care," in both cases, may be breached without negligence or intent to do harm.

Activities that give rise to liability normally involve situations in which harm to others would result should a mishap occur, yet there may also be substantial benefits to society from the activity. Because of the possibility of harm, the person conducting the activities is held responsible to see that such harm does not occur. In other words, that person must use a certain standard of care in conducting those activities such that the standard reduces or prevents the possibility of harm. Moreover, because a person performing such activities is usually in a better position to understand the dangers involved in an especially hazardous situation, it is reasonable to hold that person strictly accountable if someone is harmed.

Activities that impose strict or absolute liability include the following:

1. Performing a reasonable activity in an unreasonable setting. An example might be the storing of large quantities of a highly flammable substance in a highly populated area.

2. Keeping animals known or presumed to be dangerous. Wild animals, regardless of the length of time in captivity, are known to be dangerous. A person whose business is providing wild animals for use in promotional activities, for example, is held liable if one of the animals injures someone.

3. Exposing one's employees to injury or disease. Society has decided that it is unfair to expect workers to bear the costs of illnesses and accidents associated with the production of goods and services. Thus, the loss of wages, medical expenses, and rehabilitation costs associated with these occurrences are instead borne by the employer, to be added to the cost of the product and paid ultimately by the consumer of that product. Under workers compensation laws, the employer is liable for the employee's injuries, regardless of fault.

4. Harming persons or damaging property on the ground while operating an aircraft is another area in which strict liability is assessed. This

is an outgrowth of the concern in the early days of aviation of the extremely dangerous nature of flying. The law recognizes that aircraft do fly over other people's property and that in most situations the owners of the property overflown have no effective method of preventing it. This being so, the aircraft's operator must be held accountable for any injury or damage caused by the aircraft to those on the ground.

5. Producing or marketing goods or services that contain a defect imposes liability on the seller. If a soda bottle explodes because of a defect, creating a loss, the fact that the bottler took "reasonable care" is not allowed as a defense.

Negligence

Negligence, the third (and most common) classification of torts, differs from intentional torts and strict liability in that it involves a careless rather than purposeful invasion of another's rights.

"Negligence" is "the omission to do something which a reasonable person, guided by those considerations which ordinarily regulate the conduct of human affairs, would do, or doing something which a reasonable and prudent person would not do."[1] This definition is called the "prudent person rule." Negligence can arise from what a person does or from what a person fails to do. The actions of a prudent person against which other actions are measured are based on considerations that *ordinarily* regulate human conduct. The criteria against which actions are measured are therefore subject to change. Comparisons are made against what is considered appropriate in this society, in a local area, at this time.

The prudent person is intended to be a peer. An attorney's actions would be measured against those of another attorney, and a brain surgeon's actions would be measured against what a reasonable brain surgeon would have done in similar circumstances. So a person whose only medical training was a course in first aid would not be held to the same level of expertise as a medical doctor.

The implication of such comparisons is that the higher the level of experience, education, or skill involved, the higher the standard of care against which actions will be judged. So a producer who advertises in the yellow pages under the heading "Insurance Consultant" could be raising the standard of care against which his or her actions are judged. An action considered reasonable when performed by a producer could be considered unreasonable or negligent if performed by a consultant.

The definition of "negligence" is worded in terms of a "prudent person" and in terms of "those considerations that ordinarily regulate the conduct of human affairs." The definition also establishes a standard (what a prudent person would do in similar circumstances) against which conduct can be measured. Judges and juries are left to decide what a prudent person would have done in similar circumstances.

Such a definition is of great value because it is adaptable to the changes in our society and in the nation's economic system. But such adaptability is paid for in the vagueness of the definition. A more specific definition

I. Tort Law
   D. Invasions of Rights Protected by Tort Law
   E. Breach of Duty Equals Invasion of a Right
   F. Sources of Liability
   G. Statutes Affecting Determination of Negligence

would make the jury's job much easier, but the concept would be less adaptable to change.

Vagueness is sometimes perceived as a cause for concern, and lawmakers often try to set up an unequivocal definition of negligence. For example, such a definition might answer questions concerning what precautions a reasonable and prudent person would take to protect neighbor children from his or her backyard swimming pool. Is a four-foot fence enough? Should the fence be chain-link, or is a wooden one adequate?

A community could decide to make an effort to answer those questions, thus more specifically defining a standard for behavior, by passing an ordinance relating to fencing swimming pools. The ordinance could require all private residential swimming pools to be fully enclosed with a chain-link fence at least four feet high with a securely fastened gate of the same or similar materials. A member of the community would therefore know what a prudent person would do; he or she would do as the ordinance requires. In establishing the conduct of a prudent person, such statutes more specifically define negligence by setting up a standard of behavior.

Another ordinance might require all sidewalks to be cleared of snow by 10 A.M. following a snowfall. If a pedestrian were injured three days after a snowfall by falling on an icy, snow-covered sidewalk, the task of deciding what a prudent person would do and thereby determining the presence of negligence is made easier. Some states have modified the definition of negligence as determined by the common-law prudent person concept by establishing the doctrines of contributory negligence and comparative negligence. (Those two doctrines are described later in this assignment.)

The following conditions must be present for a right of action for negligence to exist and to prove negligence:

1. A legal duty to use care
2. A failure to use care
3. Injury or damage
4. **Proximate cause**, which is a cause that in a natural and continuous sequence, unbroken by any new and independent cause, produces an event, and without which the event would not have happened

If care is not owed, it is not negligence to fail to use care; if no damage results, this failure was of no consequence.

Exhibit 2-2 illustrates that negligence can arise from a failure to act or from a careless act. A person renting boats could be held negligent for failure to provide safety equipment in the boats or for failure to properly maintain the boats to make them seaworthy. One is not normally required to go to the aid of someone in distress, but a lifeguard at a beach could be held accountable for failure to act to save a drowning swimmer at that beach.

Exhibit 2-2
Negligence

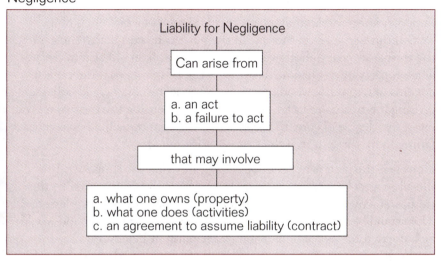

Sources of Liability

Exhibit 2-2 indicates that liability can arise from the following three sources:

1. What is owned (property)
2. What is done (activities)
3. What is agreed (contract)

Property Ownership

The existence of real and personal property makes it possible for the property to become an instrumentality that injures someone or damages other property. Over the years, courts have decided that the level of care depends on whether the person entering the land is a trespasser, a licensee, or an invitee. Alternatively, courts have applied a general standard of "reasonableness" to avoid categorizing the injured parties.

Some jurisdictions have all but abolished the distinctions between trespassers, licensees, and invitees. Producers should be aware of how and if these distinctions are made in the states in which they do business.

Trespassers

Trespassers are people on another's property for their own purposes without the owner's permission. Their presence is of no value to the owner. Trespassers actually have temporarily appropriated the property for their own use. In this case, the law states that the owner owes the trespasser nothing. Thus, since there is no legal duty to use care, the failure of the owner to provide care would not be considered negligence. In this case, the chain of conditions required to establish negligence is broken because the first condition does not exist.

There are two exceptions to the standard of care owed to trespassers. First, a property owner cannot deliberately set a trap. Second, a property

I. Tort Law
   E. Breach of Duty Equals Invasion of a Right
   F. Sources of Liability
   G. Statutes Affecting Determination of Negligence

II. Agency

owner owes a duty to protect small children who might not understand that they are trespassers.

Suppose, for example, that a person cuts across someone else's property several times a week on the way to the bus. As he cuts across the garden, the trespasser hears a hollow sound as he steps on an old cistern cover. The property owner had no duty to tell the trespasser that the cistern cover is old, that the wood is rotten, and that the cover could collapse, causing the trespasser to fall into the cistern. Because the trespasser is not owed this degree of care, the property owner cannot be held negligent for failing to fix the cistern if the trespasser is injured.

However, the landowner cannot deliberately trap the trespasser. It is illegal to set a bear trap, for example, on the path usually taken by the trespasser, cover it with leaves, and hope to teach the person a lesson. This would be an attempt to deliberately harm the trespasser and would be a use of force out of proportion to the harm inflicted. In Iowa, a landowner who was frequently robbed set up a device that discharged a shotgun when his window was opened. The resulting blast, which injured a burglar coming through the window, was considered excessive.

The second exception rests in the principle that all members of society owe a duty to children to protect them from harm. Much of the law involving minors is based on the idea that children must be protected from themselves and from actions they do not realize will harm them. Property owners owe a duty to small children to keep them safe even when these children are trespassing. This principle comes into play when something exists that the landowner knows will attract children to his property. This "something" is known as an **attractive nuisance** and is especially important when conditions involve children too young to read "No Trespassing" or "Warning" signs. The most common example of an attractive nuisance is a swimming pool. A homeowner should realize that a pool would attract children and that many children cannot swim and could drown. The homeowner has a duty to protect children from their own inexperience. The pool should be securely fenced and locked when not in use. Other examples of items attractive to children could be ladders to climb, animals to pet, and machinery to start. If a child trespasses on property as a result of an attractive nuisance and is consequently hurt, the property owner could be held to be negligent even though the child is a trespasser.

Licensees

Licensees are people on another's property for their own benefit and who can be assumed to have implied permission to be on the property. Licensees include door-to-door salespeople and delivery people, those needing emergency aid or assistance, police officers, and firefighters. Social guests are classified as licensees in most states. The difference between the licensee and the trespasser is that a licensee, although on another's property for his or her own benefit, has the property owner's implied or expressed permission to be there. This is because our society recognizes the virtue of work and the necessity of reasonably free and open travel, often including the need to enter the property of others. Reasonable care would require the removal of hazards where appropriate or the posting of signs warning of these hazards (such as the previously described old cistern cover) if their removal is not appropriate.

Invitees

An **invitee** is someone on a property for his or her own benefit and for the property owner's benefit. An invitee is owed a greater degree of care than reasonable care. The landowner should actively seek out hazards and remove them. If this is not possible, care should be taken to post signs warning of those hazards. There should be indications of some positive action to protect the invitee, action to indicate that care was taken. For example, the previously described cistern should be filled in or barricaded in such a way as to attempt to prevent an invitee from accidental harm. Invitees would include customers of a commercial establishment, government representatives, public utility workers such as meter readers, and others whose presence would benefit the landowner. Social guests are considered to be invitees in some states.

Activities

In addition to what one owns, what one does (activities) can also negligently injure or damage the property of another. Again, in order for negligence to exist, a chain of circumstances must also exist: there must be a legal duty to use care in one's activities, a failure to perform this duty, and resulting damage or injury.

Personal activities, such as operating a boat, fishing, playing golf, and riding a bicycle, can be negligently performed. Those who engage in business activities also have an obligation and a responsibility to the public not to let these activities harm them.

Shifting Responsibility by Contract

In addition to what one owns and does, one can agree to be liable for negligence. This agreement typically takes the form of a legal contract through which a duty or an obligation of one party is assumed by, or shifted to, another. Under such a contract, the failure of the second party to perform that duty can be the basis for negligence if that failure has brought harm to someone. Because of the contract, the responsibility for negligence is shifted from the first party to the second.

For example, a lease of premises agreement might shift the burden for building maintenance from the landlord to the tenant and require the tenant to hold the landlord harmless for any liability arising out of faulty maintenance. A subsequent boiler explosion caused by faulty maintenance would be properly appraised as a function and responsibility of the landlord except that the tenant has assumed this responsibility by contract.

In addition to lease of premises agreements, railroad sidetrack agreements and other hold harmless agreements are examples of liability exposures assumed by contract.

Statutes Affecting Determination of Negligence

Some states have modified the definition of "negligence" as determined

I. Tort Law
   F. Sources of Liability
   G. **Statutes Affecting Determination of Negligence**
II. Agency
   A. **Scope of Agency**
   B. Agency in Property-Liability Insurance

by the common-law prudent person concept by establishing the doctrines of contributory negligence and comparative negligence.

Contributory Negligence

The concept of negligence can be applied with relative ease in situations in which one party is clearly at fault and one is not at fault. When both parties are at fault to a degree, the concept begins to break down. The doctrine of **contributory negligence** states that if each party is to some degree at fault, then each must bear responsibility for its own injury. In an auto accident, if one party was intoxicated under state law and the other was speeding, then both would be required by the doctrine of contributory negligence to pay for their own damages.

A major defect in the contributory negligence doctrine is that the degree of negligence imputed to one party might be very small yet still sufficient to require each party to bear the burden of his or her own damages. One party might have been driving recklessly at high speed under the influence of alcohol. The other party might have been daydreaming for a moment. In theory, each was negligent, and each should bear his or her own loss. Thus, the concept, designed to create equity in situations in which both parties are responsible, often operates to the detriment of the party who was responsible in a very small way. It does not account for the differences in degrees of negligence.

Comparative Negligence

The concept of **comparative negligence** attempts to assess the relative responsibility of the parties involved in an accident or a harm-causing situation. Assume Party A is held responsible for 60 percent of the blame and Party B for the remaining 40 percent. Party A is thus held responsible for 60 percent of Party B's damages. Depending on the jurisdiction, Party B may be responsible for 0 or 40 percent of Party A's damages. Damages allocated between the parties on this basis would more fairly and accurately reflect the degree of responsibility of each party.

Because comparative negligence statutes appear to operate more equitably than contributory negligence statutes, nearly all states have passed them. Such statutes do not, however, eliminate all the problems of establishing responsibility for damages. It can be difficult to assess whether negligence is shared and the correct percentage of blame allotted to each party.

Marketing Tip

As noted earlier, producers must become familiar with the laws of the states within which they operate. This is obvious in the preceding material about contributory and comparative negligence—these two concepts vary by state and might affect the coverages that producers recommend to their clients. Producers who can explain to their clients the differences between contributory and comparative negligence, along with other legal concepts, will have additional sales opportunities.

> **E&O Alert!**
>
> Producers must also remember that they should refer clients to a lawyer for specific answers to legal questions.

Vicarious Liability

Vicarious liability exists when the negligence of one party is imputed to another. Vicarious liability often arises in the context of an agent-principal relationship, which will be discussed later in this assignment.

Vicarious liability can arise from specific statutes defining this relationship. Some states have passed family automobile or family purpose statutes wherein the negligent use of the motor vehicle by a family member is imputed to the head of the household owning that vehicle.

Agency

When the words "agent" and "agency" are used in the following discussion, they are used in the legal sense. Party A (the agent) is acting on behalf of Party P (the principal). Insurance producers do use the word "agent" to correctly describe their legal position with their insurance companies. But unless specifically mentioned, "agent" and "agency" here have the broader meaning.

A relationship of **agency** exists when one party represents or acts for another as directed. One party, the **principal**, delegates responsibilities to another, the **agent**, who acts under the direct orders of the principal. An employer-employee relationship is one example of agency. Partners and independent contractors can also have agency relationships with other partners and subcontractors.

Scope of Agency

The relationship between an agent and the principal is usually limited to the authority given to the agent by the principal. An agency relationship does not make the principal responsible for all acts of the agent. Only those acts undertaken within the scope and intent of the agreement would be involved.

An agency situation is usually established for a specific purpose. For example, a person agrees to represent an insurance company in marketing its products. A real estate agent agrees to act for a homeowner for the express purpose of selling the property. The principal is not involved in other aspects of the agent's activities and is not responsible for these other activities. An insurance company, for example, would not be liable for the negligent operation of a speedboat that one of its agents operated as a hobby.

I. Tort Law
II. Agency
   A. Scope of Agency
   B. Agency in Property-Liability Insurance

Dual Agency

An agent should not act against the interests of the principal. This requirement suggests that an agent should not represent another party within the scope of that agency. It is difficult for an agent to act with faithfulness when representing two adverse parties. The agent is obligated to act with loyalty, in the best interest of the principal. This cannot be accomplished when what the agent would do for Principal X could be detrimental to Principal Y.

The agent can, however, act for both parties in a transaction when each has the full facts of this representation and when such representation does not conflict with the interests of either party. To maintain a **dual agency** role requires full disclosure and a situation in which the agent can maximize the advantage to both parties.

Agency Formation

The creation of an agency relationship is normally deliberate and written. An expressed agency agreement usually outlines the duties and responsibilities of each party. This is the case with insurance agents.

Such formality is not a requirement. One may agree to be an agent without any consideration. The agreement may be oral. Agency is sometimes created unwittingly. If one sends another to the grocery store to make a purchase, an agency relationship has been formed.

Agency by Appointment

Agency by appointment is the usual method of forming an agency relationship. Party P, the principal, appoints Party A, the agent, to act on Party P's behalf in a particular endeavor, for example, selling insurance, buying property, and so on. There is usually a written agency agreement outlining the duties, responsibilities, limits of authority, and area of endeavor. Consent is a necessity. The agency relationship is formed by choice, and the agent must agree to the arrangement. Even when one party goes to the store for another party, the agent has agreed to the appointment. The first party realizes and tacitly agrees that the act of going to the store is an act done on behalf of the other.

Agency by Estoppel

The law can impose an agency relationship in some cases even though the parties do not consent to it. Suppose someone acted to suggest or imply that an agency existed, and a third party relied on these acts to his detriment. For example, a principal has business cards printed indicating that some well-known person was acting as his or her agent. If a third party acted on that knowledge, the principal would be estopped (prevented) from denying the agency relationship. **Agency by estoppel** protects third parties from harm when a principal creates the appearance of an agency relationship.

Agency by Ratification

If someone represents himself or herself as the agent of another party, that party can deny that a relationship exists and refuse to confirm any relationship or transaction. If that party ratifies or confirms the transaction, however, an agency has been established. **Agency by ratification** affirms that agency has in fact existed and accepts the previous acts as the acts of an agent on behalf of a principal. Normally, ratification would be effective back to the date of the original transaction that implied agency.

Authority of Agents

The scope of an agent's authority may be actual or apparent. Actual authority may be express or implied.

Express Authority

An agent's **express authority** is whatever is agreed to (usually in writing) by the agent and principal. Most property-liability insurance producers have authority, within expressed limits, to make or to modify contracts of insurance and to perform all other activities necessary to insurance production.

Implied Authority

No agency contract can account for every possible contingency. So the agreement between agency and principal stipulated in the agency contract is broadened by law and by custom to include other acts deemed necessary to carry out the agent's express authority. An agent should be able to believe that any actions that are in accord with accepted custom are implied to be within the scope of authority granted. This authority is known as **implied authority**.

Implied authority can also arise from the principal's conduct, which could be construed by the agent as the principal intending to confer such authority. To illustrate, suppose Agent A has for years bound property exposures without any limitation on value and with no objections from the insurance company. Agent A has, by implication, the right to continue to do so until some expression from the company alters this situation.

Apparent Authority

Few members of the public know the extent of the express and implied authority that exists in relationships between agents and their principals. How many policyholders have seen the agency contract in force between a producer and the insurance company? In general, the public can usually depend on the law to correct any harm created by defects in agency authority when the principal creates the appearance that the agency is operated according to the accepted customs and traditions of that business. For example, when an insurer directs a customer to a producer who sits in front of the customer, fills out an application, requests the customer's signature in three places, and asks for and receives a check for the initial premium, the customer can reasonably assume that the coverage has been placed into effect, even if the producer did not have binding authority from the insurer. In the event of a claim, the customer would expect coverage on the basis of **apparent authority** because it appeared to the customer that the agent had the authority to bind coverage.

I. Tort Law
II. Agency
   A. Scope of Agency
   B. Agency in Property-Liability Insurance

Yet third parties cannot always depend on appearances created by the agent. The public must act as reasonable and prudent persons would when acquainted with the customs and nature of the business, being on guard to note situations that are special or unusual. When a producer acts in a way that causes doubt about his or her relationship to an insurer, the third party has the duty to ascertain the extent of the agent's authority by a direct inquiry to the insurer. The insurer can then either deny or ratify the agent's actions.

Duties in Agency Relationships

Along with the powers and authority of agency come the duties and liabilities that are either imposed by the agreement or implied by law. Agency is a relationship involving a high degree of trust. There must be confidence that this trust will not be betrayed.

Because of the importance of trust in an agency relationship, the courts must be certain that the agent does not take advantage of the agency relationship. To do so, the law imposes a higher standard of conduct on the agent than would be expected in usual business dealings.

This special relationship requires the following of the agent:

- Loyalty
- Obedience
- Reasonable care
- Accounting
- Relaying information

Breach of these duties is a breach of the implied terms of the agreement, and any violation of these duties by the agent can terminate the agency agreement, can cause potential liability for damages, or both.

Termination of Agency

The agency relationship between an agent and a principal can be terminated in several ways:

- Lapse of time
- Accomplishment of purpose
- Revocation or renunciation
- Death or loss of capacity
- Impossibility or changed circumstances

Lapse of Time

An agency agreement is often in effect for a specific period of time. When this period expires, the agency relationship is dissolved. When no time limit is specified, a "reasonable" time, which may be indefinite, applies.

Accomplishment of Purpose

If the agent's responsibility is to perform a specific task, then the relationship is finished when the task has been accomplished. Agency exists between a real estate agent and the homeowner when a contract is signed to have the real estate agent represent the owner in the sale of property. When the property is sold and all aspects of the sale are completed, the agency relationship is ended.

Revocation or Renunciation

The principal can revoke the relationship at any time by any act that indicates that the agent can no longer exercise authority. The agent must be notified. Improper termination can be a cause for action by the agent against the principal for damages, but this does not mitigate the principal's power to end the agency relationship.

The agent can terminate the agreement through "renunciation of authority." Although this can be a breach of contract that exposes the agent to damages, it does not alter the power of the agent to terminate the agreement.

The ability to revoke or renounce the agency relationship demonstrates the importance of the distinction between the *power* to terminate and the *right* to do so. By its nature, the operation of an agency relationship requires open, honest, and effective cooperation between two parties. So even though one party has the *power* to terminate, courts may allow damages for improper use of that power.

Death or Loss of Capacity

The death of either party automatically terminates the agreement. Since death is a matter of public record, there need be no special notice to the agent or to the public. An exception to this rule lies in the necessity for banks to accept and process checks and deposits until notified. Checks drawn before death and monies collected before death can still be processed after death until the financial institution receives notification. This allows the ordinary processes of commerce to continue in an orderly fashion.

Impossibility or Changed Circumstances

When the subject for which the agency was formed no longer exists, the agency no longer exists. An agreement with a real estate agent to sell a home is no longer valid when the residence has been destroyed by fire.

Changed circumstances similarly terminate the agency. If an agent is appointed to sell the oil from an exploratory well, that relationship ends if the drilling shows that there is a dry hole.

Bankruptcy of the principal is another changed circumstance that would terminate the authority of the agent because all the principal's assets would come under the jurisdiction of the bankruptcy court.

A change of law could terminate agency if the substance or activity that is the basis of agency is no longer legal. A county that voted itself "dry" would have the effect of terminating an agency agreement involving the sale of alcoholic beverages in that area.

- I. Tort Law
- II. Agency
  - A. Scope of Agency
  - B. Agency in Property-Liability Insurance
  - C. Duties of Insurance Agents
  - D. Insurance Professionals
- III. Law of Contracts

Agency in Property-Liability Insurance

Many of the marketing personnel in the insurance field are referred to as agents. These persons typically represent the insurer in dealings with the insurance-buying public. The scope of their authority and the duties they are obligated to perform can vary greatly. The terms discussed below are widely used in the insurance field.

General Agent

General agents have authority within limits established by the agency agreement and common law to make and to modify contracts of insurance. A **general agent** solicits, accepts, and forwards applications; agrees to terms; and executes and delivers insurance policies. This agent has broad powers to represent the insurance company in a given area and for a specific line or lines of insurance.

Solicitors or Soliciting Agents

The authority of **solicitors** is normally more limited than that of general agents. They are usually confined to soliciting applications for insurance from the insurance-buying public.

Many specific statutes and state insurance department regulations cover the licensing and the authority of solicitors. If solicitors are permitted by law, they are usually considered agents of the producer rather than the insurer. Some statutes do make the solicitor a representative of the insurer in the event of a dispute between the insured and the company. The important fact is that a solicitor has less authority and fewer powers than an agent. Solicitors do not normally have the authority to do the things an agent would do, such as extend time for payments or modify or waive any other aspects of the insurance transaction.

Brokers

The word "broker" is a generic term for an agent. It is used in many states to indicate any agent who represents a number of different companies. In the strictest use of the term, however, a broker is a person who secures insurance for another party and who is the agent of that party in the transaction, not the agent of the insurer. Because of the discrepancy in the meaning of the term and in the role of the broker, a great many legal problems can arise. Consequently, statutes often specify the duties and responsibilities of brokers.

The laws of agency presume that the principal knows what the agent knows. The receipt of a premium payment by an agent is the same as the receipt of a premium payment by the principal. The broker is defined as the insured's agent, so payment to the broker would not be considered payment to the insurer. Because of the discrepancy about the function of a broker vis-à-vis the insured and the insurer, statutes have been passed to define the broker as the insured's agent except for purposes of collecting the premium, in which case the broker is considered to be the insurer's agent. So when the broker is paid, the insurer is normally considered as having received the money. These statutes permit the public to be sure that payment to the insurance broker is payment to the insurer. The broker, therefore, is the insured's agent for some aspects of the insurance transaction and the insurance company's agent for other aspects of the transaction.

Duties of Insurance Agents

Insurance agents owe their insurance companies the same duties that other agents owe their principals, specifically loyalty, obedience, reasonable care, accounting, and relaying of information. However, an insurance agent really represents both parties to the insurance transaction and is thus a dual agent.

The agent's primary allegiance is to the insurance company. All information material to the transaction must be transmitted to the insurer, all monies must be accounted for, and in every way the agent must be the faithful servant of the company. To the insured, the agent owes reasonable services and accurate information in securing the appropriate contracts at an appropriate price. The agent owes the insured his or her expertise.

Insurance Professionals

Insurance agents view themselves as professionals because their work requires competent performance and high standards of ethical conduct, education, training, and experience. But there are differing levels of professionalism, and certain terms carry different connotations of professionalism. The term "insurance consultant" implies a higher standard of professionalism than do the terms "insurance agent" and "insurance broker."

Because producers represent themselves as professionals, the standard of care against which they will be measured is higher than it would be if they did not consider themselves professionals. This higher standard of care can, consequently, subject insurance professionals to E&O claims for failing to meet that standard.

> **Check** your understanding of the *Key Words and Phrases* found in the first part of this assignment.

Legal wrong (p. 4)

Criminal wrong (p. 4)

Civil wrong (p. 4)

Common law (p. 5)

Statutory law (p. 5)

Tort (p. 5)

Compensatory damages (p. 7)

Nominal damages (p. 7)

Punitive damages (p. 7)

Injunction (p. 7)

Restitution (p. 7)

Battery (p. 7)

Assault (p. 7)

False imprisonment (p. 7)

Trespass (p. 8)

Defamation (p. 9)

Invasion of privacy (p. 9)

Strict liability/absolute liability (p. 10)

Negligence (p. 11)

Proximate cause (p. 12)

Trespassers (p. 13)

Attractive nuisance (p. 14)

Licensees (p. 14)

Invitee (p. 15)

Contributory negligence (p. 16)

Comparative negligence (p. 16)

Vicarious liability (p. 17)

Agency (p. 17)

Principal (p. 17)

Agent (p. 17)

Dual agency (p. 18)

Agency by appointment (p. 18)

Agency by estoppel (p. 18)

Agency by ratification (pp. 18-19)

Express authority (p. 19)

Implied authority (p. 19)

Apparent authority (p. 19)

General agent (p. 22)

Solicitors (p. 22)

Review the concepts presented in the first part of this assignment by answering the following questions. **Note: Acceptable answers to all questions appear at the end of this segment.**

1. How does a tort differ from a criminal wrong? (pp. 4-5)

2. How did common law develop? (p. 5)

3. What are the essential elements of the tort of negligence? (pp. 5-6)

4. Explain the three kinds of legal remedies that can be granted by the courts in tort cases. (pp. 6-7)

5. Explain the three kinds of monetary damages that can be granted by the courts in tort cases. (p. 7)

6. What are the violations of rights for which tort law provides a remedy? (pp. 7-9)

7. How does assault differ from battery? (p. 7)

8. Why have some activities been singled out for the application of strict or absolute liability? (pp. 10-11)

9. What are the common-law characteristics of a negligent act? (p. 11)

10. What conditions must be present for a tort right of action to exist? (p. 12)

11. Explain the duties a landowner owes to each of the following:
    (a) trespassers (pp. 13-14)

    (b) licensees (p. 14)

    (c) invitees (p. 15)

12. How does the attractive nuisance doctrine affect the liability of a landowner to a trespasser? (p. 14)

13. How are comparative negligence and contributory negligence different? (p. 16)

14. How may an agency-principal relationship be created? (pp. 18-19)

15. Under what circumstances might a principal be bound by the acts of an agent, even though the acts were not committed within the express authority granted to the agent? (p. 19)

16. What are the duties that an agent owes to the principal? (p. 20)

17. How may an agency relationship be terminated? (pp. 20-21)

18. How does the legal position of an insurance broker differ from that of an insurance agent? (pp. 22-23)

19. How might the liability exposure of an insurance producer be affected by being viewed as a professional? (p. 23)

Apply the concepts presented in the first part of this assignment by answering the following questions.

1. John is driving his car east on Main Boulevard at a speed of 35 miles per hour, the speed limit for the area. Elizabeth is driving her car south on First Avenue at a speed of 55 miles per hour, 20 miles per hour in excess of the speed limit. John fails to stop for the stop sign at the intersection, and the two cars collide in the intersection. Skid marks indicate that Elizabeth could have stopped in time to avoid the accident if she had been traveling within the speed limit.

    (a) What legal doctrines may be called upon to determine the liabilities of John and Elizabeth to each other?

    (b) Which necessary elements of a tort action are present in this situation?

2. Frank is an agent for the Quaking Casualty Company. Frank's agency agreement with this insurer specifically states that he does not have binding authority for automobile insurance. Brenda, who had no knowledge of the terms of Frank's agency contract, called Frank to order insurance on a new

automobile, the first she had ever owned. Frank told her that coverage was bound, that it was effective immediately, and that the policy would be issued by the Quaking Casualty Company. Brenda was involved in a serious accident in her new car within an hour after her conversation with Frank and was held liable for serious injuries to several persons.

(a) Will Quaking Casualty Company be required to provide protection for Brenda? Justify your answer.

(b) Explain the legal doctrines that will determine Frank's liability or lack of liability to (1) Brenda and (2) Quaking Casualty Company.

3. Professional Insurance Brokers, Inc., advertises extensively in local newspapers and magazines. Its advertisements stress "the professional risk management skills" of its officers and producers. What effect, if any, are the advertisements likely to have on the firm's liability for errors in the design and execution of its clients' insurance programs? Explain.

4. Professionals in many fields purchase malpractice or errors and omissions coverage. Why should such coverage be designed to protect professionals for both unintentional torts and breach of contract?

5. Bob owns a large corner building lot in a well-developed residential neighborhood. He has had the foundation excavation begun, but the construction had to stop because of cold weather. The hole is not protected by fencing, nor is there a sign warning of it. What responsibility, if any, does Bob have to each of the following persons while on his land? Explain your answer.

(a) A building inspector for the local municipality

(b) A six-year-old taking a shortcut home from school

(c) Several teenagers who meet there to smoke

(d) The contractor who is building his house

Read the definitions of the *Key Words and Phrases* that follow. Being familiar with these important words will help you better understand the second part of this assignment.

Competent parties	The parties involved must be legally capable of entering into a contract
Conditional contract	A contract that depends on an uncertain condition or event
Contract of adhesion	A contract in which one party has no bargaining power and must adhere to the agreement as written
Utmost good faith	An obligation to deal in complete honesty
Concealment	When the applicant hides material facts that would have led the insurer to refuse to enter into the contract
Warranty	A fact regarding the subject of a contract that is guaranteed to be true
Representation	A statement by one party that is true to the best knowledge of that party
Misrepresentation	A false statement of a material fact
Actual cash value	Replacement cost less depreciation
Apportionment clause	A clause that limits the company's liability to the same proportion of the total loss which that company's coverage bears to the total coverage on the property

Study the second part of this assignment, which includes the following sections:

III. Law of Contracts
IV. Insurance Policy Construction and Analysis

Law of Contracts

Both business and personal activities involve contracts. The insurance agent-insurance company agreement and the insurance policy itself are good examples of contracts that are part of the transactions of insurance.

Certain common-law concepts as well as specific statutes relate to contracts. Contracts can be defined as agreements enforceable by law or as promises for which the law provides a remedy for breach. This section explains the elements of any contract and the unique aspects of insurance contracts.

Elements of a Contract

Four elements are required for a valid contract:

1. Agreement
2. Competent parties
3. Consideration
4. Legal purpose

Agreement

An agreement has two components: an offer and an acceptance. One party (the offeror) must make an offer, and another party (the offeree) must accept it. An offer must include (1) an expression of the intent to make a contract, (2) sufficiently definite terms, and (3) communication of these terms to the one receiving the offer. Vague promises such as to "take care of my employees" or "for a few days" are terms too indefinite to be part of most offers. An acceptance includes the counterparts to the three elements of the offer. All acceptances must (1) be made by the person to whom the offer was made, (2) be unconditional and unequivocal (sufficiently definite terms), and (3) be communicated to the offeror. If these three requirements are not met, there is no acceptance. The offeree can counteroffer, which can lead to further counteroffers, until one party makes an offer accepted by the other.

The agreement between the parties must not be affected by fraud, duress, concealment, or mistake.

Many contracts are oral and are performed without recourse to the courts for enforcement of their provisions. When the existence of an oral contract can be demonstrated (perhaps an oral agreement by two parties made in front of competent, disinterested parties), courts find no difficulty in enforcing it if they must be involved.

However, the existence of some oral contracts can be difficult to prove. A witness might falsely state that a contract was made, and if detrimental to one of the party's interests, the alleged contract should be disallowed.

Because of problems associated with oral contracts, all states have enacted Statutes of Frauds, which provide that contracts that are particularly susceptible to perjury must be in writing. The following are six of the most common situations that require contracts to be written:

1. The sale of land
2. Agreements that cannot be performed within one year
3. Promises to answer for the debts of another
4. Promises made in consideration of marriage

II. Agency
III. Law of Contracts
   A. Elements of a Contract
   B. Unique Aspects of Insurance Contracts

5. Promises made by executors of decedents' estates to pay debts of the estate from the executors' own funds
6. The sale of personal property in which the sale price is $500 or more

Because such agreements must be in writing, fraud, duress, concealment, or mistakes are less likely to be involved. Such requirements can restrict what people can do regarding contracts, but they inevitably improve commerce between parties. Parties cannot use the courts to enforce oral agreements on the above subjects.

Generally, the insurance agent is not considered to be making an offer of insurance protection but rather to be soliciting offers for insurance from prospective purchasers. The completed application is considered an offer by the applicant. Issuance of an insurance policy in conformance with the application is considered acceptance. If the policy written is materially different from what was called for on the application, then the policy becomes a counteroffer subject to acceptance by the applicant.

Sometimes, the applicant is considered to be soliciting an offer from the insurance company if no premium or deposit payment accompanies the application. In such cases, the proffered policy is the offer, and the payment of the premium by the client is considered the acceptance.

In property-liability insurance, the client often requires immediate coverage, such as at the time of purchase of real estate. Most property-liability agents have the authority to place coverage in effect immediately so as not to expose the client to a period of time in which there is no insurance coverage on the newly acquired property. The client's request for coverage is sometimes accommodated by the producer's oral statement that the client is covered. It is clear that there is an agreement in such cases. The client's request for immediate coverage is (1) an expression of the intent to make a contract, (2) in definite terms, and (3) communicated to the agent. As such, it meets the requisites of an offer. The agent's oral expression indicating that coverage was granted is made (1) by the person receiving the offer, (2) in definite terms, and (3) to the offeror. As a result of this acceptance, agreement exists, and the first requirement of a contract has been met. This transaction of committing the company to coverage is called "binding of coverage." It may be written or oral, but it is better done in writing to prevent misunderstandings.

In most life and health situations, the agents *do not* have authority to bind coverage. In most cases, agreement is not made until an application has been presented to the company and acted upon—that is, a policy is issued, it is delivered to the client, and the premium is received. Only at this point are the requirements of offer and acceptance met.

Marketing Tip

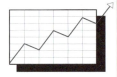

Given the many difficulties that can arise concerning whether a contract of insurance is in force, the agent must be especially careful to create an actual agreement between the parties. This suggests written rather than oral communications whenever possible. It also suggests that either premiums should be collected at the time of the transaction or definite arrangements for financing should be made. A copy of the ACORD binder form meeting the written requirement appears in Exhibit 2-3.

E&O Alert!

Written binders are also a good way to prevent errors and omissions claims. It is difficult to dispute coverage terms and limits if there is written documentation.

If a contract of insurance is in written form, it will be considered as the entire contract. It is reasonable to limit the terms of a contract to those expressed in it and not permit the allegation that additional agreements exist that could modify the written contract. A concept known as the "parol evidence rule" prevents introducing oral evidence to contradict or interpret final written contract terms. Thus, statements made by the producer before or at the time the written insurance contract is agreed to are not normally permitted by the courts to vary the written agreement. *Existing* written contracts can be modified orally.

Competent Parties

The second element essential to a contract is that the parties involved must be competent. The term **competent parties** refers to parties' legal capability or capacity to contract. Those who do not have this capability are considered incompetent.

Incompetency to contract may result if a party is (1) underage, (2) insane, (3) under the influence of alcohol or drugs, or (4) an artificial entity (a corporation) that lacks the authority to enter into certain contracts.

Generally, the law protects incompetents, who are often unable to protect themselves from exploitation, by giving them the chance to disaffirm contracts entered into while incompetent. At the same time, an objective of the legal system is to enforce legal agreements and to protect the validity of contracts and other legitimate transactions.

Underage Persons (Minors)

In most states, one reaches majority (and therefore gains the capacity to enter into contracts freely) at the age of eighteen. The law protects minors from themselves in part by permitting them to contract only for items and services "necessary" to their daily lives.

Many statutes have been passed creating exceptions to the common-law doctrine of majority. The Twenty-Sixth Amendment to the United States Constitution, which lowered the voting age to eighteen, served as a great impetus in this direction. These statutes created "majority" at different ages for different purposes. At eighteen, one could be old enough to vote but not to buy liquor.

Exhibit 2-3
ACORD Insurance Binder

©Copyright ACORD, 1993; used with permission.

The common-law concept that permits contract enforcement with a minor for those things "necessary" is in the public interest, for minors must be able to exist and thrive. "Necessaries" or "necessities" include items and services relating to the health, education, work, and comfort of the minor, and minors are liable for the reasonable value of these necessities. The requirement that the minor pay for the reasonable value of the necessary goods and/or services reflects the common-law concept that the laws of minority should be used as a "shield" to protect them rather than a "sword" to injure someone else.

Any contract for nonnecessities that involves a minor is voidable by the minor. Generally, a minor can assert minority as a defense against liability in contracts that do not involve the purchase of necessities. A minor can avoid a contract for nonnecessities at any time during minority or within a "reasonable time" after reaching majority. Such a contract is not "void" but "voidable" by the minor. A void contract can be said to "never have existed." A "voidable" contract is enforceable at the option of the minor. A minor has been held not liable under contracts of fire and life insurance by courts that have considered that contracts of insurance are not necessary. Some jurisdictions, however, have identified an age of majority for the specific purpose of purchasing life insurance. The underlying concept is that it is in the youth's best interest to buy when the rates are low and to encourage the development of the traits of thrift and saving.

Because it is not always easy to know what is necessary for a minor's health and comfort, merchants often require that a minor's legal guardians join in any agreement. Then, should the minor disavow the agreement, the adult, having also agreed, stands obligated to pay. Even in cases when the minor has the cash for a purchase, a prudent business will legitimately require an adult to join the transaction.

In addition to a contract for the necessities of life, minors can enter into, and cannot avoid on the basis of minority, certain other contracts. If a minor has married or has enlisted in the armed services, the contracts will stand. Minors cannot disavow agreements involving the obligations of a bail bond or the duties of child support.

Courts are often involved in contracts with minors. For instance, an insurance company may require the assent of the courts to any settlement offered a minor in an insurance claim. Court approval may reasonably be sought for a contract involving the performance of services by a child, such as a child actor or performer. Such approval makes subsequent disavowal of the contract by the minor a difficult task.

Insane Persons

People can be "adjudicated insane," that is, declared insane by a court of law. Any agreement entered into by such persons is void. More troublesome are contracts that persons attempt to avoid on the grounds that they were mentally incompetent, but not "adjudicated insane," when the contract was made. Contracts that involve such persons are considered voidable and normally remain in effect until actually voided by the insane party. In such cases, the insane person must show that he or she

II. Agency
III. Law of Contracts
   A. Elements of a Contract
   B. Unique Aspects of Insurance Contracts

(1) did not know a contract was being made or (2) did not understand the legal consequences of what was being done. A requirement for voiding the contract is incapacity arising from insanity, idiocy, senility, or some other mental defect. Mere mental weakness or stupidity is not sufficient to avoid a contract.

The competent party, having entered into the agreement, is bound by it until and unless it is voided by the other party. Should the contract be disavowed, the consideration (goods, services, or whatever) given the incompetent party must be returned to the other party. It is sometimes important to provide for an insane person's health and welfare. Contracts for such "necessities" for an insane person are valid. If the agreement is beneficial to the insane person, and the other party is ignorant of this situation, the insane party may not disavow it.

Persons Under the Influence of Alcohol or Drugs

Generally, the use of intoxicants or drugs will not invalidate a contract. Society obligates persons to be bound by their own acts, whether or not such acts were in their own best interests. People should bear the consequences of their folly—foolishness is no reason to escape a legal obligation. For a contract to be voided on the basis of intoxication, the same two conditions are required as for an insane person: that (1) the person was too far under the influence of alcohol or drugs to understand that a contract was being entered into or (2) the consequences of the act were not understood.

Exceptions do exist. If a person were deliberately drugged or made drunk, the party responsible should not be permitted to benefit, and the contract can be voided. Contracts for necessaries for drugged or intoxicated people are valid.

Artificial Entities

Corporations are created by the state and are considered separate entities in the eyes of the law. As a separate entity, a corporation can enter into lawful agreements and can sue, be sued, commit crimes and torts, enter into contracts, and intentionally breach contracts.

Some specifically licensed and controlled corporations are limited in the type of contracts they can make. Banks and insurance companies are good examples of businesses that are subject to such restrictions. For example, a property-liability insurer is not permitted to enter into contracts providing life insurance.

Capacity To Enter Into Insurance Contracts

Given the degree to which individuals, families, and businesses rely on the protection offered by insurance, determining the legal standing of all parties to an insurance contract is important.

Insurance Companies Insurers usually are corporations and can enter into contracts like any other corporation except for the limitations imposed by their charter powers and by insurance regulations. Insurers must normally meet financial requirements and be licensed to do business in the field of insurance in a given jurisdiction. Statutory law and insurance department regulations determine the qualifications necessary to do business.

As with contracts of any corporation, an insurance contract that exceeds or is different from the authority granted to the insurer may still be enforced against the insurer. The regulatory authority can revoke its license, and the other party can proceed to enforce the contract as written. The insurer's wrongdoing is not permitted as a defense in an action on the contract. The contracts of nonadmitted insurers (those not licensed in a given jurisdiction) are enforceable as well.

Marketing Tip

Producers should be keenly aware of the laws affecting admitted and nonadmitted insurers in their marketing area. Whenever possible, business should be placed with admitted carriers to best protect clients, and in some states this is required by law or regulation. Why?. . .

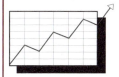

E&O Alert!

. . .Because if a nonadmitted carrier becomes insolvent, the solvency or guaranty fund in the client's state will not be available to pay claims. Also, there are many areas where the state insurance commissioner has jurisdiction over admitted carriers but has little or no authority when dealing with nonadmitted insurers. Where will the client turn for the payment of unfunded or disputed claims? Probably the errors and omissions insurer of the producer who placed the client with the nonadmitted insurer. Avoid these problems by knowing the laws.

Insurance Agents   Because the agent's act is considered the principal's act, the agent does not need contractual capacity. Even a contract entered into by an agent who is a minor, drunk, drugged, or insane cannot later be voided by the insurer so long as the incompetent agent had the ability to carry out instructions. It is the responsibility of the insurance company not to permit such a person to represent it.

Consideration

Consideration is the third essential contract element. Consideration is an exchange of something of value. It is what one person asks another to do in return for a promise. It is the bargained-for exchange.

Consideration can take the following forms:

1. A return promise
2. An act performed
3. A forbearance to act—that is, an agreement not to do something

II. Agency
III. Law of Contracts
   A. Elements of a Contract
   B. Unique Aspects of Insurance Contracts
IV. Insurance Policy Construction and Analysis

Consideration must be something of value. Sometimes one encounters in an agreement statements that are specifically designed to satisfy the requirement that consideration be present: "In consideration of the sum of one dollar, hereby conveyed, and other valuable consideration, I promise to do the following." Such a statement clearly indicates a monetary exchange and alludes to other things of value that are involved in the agreement.

As a consequence of the requirement that consideration be a part of enforceable agreements, promises to make a gift are normally not legally binding because the intended recipient neither makes a return promise nor performs any act that could be deemed consideration. Because no consideration is involved, no legally enforceable agreement exists.

Courts do not get involved in determining the adequacy of the consideration. The last thing the courts wish to do is to get involved in determining the "fairness" of contracts. Given that agreements are entered into freely and that both parties are competent, courts should not interfere relative to the fairness of the exchange. To intervene on one party's behalf would be to the disadvantage of the other. The long-settled rule applies that the courts normally "will leave the parties to a valid contract where it finds them." Exceptions may be made if fraud is suspected, when there is an unequal exchange of identical units, or when the agreement appears unconscionable. That is, courts would become involved only when there appears to be an excessively high or excessively low price for services or goods.

Insurance contracts require the presence of consideration, just like any other contract. The consideration given by the insurance company is its promise to indemnify the insured upon the occurrence of an event insured against. The consideration given by the insured is payment of the premium or the promise to pay the premium at a later date. In property-liability insurance, prepayment of the premium is not required as a condition of the agreement, but the premium does become an obligation as soon as coverage attaches (when the policy is in full force and effect). This implied obligation arises out of the acceptance of the policy even in the absence of an express agreement to pay the premium.

In life insurance, the insurance does not normally take effect until the first full premium is paid. There is, however, no duty on the part of the insured to pay any premium beyond the first one. Policies containing provisions for developing cash values also contain provisions to extend the effect of the policy by using these values to continue the contract in force should the policyowner not do so. Thus, values accrued in the policy can be returned to the owner in the form of an extended period of coverage.

Legal Purpose

The fourth element essential to a contract is legal purpose. Contracts must be consistent with public policy. If the subject of some agreement between two parties is illegal, the law should not be used to enforce the conditions of that agreement. So even though there is an agreement, it is not a contract. It is not an "agreement enforceable by law." Thus, contracts to commit crimes, contracts harmful to the public interest, agreements calling for excessive rates of interest (usury agreements), and wagering agreements are not contracts because such agreements have no legal purpose.

Illegality in insurance contracts is not a serious problem. Certain situations do exist, however, that may void an insurance policy. Public policy requires an insured to have an insurable interest in the life or property insured. This requirement demonstrates that some honest, legal damage can occur to the insured should a loss caused by an insured peril occur. If no such interest exists, the contract is unenforceable. For example, insurance obtained on illegal property is not valid because there can be no insurable interest in illegal property (such as flamethrowers, heroin, and marijuana). In addition, no insurance contract will remain valid if the wrongful conduct of the insured causes the operation of the contract to violate public policy. Thus, arson by an insured would render the contract unenforceable and would preclude recovery under the contract. An insurance contract cannot protect one against the consequences of his or her illegal act.

Form Required by Law for Insurance Contracts

In property-liability insurance, policy form and wording could be required by statute or insurance department rule. In cases in which oral contracts are valid, the law presumes that the agreement follows any required form and wording.

In life and health insurance, no standard form is required, but statutes and insurance department regulations require each policy to contain certain standard provisions. For example, life insurance policies must contain standard wording to treat such situations as suicide, grace periods, and incontestable clauses.

Unique Aspects of Insurance Contracts

All contracts must have an agreement, competent parties, consideration, and a legal purpose. Some must also be in a required form. Insurance contracts have all these elements and also have features that make them unique. These features are discussed below.

Conditional Contracts

Insurance contracts are **conditional contracts**. That is, they depend on an uncertain condition or event. Normally, contracts involving a promise must eventually be fulfilled—the work is eventually done; the event ultimately takes place. In property-liability insurance and in term life insurance, the contingency insured against might never occur. Consequently, performance under the contract might never be required.

Contracts of Adhesion

Many contracts are products of a bargaining procedure that includes an offer, counteroffers, and many changes, until a final agreement is reached. Price, terms, and conditions are all subject to this negotiating process.

II. Agency
III. Law of Contracts
   A. Elements of a Contract
   B. **Unique Aspects of Insurance Contracts**
IV. Insurance Policy Construction and Analysis

This is normally not the case with insurance contracts. There may be options and choices, such as full coverage or a deductible, named perils or "all-risks" coverage. By and large, however, the general form of the contract is fixed. The insured has no opportunity to object to or change, for example, the definition of "who is an insured" in Section I of the personal auto policy. The insured must either take it or leave it. This is especially true for a required form. The insured must *adhere* to the agreement as written, and so it is called a **contract of adhesion**.

This aspect of insurance contracts is important to the insurance-buying public because of the way in which courts view contracts of adhesion. Courts consistently have taken the position that because the insured had nothing to do with the wording of the contract, any inconsistency or ambiguity should be held strictly against the maker of the contract, the insurance company, and strictly in favor of the insured. This presumes that any difficulty in determining the true meaning of the insurance policy has to be the insurer's fault.

Today's trend toward simplifying policies by using readable language makes it likely that the court will reinterpret many provisions, and it may be many years before an insurance company may rely on a certain term to be judged "clear and unambiguous." For example, the courts' inability to agree on the clear meaning of "occurrence" in the general liability forms led to the introduction of both the "claims-made" commercial general liability form and the general aggregate limits provisions (described in subsequent assignments).

Contracts of Utmost Good Faith

Utmost good faith places on the applicant and the insurer the obligation to deal with each other in complete honesty.

Insurance especially requires a complete history and disclosure of all relevant facts between the parties because the very nature of the contract involves a promise, not a product. In addition, claims often involve human actions or failures rather than a defective product. Also, performance of insurance promises often involve people who were not involved in making the product. The beneficiary of a policy must rely on the good faith of the life insurance company. The general public must depend on the insurance company to handle a liability claim fairly. The long-term nature of many insurance policies also increases the need for utmost good faith. Because of those public policy considerations, it is deemed in the public interest to require that the parties to an insurance contract act in utmost good faith.

Concealment

Utmost good faith requires disclosure on the part of the applicant of all material facts relative to the transaction. Many aspects of the transaction involve fact, but failure to disclose all facts is not necessarily important or even required. Only those facts that are *material* to the contract must be disclosed. In the context of a contract, a material fact is an item of information on which someone relies in making a decision to enter into a contract. If an applicant were to conceal material facts that would have led the insurer to refuse to enter into the contract (such as past losses or dangerous hazards), then this **concealment** would make the policy voidable by the insurer.

Warranties and Representations

A **warranty** is a fact regarding the subject of a contract that is expressed or implied to be true. To warrant something is to promise the truth of what is said. A **representation** is a statement by one party that is true to the best knowledge of that party. A fact warranted to be true is guaranteed to be true. A fact represented to be true is not guaranteed to be true.

A **misrepresentation** is a false statement of a material fact made with the knowledge of the person making the statement. Misrepresentation has the same effect as concealment. Whereas *concealment* is silence, misrepresentation is spoken. In both cases, the contract becomes voidable by the other party.

Representations are normally affirmative statements made in connection with the application for insurance and are not normally a part of the contract. It is rare that statements are considered warranties. To do so would place too great a burden on the applicant and lead to contracts being voided to the detriment of an innocent policyholder. Warranties are found chiefly in ocean marine insurance in which, because of the distances involved and the inability of the insurer to inspect the insured object, the insurer must rely on the truth of the statements. The facts of such issues as the seaworthiness of the vessel, the directness of the route taken by the ship, and the legality of the cargo must be warranted. Here, the simple fact of error breaches the warranty and voids coverage. A misrepresentation must be material, false, and made with the intent to deceive to make the contract voidable.

Contracts of Indemnity

To indemnify a person is to restore the person to the same financial position occupied immediately before the loss. To indemnify is to make a person financially "whole" again with neither a profit nor a loss. If the insured suffers a not-paid loss, the insured is not indemnified. If the insured profits by receiving a sum greater than was lost, the insured is not indemnified.

Insurance contracts are meant to be contracts of indemnity, a means through which the injured party is financially compensated for the loss suffered. An insurance company, for example, will not usually go into the marketplace to replace a demolished vehicle with another of the same condition, make, and model. Rather, the insurer will pay a financial amount equal to the value of that vehicle excluding, of course, any deductibles. The concept of indemnity is the very essence of insurance. It is what makes insurance work.

Insurable Interest

To be indemnified, a policyholder must have an insurable interest. This is defined as a relationship between the insured and the event insured against of such a nature that the occurrence of that event will cause

II. Agency
III. Law of Contracts
   A. Elements of a Contract
   B. Unique Aspects of Insurance Contracts
IV. Insurance Policy Construction and Analysis

financial loss to the insured. In other words, the insured must have some right, relationship, or interest in the subject covered by the insurance contract and will be hurt financially if a loss occurs. If the policyholder does not have an insurable interest and therefore will not suffer a financial loss, there cannot be indemnity. The requirement of insurable interest accomplishes three things: (1) it helps to establish the upper limit of a loss, (2) it prevents wagering (moral hazard), and (3) it reduces morale hazard.

The maximum limit of a loss sometimes is the *extent* of the insurable interest. A person owning a one-third share in a building can suffer the loss of only one-third the value of the building if it is destroyed. Although the total loss is suffered by all owners, a part owner can only suffer the loss of his or her share. Thus, the extent of the interest establishes the extent of that person's loss.

If one were to insure a neighbor's house, no real chance for financial loss exists because only the owner would suffer in the event of loss. Thus, buying insurance on a neighbor's house could only be to wager, or gamble, on the chance such a loss would occur. Because the goal in gambling is to win the bet and to make a profit, one could be tempted to cause such a loss, creating a moral hazard. If an insurance company does not offer a policy in situations in which the buyer's only interest is in the profit to be made should the accident happen, fewer losses should occur. Thus, only the owner can legitimately purchase insurance on that property.

Requiring an insurable interest also helps to reduce morale hazard. Morale hazards, such as poor housekeeping and carelessness, arise from the attitudes of the insured and are likely to increase the probability or severity of loss. Because the concept of insurable interest requires a relationship whereby the insured will suffer should a loss occur, the tendency toward such an attitude is lessened.

Actual Cash Value

To be indemnified, one must be able to determine the extent of the loss. What was the value of the property lost? In order to be indemnified, one should collect the actual cash value of the property should it be damaged or destroyed. **Actual cash value** is generally taken to mean the current replacement cost of the property minus depreciation. Depreciation includes any loss of value, whether due to wear and tear, age, obsolescence, or any other cause. The actual cash value of a ten-year-old roof, costing $4,000 to replace, would be $2,000, given an expected useful life of twenty years.

In some situations, value is more difficult to determine. Antiques, for example, often have values that can be measured only after an involved process of appraisal. In some cases, it makes sense for the insured and the insurer to come to a prior agreement as to the value of an object. Those agreements are known as "valued policies." They might be considered an exception to the indemnity concept because value normally changes with time, and the best determination of value would therefore be at the time of the loss, not when the policy was taken out. An insured collecting a predetermined value could actually profit if the true values had gone down by the time of loss or could suffer a loss if values had risen. Conversely, a valued policy can be viewed simply as a pre-agreement as to what sum would constitute true indemnity. Either way, valued policies are commonly used.

Some states have valued policy laws. Such statutes require that in the event of a total loss to real property, the face amount of the contract must be paid. This is to ensure that the policyholder receives the amount of protection for which he or she paid premiums. Such laws would preclude, for example, an insurance company's collecting premiums on a value of $300,000 on a residence, then at a total loss saying its actual cash value was only $150,000. If the insured paid premiums on one value, then a total loss should result in a payment of that value. Insurance companies are generally uncomfortable with such laws because constantly updating appraisals of insured properties is virtually impossible. Many view such a settlement in excess of the actual cash value of the property as a violation of indemnity. Producers in valued policy states must determine values at risk accurately.

Policies that insure for the replacement value of property can also be viewed as violations of indemnity. Indemnification requires that depreciation be taken into account. If the full replacement cost of property is paid in times of rising costs and inflation, the insured has profited to the extent depreciation would have lowered the payment. Replacement cost loss settlements do more than indemnify because they replace old property with new property.

Yet insurers are concerned with policyholders receiving adequate, satisfactory settlements at the time of loss. If depreciation takes too great a share of the value, the settlement is inadequate for the insured to replace the property. Thus, the property owner must find extra funds to obtain comparable property.

Insurers encourage people to insure to value. In this way, insurance companies get a premium that more adequately reflects the risk and values involved. One method to encourage applicants to insure to value has been to insert a clause in homeowners policies that permits the settlement of losses without regard to depreciation if the policyholder is carrying at least 80 percent of the replacement cost of the dwelling. Many insurers also use policy provisions that automatically adjust the amount of insurance to reflect the rising value of property.

Other Insurance

Another policy provision that supports the indemnity principle is the "other insurance" clause. Different provisions apply when other additional insurance is involved on real and personal property. For example, an **apportionment clause** generally works to limit the company's liability to the same proportion of the total loss that company's coverage bears to the total coverage on that property from all insurers, thus allocating loss costs equitably among the insurers. Such provisions prevent multiple payments for the same loss, which would result in the insured's "profiting" from carrying duplicate policies with several insurers.

II. Agency
III. Law of Contracts
   A. Elements of a Contract
   B. Unique Aspects of Insurance Contracts
IV. Insurance Policy Construction and Analysis
   A. Policy Construction
   B. Policy Analysis

Transfer of Rights of Recovery

The typical insurance policy requires the assignment of any rights of recovery the insured may have against a third party to the insurer, to the extent of the insurer's payment to the insured. This helps effect indemnity by preventing the insured from collecting from the insurance company and from a third party. It also provides equity by permitting the insurance company to be reimbursed for any payment it had to make because of the negligence of a third party. Enforcing rights of recovery ultimately results in the responsible party bearing the loss.

Insurance Policy Construction and Analysis

To this point, the purpose of the text has been to establish a foundation of general and insurance contract principles. This section shows how that foundation is built on in the construction of standard insurance policies and how it forms the practical basis for a task the producer will need to perform almost daily: the analysis of coverage provided in a given policy for a specific loss situation.

Policy Construction

Insurance policies consist of five parts:

1. Declarations
2. Insuring agreement
3. Exclusions
4. Conditions and miscellaneous provisions
5. Definitions

Many policies also include endorsements. In many cases, policies do not use those specific section titles. Still, every clause or provision of an insurance contract fits into one of those categories.

Declarations

The declarations appear as a separate form or as the first page of the policy. This section personalizes the policy. Information necessary for any insurance policy includes the name and address of the named insured, the policy inception date, the amount(s) of insurance, and the premium. Other information to be entered varies by type of policy and can include property and its location or other subject of insurance, identification of lender interests such as a mortgagee or lienholder, and deductibles.

The importance of correct information in the declarations is emphasized by a policy condition that appears in many forms:

> **Policy Toolbox**
>
> Declarations: By acceptance of this policy, the named insured agrees that the statements in the declarations are his or her agreements and representations, that this policy is issued in reliance upon the truth of such representations, and that this policy embodies all agreements existing between himself or herself and the company or any of its agents relating to this insurance.

The courts protect an insured should an insurer attempt to apply this condition too narrowly. For example, a minor error in the description of the exposure that does not affect acceptability or the premium charged would not provide a supportable basis for the insurer to deny a claim. The declarations should, however, be completed accurately.

Insuring Agreement

The insuring agreement describes the policy coverage in broad terms. If coverage for an accident or loss is to be included, the basis of payment must be included in the insuring agreement. Generally, the insuring agreement appears immediately after the declarations or at the beginning of the printed provisions of the policy.

Exclusions

Exclusions limit the coverage described in the insuring agreement. Exclusions have been classified in numerous ways, but they all serve one of three purposes: (1) to exclude coverage because a different form of insurance is more appropriate, (2) to exclude coverage because the premium charged does not include the exposure, or (3) to exclude coverage for exposures that are uninsurable.

For example, a business owner may wish to insure against liability for injuries or damage at the business premises. The insuring agreement might broadly state that any liability arising out of the location is covered. Then, the exclusions would eliminate any coverage for injuries to employees (because the insured should have workers compensation insurance for such exposures) or coverage for any automobiles, aircraft, or boats (because those are subjects for auto, aviation, and marine coverages).

As an example of the second purpose of exclusions, the exclusions might provide that no coverage exists for damage to property of others in the insured's care, custody, or control, or for pollution or contamination of the air, earth, or water, or for injury or damage intentionally caused by the insured.

Examples of the third purpose of exclusions include war (because of the catastrophic nature of that exposure) and intentional injury (because that would violate public policy).

III. Law of Contracts
IV. Insurance Policy Construction and Analysis
   A. Policy Construction
   B. Policy Analysis

Conditions and Miscellaneous Provisions

Conditions and miscellaneous provisions usually appear together under the title "Conditions" or "General Provisions." Insurance policies are conditional contracts. The conditions with which the insured must comply, if the insurer is expected to perform, appear in this part of the policy. The insured may be required to give prompt notice of loss to the insurer, to cooperate in various aspects of the claim, to furnish proof of the loss, and to perform or refrain from performing other acts. Other provisions include what have been called "ground rules of the game." Examples of such provisions are how the policy may be canceled, how the policy will apply if other insurance exists, how disputes between insurer and insured will be resolved, and the insurer's rights of recovery against third parties.

Definitions

In many policies, a section entitled "Definitions" is included. Here, words and phrases used throughout the policy are fully defined. Wherever those words and phrases appear, they are printed in boldface type or sometimes in quotation marks to remind the reader that a definition applies.

Endorsements

Today, most insurance policies have endorsements attached. Endorsements modify any of the five basic policy parts.

Marketing Tip

Whenever endorsements are added to a policy, the terms of the endorsements supersede the terms of the policy to which the endorsements are attached. Producers must understand this important concept and explain it to their insureds.

Many insurers file their own forms or endorsements that modify basic policies that are filed by ISO, AAIS, or other such organizations. The purpose of these company-filed endorsements is often to broaden coverage for a marketing advantage, and producers should use their broader coverages to better protect their clients.

E&O Alert!

But coverage restrictions can also apply. If a restricting endorsement were added to a policy (excluding a cause of loss or limiting the dollar amount on certain property, for instance), the insured must be advised that the standard policy language is no longer applicable. Producers should be familiar with the standard policy language of all policies that they sell. Producers must also review each policy sold before delivery to the client to ensure that unanticipated restrictions do not apply.

Assignment 2—Insurance and the Legal System /2-47

Policy Analysis

"Policy analysis" is defined in this text as the process of determining whether and to what extent a specific loss is covered under a specific policy. A method of policy analysis involves posing certain questions in a certain order. One set of questions is used for any "first party" or property contract, another for a "third party" or liability contract. The questions are based on the assumption that there are no peripheral problems such as the insured's failure to comply with policy conditions, the policy's being voidable because of a concealment or misrepresentation by the insured, or the loss occurring at a time not within the policy period.

Throughout AAI 81 and AAI 82, policy language is presented and discussed. All producers must have a strong working knowledge of this language, but memorization of the language is not necessary. Why? The wording will periodically change, and policy language will vary among different insurers, especially in those endorsements mentioned in the Marketing Tip above. The skills that producers should gain from reading and analyzing policies in the AAI program are learning how to use the policy as a tool to design the best coverage program for clients and mastering how to answer their questions. In other words, producers must apply their knowledge of the policy to everyday working needs.

Policy Toolboxes appearing in the insurance assignments of AAI identify the language of the insurance policy being reviewed and provide interpretation and application opportunities. The policy is a contract that must be adhered to by both the insured and the insurer. Producers can use their knowledge of this contract to earn the trust of their clients and the respect of their insurers. The following section presents a series of questions that AAI students should use when studying the policies and when assisting their clients.

The following questions should be asked to determine coverage for a loss situation under a *property* insurance policy:

1. To establish whether *any* coverage is provided:
   a. Was the person or organization that suffered the loss protected under the policy?
   b. Was the damaged property "covered property" at a covered location?
   c. Was the loss caused by a covered peril?
   d. Are the cause and effect free of all exclusionary provisions?

2. If the answer to all of the above questions is yes, ask the following questions to establish the *degree* of coverage:
   a. What valuation basis applies to the property?
   b. Is there other insurance? If so, how does this policy interact with others?
   c. Does a deductible apply?
   d. What is the limit of coverage?

2-48 / Foundations of Insurance Production: Principles of Insurance

The following questions should be asked to make a determination on a loss situation under a *liability* insurance policy:

1. Is the person against whom claim is made an "insured"?
2. Does the insuring agreement apply to what happened?
3. Does an exclusion apply?
4. Is there other insurance? If so, how does this policy interact with others?
5. What is the limit of coverage?

This method is comprehensive but not foolproof. For example, liability insurance is normally written without a deductible, but there *can* be a deductible.

Memorizing this or any other method of policy analysis is not necessary. Rather, it is important to develop a basic understanding of the key issues and the order in which they should be addressed. Producers who have not learned an organized approach to policy analysis will go about it haphazardly. Looking at the questions in reverse order shows the importance of asking the questions in a certain order. Why be concerned over the amount of insurance if the loss is excluded? Why bother even to look at the exclusions if coverage is not basically provided by the insuring agreement?

The successful producer must develop a reasonable degree of expertise in policy analysis. He or she should also be able to respond intelligently to an insured's coverage questions. More important, however, is the process of relating contract provisions to an insured's exposures in order to formulate a sound insurance program. Product knowledge and the ability to use it responsibly and profitably are the emphasis of the remainder of the AAI 81 course and all of AAI 82.

Check your understanding of the *Key Words and Phrases* found in the second part of this assignment.

Competent parties (p. 33)

Conditional contract (p. 39)

Contract of adhesion (p. 40)

Utmost good faith (p. 40)

Concealment (p. 41)

Warranty (p. 41)

Representation (p. 41)

Misrepresentation (p. 41)

Actual cash value (p. 42)

Apportionment clause (p. 43)

> **Review** the concepts presented in the second part of this assignment by answering the following questions.

20. What elements must be present for a valid contract to exist? (p. 31)

21. In the negotiation of property-liability insurance contracts, who usually makes the offer? (p. 32)

22. What is the usual consideration for an insurance contract on the part of (a) the insurance company and (b) the insured? (pp. 37-38)

23. What is the significance of the fact that insurance policies are contracts of adhesion? (pp. 39-40)

24. What is the difference between a warranty and a representation? (p. 41)

25. Which insurance policy provisions reinforce the principle of indemnity? (pp. 41-44)

26. What are the functions of the five parts of an insurance policy: (pp. 44-46)

27. Why are there exclusions in insurance policies? (p. 45)

28. Describe the process of policy analysis for (1) property and (2) liability policies. (pp. 47-48)

Apply the concepts presented in the second part of this assignment by answering the following questions.

6. To quote the judge presiding over a suit in a disputed claim, "The exclusion is vague and ambiguous and therefore unenforceable against the insured."
   (a) What unique aspect of insurance contracts is the judge's decision based on?

   (b) Why does the aspect identified in (a) have such importance to insurance contract disputes?

7. Bill is an agent for Kindling Fire Insurance Company. He submits an application to Kindling for property insurance covering a large building owned by Sam and Jim, Sam's son. Although Bill is aware that Jim has recently been paroled from a prison sentence for arson, he does not inform Kindling of that fact. After the policy is issued, the building is destroyed by a fire of unknown origin. When investigating the claim, Kindling discovers that Jim has a history of arson. Kindling denies the claim on the grounds of concealment, and Sam and Jim sue.
   (a) Should Kindling succeed in its denial of the claim? Explain the legal rules that support your answer.

(b) Would your answer be different if Bill had been a broker? Explain.

(c) If Kindling is required to pay the claim, does it have any right of action against Bill? Explain the legal rules that support your answer.

Summary

The legal foundations of tort law arise from common law as modified by statutes. The essential elements of a tort are a right not to be harmed (or a duty to refrain from causing harm), a violation of the right or duty, damage as a result of the breach of duty, and no justification for the breach of duty. The breach of duty may arise from intentional acts, acts that society considers inherently dangerous, or unintentional acts. Negligence is measured by what a prudent person would have done in a similar situation.

Agency is the relationship created when one party, the agent, agrees to act on behalf of another party, the principal. Agency is created by appointment, estoppel, or ratification. Agents have express, implied, or apparent authority from their principals. Agency may be terminated by lapse of time, accomplishment of purpose, revocation, renunciation, death or loss of capacity, impossibility, or changed circumstances.

The law of contracts requires each contract to have certain elements to be valid. Those elements are agreement, competent parties, consideration, and a legal purpose. Insurance contracts, in addition to the essential elements, have certain unique characteristics. They are conditional contracts, contracts of adhesion, contracts of utmost good faith, and contracts of indemnity.

The assignment concluded with an illustration of how contract principles form the foundation for analyzing policy construction and coverages provided according to the loss situation. Throughout AAI 81 and AAI 82, this method of analysis becomes more meaningful as students learn exactly what is provided by the various kinds of coverages.

Chapter Note

1. Seymour D. Thompson, *Commentaries on the Law of Negligence*, rev. ed. (Indianapolis, IN: Bobbs-Merrill Co., 1901-1914), I.2.

Risk Management and the Producer
Assignment 3

Assignment Objectives

After completing this assignment, you should be able to:

1. Given a case, apply the risk management process and recommend the appropriate techniques to address the specified exposures.

   To achieve the assignment objective listed above, you should be able to do the following:

   a. Contrast the various goals of risk management.
   b. Identify, describe, and give examples of the elements of a loss exposure.
   c. Illustrate each of the steps in risk management and the techniques and methods that may be used in each step.
   d. Explain the techniques of probability useful in risk management.

2. Explain the importance of risk management to insurance selling.

3. Define or describe each of the Key Words and Phrases for this assignment.

Assignment Outline

I. Selling and the Shift to Risk Management
   A. The Risk Manager's Role
   B. Goals of Risk Management
   C. Elements of a Loss Exposure
II. The Risk Management Process
   A. Exposure Identification and Analysis
   B. Formulating Alternatives for Dealing With Each Exposure
   C. Selecting the Apparently Best Technique or Techniques
   D. Implementing the Chosen Techniques
   E. Monitoring Results and Modifying the Program
III. The Wilson Case
IV. Summary

Assignment 3
Risk Management and the Producer

Orient yourself to this assignment by reading the following introduction.

This assignment introduces the subject of risk management to the producer. The intent of the assignment is to show how the producer can use risk management in sales efforts to satisfy clients' needs. All types of organizations as well as families need to treat their loss exposures, and treatment techniques include more than insurance. Keep in mind throughout this assignment that insurance producers must be prepared to provide total risk management services to their clients in addition to selling insurance coverages.

Risk management is a process designed to systematically manage the accidental losses (sometimes referred to as "pure losses" or "pure risks") of an organization. Management of business risks is the role of financial, marketing, sales, and production personnel, as well as general management. Almost everyone on the management team has responsibility for managing business risks through such activities as budgeting, supervising production, and arranging financing. The risk management professional is directly responsible for managing accidental losses and loss exposures, but the entire management team also shares in this job.

Although the risk management process can be quite complex, it need not be. The fundamentals of what is called risk management have been practiced throughout the ages. The citizens of a medieval town who fortified its perimeter with walls were practicing "loss prevention," although they hardly would have thought of their work in those terms.

Only in the last few decades has the process of risk management been studied, classified, and refined. As the practice of risk management has expanded and grown, the difference between pure risks and speculative risks has tended to blur, and the management of accidental losses has broadened to include the management of the adverse effects of any unplanned events that could interfere with an organization's objectives. There is a growing recognition that business risks cannot be totally excluded from risk management because speculative and pure risks are inextricably intertwined. An individual or organization acquiring an asset or undertaking an activity in speculative hope of gain also assumes the pure risks loss associated with that asset or activity.

Risk management is thought of by some as a science, but it is also an art, relying heavily on experience and intuition. Whether those practicing risk management are company executives, individuals planning for themselves, or producers working with clients, the goal is the same: to minimize the effects of exposures to loss. In other words, their goal is to manage loss exposures. For every risk management professional relying on computers to assist with the decision making, there are two, or five, or a hundred who pencil their solutions on the backs of envelopes. Risk management is not just a systems approach for large corporate buyers of insurance. The concepts can be used by smaller firms, political subdivisions, families, and even individuals. When mastered, the risk management approach can be an invaluable needs-based sales technique to assist a producer in doing a better job for the client, the producer, and the insurer. The value of risk management to the producer is that it takes a "needs approach" that places the producer in the position of *working with the client* instead of *selling to the client*.

This assignment will introduce the fundamentals of risk management and will apply those fundamentals to sales. When reference is made to a risk manager or risk management professional, the title should be taken in its broadest meaning to include anyone with risk management responsibility.

Read the definitions of the *Key Words and Phrases* that follow. Being familiar with these important words will help you better understand the first part of this assignment. *Key Words and Phrases* appear in bold in the text when they are defined.

Risk management	A process designed to systematically manage an organization's accidental losses
Insurance management	Involves the purchase of insurance, maintenance of policies, reporting of claims, and so on
Pre-loss goals	Goals to be accomplished before a loss, involving social responsibility, externally imposed goals, reduction of anxiety, and economy
Post-loss goals	Goals to be accomplished after a loss, including social responsibility and financial goals
Elements of a loss exposure	Include items subject to loss, causal forces (perils), and the financial impact of the occurrence
Exposure identification methods	Five methods identify exposures: surveys, flowcharts, financial statements, personal inspections, and loss histories
Flowchart	A graphic representation of a business activity in its basic components as values flow in, are processed and increased in value, and flow out
Probability	The chance of an occurrence or loss

Study the first part of the assignment, which includes the following sections:

I. Selling and the Shift to Risk Management
II. The Risk Management Process

Selling and the Shift to Risk Management

Insurance is often sold on the basis of quoting individual policies instead of through an examination of the client's insurance needs. Competition for an account has often proceeded on the same basis. Imagine a prospect with property and liability exposures and a stack of current insurance policies. If a producer wants to compete for the account, the traditional approach is to pick up the expiration dates and coverages of the stack of insurance policies and develop another stack of more or less similar policies to be offered for a lower price. The problem with that insurance selling approach is that the errors and oversights of the first producer are repeated by the second producer. Coverage could continue to be inadequate or improper, though the producers and insurance companies change. The producer today cannot afford to use such a policy replacement technique. Clients need help in determining what to insure and how much insurance coverage they need. Producers can use the risk management process to determine what clients need to insure and for how much coverage. This section examines the risk manager's role, the objectives of risk management, and the elements of a loss exposure.

The Risk Manager's Role

In a corporate setting, risk management decisions often are made by a full-time risk management professional. Generally, the risk management department is located at the company home office and serves as a staff or advisory department of the controller, treasurer, or personnel manager. The risk manager occasionally reports directly to the president of a company. The location of the risk manager, who could also be called "Director of Risk Management" or "Vice President for Risk Management," is often determined by where the insurance purchasing was done in the company before risk management came into being. But risk management is a broader concept than **insurance management**, which involves only the purchase of insurance, maintenance of the policies, reporting of claims, and so on. Risk management encompasses all of those activities and more. The producer working with a new prospect should always determine who will make the buying decision. In a company with a full-time risk manager, the buying decision will probably be made by that person or by the staff of the risk management department.

3-4 / Foundations of Insurance Production: Principles of Insurance

I. Selling and the Shift to Risk Management
   A. The Risk Manager's Role
   B. Goals of Risk Management
   C. Elements of a Loss Exposure

Typically, only large organizations have risk management professionals on staff. Risk management decisions in smaller organizations are frequently made by an owner, a controller, or a general manager. Those individuals might or might not be aware that they are the *de facto* risk manager for their organizations. In a family, the risk management function is generally performed by the head of the household.

Experienced producers usually find that dealing with a person designated as the risk manager is a pleasure because that person understands the insurance marketplace, knows coverages, and recognizes the importance of what the producer is trying to do. For an inexperienced producer, however, a risk manager can be a nightmare in the same way an experienced trial lawyer can be a formidable adversary to a new attorney. When an organization has no risk manager, one of the responsibilities of the producer is to educate the customer in the concepts of risk management so that the client can make sound risk management decisions.

The risk management process identifies loss exposures (needs) of people and organizations and then offers solutions to those needs. Knowing the risk management process gives the producer the ability to "talk the same language" as a professional risk manager in large organizations and the ability to become a vital part of the management team of smaller organizations—including families. In other words, the producer can act as the risk management professional for smaller clients or can consult with risk management specialists of larger firms. In either role, the producer must understand the goals of the risk management process.

Marketing Tip

The preceding paragraph suggests that a producer can become a part of the small client's team when acting as that client's risk management professional. This is a very important point, and a producer can often become a part of the risk management team with larger clients as well. How will this help to increase sales? Well, as a part of the decision-making team, the producer will be viewed as a problem solver and not just an outsider trying to sell insurance. Prospects and clients will appreciate suggestions for dealing with exposures that do not necessarily require the purchase of insurance, yet insurance is often the best alternative for the exposure. By using the risk management approach to provide clients with the best possible service, producers will increase sales.

E&O Alert!

The advantages gained in becoming a team member come with responsibilities. If a producer fails to identify an exposure or underestimates its severity, the client might hold the producer accountable for uninsured or underinsured consequences. The producer who acts as a risk manager should be aware of this possible outcome. The best way to reduce this E&O exposure is to have the

> client thoroughly review all recommendations and make all decisions regarding insurance, retention, and other suggested risk management techniques. This approach might not prevent an E&O claim from being made, but it should help to minimize the impact of any claim.

Goals of Risk Management

Whether the person responsible for risk management is a corporate officer, the head of a family, an individual, or the producer, certain universal goals can be identified. Each person making risk management decisions selects from among the possible goals to set policy and to mold a risk management program. Often in large firms the goals are set in conjunction with top management and specified in a formal policy statement on risk management. For smaller companies and families, the goals might be the same, but they will rarely be found in writing. Rather, a conversation between the producer and the decision maker will develop some broad guidelines for the risk management program.

The goals of risk management can be divided into two phases. Those to be accomplished before a loss (**pre-loss goals**) constitute the first phase. Those goals to be met after a loss (**post-loss goals**) are the second phase. Goals can conflict with one another as they represent alternatives from among which the risk manager must choose, and there are always tradeoffs to be considered.

Pre-Loss Goals

Pre-loss risk management goals include social responsibility, externally imposed goals, reduction of anxiety, and economy.

Social Responsibility

For a large organization, social responsibility might consist of a commitment to minimize disruption in the community if a major loss occurs. Social responsibility could also be seen in a company's catastrophe plan that places a high value on human safety as opposed to protecting the physical assets of the firm. For a family, the objective of social responsibility could simply be "being good neighbors."

Externally Imposed Goals

Often, demands are made upon an entity by a government agency, by business arrangements, by customers, or by others; and meeting these demands is often a primary goal of a risk management program. For instance, customers might require certificates of products liability insurance from a manufacturer, so arrangements must be made for such certificates even if the products exposure is treated by using risk management devices other than insurance. A banker loaning money to a family for a home or a car requires evidence of suitable insurance before releasing the funds. The laws of each state require that employees be protected by a workers compensation policy or by a suitable program of self-insurance. The nature of the externally imposed goals often play a major role in determining the make-up of the risk management program.

I. Selling and the Shift to Risk Management
   A. The Risk Manager's Role
   B. Goals of Risk Management
   C. Elements of a Loss Exposure

Reduction of Anxiety

The so-called "good night's sleep" is an important pre-loss goal of a risk management program. In fact, a major role of the risk management process is to remove financial uncertainty concerning loss exposures. By removing or minimizing uncertainty about loss exposures, the risk manager can concentrate on business operations or family plans. Each person and each organization have a different level of tolerance for anxiety—a different threshold at which worry sets in. For example, a venture capitalist in a high-technology industry probably has the ability to gamble on certain exposures because such a person is comfortable with speculating on the outcome of a new company or its experimental product. A banker is probably at the other extreme, because his or her career depends on being certain that loans are repaid, and bankers would like to view lending as risk-free. Likewise, the head of a household with five or six dependents living on a moderate income will probably be more conservative about assuming loss exposures than a well-to-do single individual with no family responsibilities.

Larger organizations have the ability to absorb losses without causing anxiety because even if the dollar amounts are sizable, the size of the loss relative to the net worth or gross sales of the organization might be small. There comes a time, however, when a loss would be large enough to hurt. For a low-income family, the loss of $100 might be catastrophic, while for a major manufacturer or financial institution, the loss of hundreds of thousands of dollars might have relatively little importance. Near the break point anxiety sets in because at that stage an entity is destroyed financially. The producer must work to minimize the possibility of the anxiety caused by the threat of such an eventuality.

Economy

The fourth pre-loss goal to be considered is the cost of the risk management program. No matter how concerned a business or family might be about social responsibility, externally imposed goals, or reduction of anxiety, the resources available to fund the risk management program will be a very important consideration. The cost of the program, which includes insurance and expected retained losses, must be kept to a minimum consistent with the other goals. Conflicts among the pre-loss goals necessarily arise from the restrictions imposed by limited financial resources.

Post-Loss Goals

Post-loss risk management goals include, again, social responsibility and meeting the organization's financial goals.

Social Responsibility

This goal is similar to the pre-loss goal of the same name. After a loss, it is still important to consider the community. For instance, a company's post-loss goal might be to keep as many employees on the payroll as possible despite major damage to the office or plant.

Financial Goals

These post-loss goals are stated in terms that apply to business enterprises, but the producer can adapt them so that they apply to organizations that exist other than for profit and to families or individuals.

Financial post-loss goals usually include survival, operational continuity, earnings stability, and sustained growth.

Survival   In the worst loss situation, the minimum financial goal is to continue to exist as a going concern after a loss. In other words, the goal is to avoid the point at which the business must be liquidated. In terms of a family, this goal means avoiding personal bankruptcy.

Operational Continuity   This post-loss financial goal is more difficult to achieve than mere survival. It means the entity will continue to function at a near-normal level despite a loss. Continuing operations as closely as possible to levels that preceded the loss is expensive because it requires back-up resources that, in order to be available following a loss, must be virtually idle before a loss.

One way to achieve operational continuity is to make an agreement to exchange the use of facilities in the event of damage. For example, a bakery might make an agreement with a pizza restaurant to use baking equipment if either firm suffers a loss. That arrangement might be possible when firms are not direct competitors but employ similar technology or processes to make their product. In highly competitive industries, such agreements might not be possible or desirable. For a family, operational continuity means the ability to provide food, clothing, and shelter similar to those the family enjoyed before a loss.

Earnings Stability   Earnings are the difference between revenues and expenses—the profits of a business enterprise. For a business, the earnings stability goal is the intention to maintain earnings following a loss at their level before the loss. Steps such as laying off the work force, reducing or eliminating the purchase of raw materials, and even not consuming energy when a facility is closed for repairs are examples of how expenses could be reduced to minimize or eliminate the effects of a drop in sales. For public corporations, stability of earnings might be critical to the firm's ability to attract capital in the future. For an individual or a family, the goal is to meet extra expenses necessitated by a loss without decreasing the financial resources available to the individual or family before the loss.

Sustained Growth   Sustained growth means continuing any plans for business expansion that were in place at the time of the loss. This is the most difficult and expensive post-loss goal to achieve, but it is possible to accomplish if vast resources are committed in advance to the risk management program.

Conflicts Among Goals

One can see that post-loss financial goals might, by their very nature, conflict with one another because they represent alternative financial goals. Spending money now for back-up facilities, for instance, could

I. **Selling and the Shift to Risk Management**
   A. The Risk Manager's Role
   B. Goals of Risk Management
   C. Elements of a Loss Exposure
II. The Risk Management Process

decrease earnings if the wrong choices are made. Post-loss goals might also conflict with pre-loss goals. Economy of operations is certainly in conflict with the expense of nonproductive back-up resources. It is up to the producer to help to resolve these conflicts in the development of a risk management program.

The pre-loss and post-loss goals are real concerns to full-time risk management professionals but might be academic to the average family. Few individuals make conscious risk management decisions about such things, and it is doubtful that any but a few heads of households or managers of small businesses have ever consciously thought about pre-loss and post-loss goals. Even some larger enterprises have done surprisingly little to plan for losses, let alone a catastrophe. The ideal risk management program is one that has been formulated, tested, and modified over a long period of time and formalized into a risk management manual. Such programs can be very complex, but the producer will rarely encounter such comprehensive risk management planning except in the largest organizations that employ a full-time risk management professional.

Marketing Tip

There is a lack of knowledge about risk management in society at large, and this offers the producer an unparalleled opportunity. Because the concepts are not widely known, the producer who thinks in risk management terms and works with prospects and clients from the risk management point of view will stand out from the crowd. The producer will be more than a salesperson; he or she will be a need satisfier. (Needs, in the risk management context, are loss exposures, the effects of which must be minimized.)

Elements of a Loss Exposure

Each pure loss exposure contains three elements that can be viewed separately. These **elements of a loss exposure** are (1) the items subject to loss, (2) the causal forces (perils), and (3) the financial impact of the occurrence.

Items Subject to Loss

There is no one correct way to categorize "items subject to loss." The general discussion of risk management in this assignment uses the four categories listed below:

1. Physical assets
2. Loss of use of physical assets
3. Legal liabilities
4. Human assets

A loss is a reduction in value, a decrease in income, or an increase in expense.

Physical Assets

Property such as buildings, office equipment, home furnishings, livestock, automobiles, or anything tangible that has exchange value is considered in this category. The list of physical assets is virtually endless, but for the purposes of further illustration, an apartment building is a good example.

Loss of Use of Physical Assets

When a physical asset is damaged or destroyed, its use is impaired, and net income can decline in two ways: revenue can be reduced, or the expense of continuing operation during the period of restoration can be increased above what would have been normal had no damage occurred. In the case of damage to the apartment building, the rental income to the owner might be reduced if tenants move out following a fire. If an attempted burglary makes locking the main entrance impossible, the owner might have to temporarily hire a security guard to protect the premises, and that would increase operating expenses.

Legal Liabilities

These obligations could be benefits due employees under a state workers compensation statute, or they could be the duty under common law not to be negligent. In the case of the apartment building, the owner might have a property manager, and in most states that manager would be an employee within the definitions of a workers compensation law. As such, the manager would be due mandated benefits in the event of a work-related injury. In addition, the owner of the apartment building owes the general public the obligation to operate with a certain degree of care. If—as a result of failure to repair a broken step—an injury occurs, the landlord could be held liable to the injured person for the costs of the injury.

Human Assets

This category, which includes sickness, disability, and premature death, refers to the exposure of the apartment owner and his or her heirs or employees arising from these eventualities. If the owner becomes sick and then dies, there will be medical bills, and there may be taxes to pay because of the value of the apartment building in the owner's estate.

Causal Forces

The forces that cause losses are known as perils or causes of loss. Perils can be grouped into three categories: human, economic, and natural causes.

Human Causes

These are people-related causes of loss. Vandalism or arson, resulting in damage to an apartment building or injuries to the tenants, are examples of human causes of loss.

Economic Causes

Changing economic conditions can cause loss. If a recession results in unusually high unemployment in the area where the apartment building

I. Selling and the Shift to Risk Management
   B. Goals of Risk Management
   C. Elements of a Loss Exposure
II. The Risk Management Process
   A. Exposure Identification and Analysis
   B. Formulating Alternatives for Dealing With Each Exposure

is located, families might move away to find jobs elsewhere, leaving the building empty.

Natural Causes

Earthquake, flood, and other forces of nature could damage or destroy the apartment or injure the tenants.

Financial Impact

The third element in a loss exposure is the financial result of the loss. The item subject to loss is damaged by some cause, and there is a resultant economic or financial impact. In the case of the apartment building, the economic impact of a fire would be the cost of repairs and possibly the loss of rents. If injuries resulted as well as damage to the physical asset, workers compensation benefits might be due the manager, and other economic losses might include court awards in favor of injured tenants.

The Risk Management Process

The risk management professional goes about the task of minimizing loss exposures by first identifying and analyzing those exposures. The second step is to formulate alternatives for dealing with each loss exposure. The third step in the risk management process is to select the apparently best technique or combination of techniques for dealing with each loss exposure. Fourth, the chosen technique or combination of techniques must be implemented. Finally, the results must be monitored and the techniques modified as necessary—in effect, starting the process all over again. Exhibit 3-1 identifies the components of the risk management process that will be discussed in the remainder of this assignment.

Exposure Identification and Analysis

In order to treat a loss exposure, the risk management professional must first identify it. That is why mere replacement of one stack of policies with another is not a needs-based sales approach. The risk management approach attempts to first identify a prospect's needs and then determine the best method or methods to meet those needs.

Methods of Exposure Identification

Risk management professionals are charged with the specific responsibility of exposure identification. The producer is often actively involved in exposure identification even when there is a full-time risk manager. When there is no risk manager, the role of the producer becomes critical because the owner of a small business or the head of a household will rely

Exhibit 3-1
Steps in the Risk Management Process

Identification

Types of exposures	Methods of identification
Physical assets Loss of use of assets Legal liabilities Human assets	Surveys Flowcharts Financial statements Records and documents Personal inspections Loss histories

Analysis

Goals	Significance

Social responsibility
External responsibilities
Reduction in anxiety
Economy
Financial goals
  Survival
  Operating continuity
  Earnings stability
  Sustained growth
	Loss frequency
	Loss severity

Formulating Alternative Techniques

Risk control (To stop or minimize loss)
Exposure avoidance Loss prevention Loss reduction Segregation of loss exposures—separation or duplication Control-type contractual transfer

Risk Financing (To pay for loss)	
Retention	Transfer
Current expensing of loss Unfunded reserve Funded reserve Borrowing Affiliated captive insurer	Financing-type contractual transfer Insurance

Selecting the Apparently Best Technique(s)

Choosing Selection Criteria
Insurance method Minimum expected cost method

Implementing the Chosen Technique(s)

Deciding what should be done
Deciding who should be responsible

Monitoring Results and Modifying the Program

Purpose	Control Process
To ensure proper implementation To identify and adapt to change	Establishing standards of performance Measuring actual performance Evaluating results Modifying program or standards as needed

I. Selling and the Shift to Risk Management

II. **The Risk Management Process**

   A. **Exposure Identification and Analysis**

   B. Formulating Alternatives for Dealing With Each Exposure

on the producer to assist—or to take the lead—in this stage of the risk management process. Both the full-time risk manager and the producer who must act as a risk management professional on behalf of a client can turn to outside experts for assistance. For instance, most fire departments will inspect a location, point out fire hazards, and even recommend corrective action. Police departments often include crime prevention as one of their services. (Attorneys and accountants can be of invaluable assistance, and, of course, there are a multitude of consultants, vendors of safety services, and others, including insurance companies, who through their loss control departments could assist in exposure identification as part of their services in conjunction with providing protection.) Assistance from insurers is, of course, limited to the areas of insurance coverage provided by the insurer—workers compensation, general liability, and so forth.

Five commonly used **exposure identification methods** are (1) surveys, (2) flowcharts, (3) financial statements, (4) personal inspections, and (5) loss histories.

Surveys

Many producers and risk management professionals use checklists, survey forms, and/or questionnaires to systematically search for exposures to loss. Two partial examples of those forms are presented in Exhibit 3-2 and Exhibit 3-3. Insurers providing errors and omissions coverage believe the use of surveys of exposures, combined with a personal inspection by the producer, is the minimum effort owed by the producer to the client.

Exhibit 3-2 is a list of terms tying the "items subject to loss" (Subjects of Insurance) with "causal forces" (Perils) and appropriate insurance contracts. It is deceptively simple. Such an aid to exposure identification is useful only if the complete meaning and full implications of each word are known to the user. Exhibit 3-3 is a "Contents Schedule" from "The Fact Finding Questionnaire for Risk Managers" by Bernard John Daenzer, CPCU, published by Risk and Insurance Management Society. Mr. Daenzer's questionnaire runs over eighty pages and is one of the most detailed survey forms ever published.

Many insurance companies distribute checklists, but for the most part these are geared to *selling insurance* rather than *identifying exposures*. In fact, many insurance checklists are little more than a set of insurance applications designed to develop underwriting data.

Producers should seek out checklists, survey forms, or questionnaires that suit the needs of the clients they solicit and serve, or they should modify forms provided by insurers so that those forms enable them to obtain the needed exposure information. A true survey form is not an application for insurance. Applying for insurance coverage is frequently a major part of the risk management process, but it is one of the last steps in the process and should not be confused with the process of exposure identification.

Exhibit 3-2
Short Checklist for Commercial Accounts

Subjects of Insurance	Perils	Insurance Contracts and Other Considerations
1. LOSS OF PHYSICAL ASSETS		
On Premises	Fire, ECE, V&MM	ACV or Replacement (Functional R/C?)
Off Premises (incl. Foreign)	Sprinkler Leakage	Selling Price/Market Value
In Storage Elsewhere		Stipulated/Agree Amount
In Process Elsewhere		Basis for Property Values (Appraisal?)
		Review method of account (FIFO/LIFO)
In Transit/Mail	Earthquake	Check Items excluded from Property Policy (foundations, landscaping, underground piping and wiring, etc.)
	Earthquake SL	
		What Co-Insurance?
		Does Buyer understand potential Penalty?
Buildings	Flood/Mudslide	DIC "All Risk" Insurance
		Is DIC parallel to basic perils (i.e. covered property BI, ordinance etc.)
	Sewer Backup	Blanket all property exposures—direct and indirect
		HPR Eligible (?)
Equipment	All other Perils ("All Risk")	Joint Loss Clause
Stock		Vacancy Permit Required?
Tenants Improvements	Ordinance Coverage (Demolition/Increased Cost of Construction/ Contingent Liability)	(Check lease for original allowance, requirements to replace TI's)
Installment Sales		Cost of Inventory an Appraisal
Fine Arts	Consequential Damage/Spoilage	Floaters/Marine
Property of Others/Customers/ Employees		Mortgagees & Loss Payees to be named
		Reporting/Non-Reporting of Values
Patterns & Dies	Political Risks abroad	Import/Export Embargo/Expropriation
Plate Glass	Breakage	Lettering, alarm tape, special glass? Measurements
Boilers & Machinery	Breakdown/Explosion	Limit of Insurance; Broad Form, Comprehensive Form; Failure of Power, Consequential Loss; Joint Loss Clause; Expediting expenses
Production Machinery	Increased Cost (Bldg. & Objects). Demo, Contingent	
Computer	Usual direct damage perils	Computerized Production Machinery?
Hardware		Computer Virus
Software	Breakdown	Business Income/Extra expense
Media	Electronic Injury/ Power Surge	Joint Loss Clause
Data	Unauthorized Access	
	Errors & Omissions	

This chart (page 1 of 4) was prepared by and is reproduced with the permission of Stephen Horn II, CPCU, ARM, AAI.

Exhibit 3-3
Contents Schedule

CONTENTS SCHEDULE

Schedule number: _____
Location number: _____
Building number: _____

1. Machinery, equipment, tools, and dies:
   a. Replacement cost new _____
   b. Actual cash value _____
   c. Basis for (b)—obtain appraisal if available _____
   _____
   d. Any mortgage?
   Name _____
   Address _____
   _____

2. Furniture and fixtures, equipment, and supplies:
   a. Replacement cost new _____
   b. Actual cash value _____
   c. Basis for (b)—obtain appraisal if available _____
   _____
   d. Any mortgage?
   Name _____
   Address _____
   _____

3. Improvements and betterments:
   a. Date installed _____
   b. Original cost _____
   c. Replacement cost _____

This schedule (page 1 of 3) was prepared by and is reprinted with the permission of the Risk and Insurance Management Society.

Marketing Tip

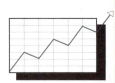

Many producers use checklists of exposures to identify commonly occurring exposures. Those checklists might not, however, keep up with changes in laws and insurance coverage. One example of a recent law that has had a tremendous impact on liability exposures is the Americans with Disability Act (ADA), yet the exposures created by this law are not necessarily identified on the checklists. Producers familiar with the law and the responsibilities it places on employers would, however, identify the new property and liability exposures without the checklists. What is the bottom line? Although checklists might be useful, producers must stay current on laws and their effect on clients' exposures—and a personal inspection is a necessity to identify exposures to loss.

E&O Alert!

Checklists can create E&O problems. As noted above, not every exposure will be identified on a checklist. Even if the checklist is thorough, if it is not completed on a regular basis, new exposures will not be identified. Any mistakes or oversights in completing the lists will further expose the producer to an E&O claim. Producers can use checklists as a risk management tool but not as the only tool, and care should be used to properly identify and address all of a client's exposures.

Flowcharts

A flowchart of an organization's operations often helps a risk manager or producer identify exposures to loss. A **flowchart** is nothing more than a graphic representation of a business activity in its basic components as values flow into the process, are processed and increased in value, and flow out. Flowcharts can be exceedingly complex or relatively simple. Exhibit 3-4 is a simplified flowchart for a winery that grows its own grapes.

Exhibit 3-4
Flowchart for a Winery

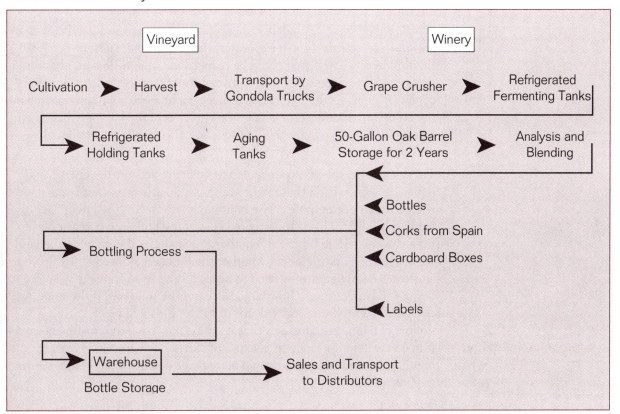

This flowchart was prepared by and is reproduced with the permission of Stephen J. Horn II, CPCU, ARM, AAI.

In this case, the flowchart reveals certain bottlenecks in production. For example, the grape crusher is vitally important because production cannot continue if that single piece of machinery breaks down. The bottling line is another key piece of equipment that could be difficult to

I.	Selling and the Shift to Risk Management
II.	The Risk Management Process
	A. Exposure Identification and Analysis
	B. Formulating Alternatives for Dealing With Each Exposure

replace quickly if damaged or destroyed. This flowchart also illustrates certain exposures beyond the winery's control. For example, suppose the bottle or box manufacturer sustains a loss and is unable to supply the winery. Are alternative suppliers available? The flowchart by itself is useful, but to gain maximum benefit from a flowchart, one must use it in conjunction with other methods of exposure identification.

Financial Statements

Company financial statements can be of assistance in identifying exposures to loss. The entries on those statements can suggest exposures to potential loss, which deserve further analysis through the detailed records underlying the financial statements. The balance sheet, the income statement, and the statement of cash flows are most commonly used.

Although financial statements are useful in identifying exposures, they are only one example of a larger, more general source of information. That more general source encompasses all the records and documents of an organization, not just those expressed in financial terms. Virtually all documents that tell something about the operations of an organization, such as contracts, correspondence, minutes of meetings, and internal memoranda, also tell something about the organization's loss exposures. For instance, analysis of a lease can highlight obligations concerning repair of the property if it is damaged or destroyed.

The Balance Sheet A balance sheet shows the assets and liabilities of an entity. In searching for loss exposures, the risk management professional should identify assets that could be reduced in value by loss and liabilities that could be increased by loss. Either of those changes will reduce the company's net worth. The balance sheet might show a building owned by the company (found in the fixed assets portion of the balance sheet). An amount will be shown for the building and also for the accumulated depreciation.

Those amounts shown on the balance sheet are accounting entries and represent information that might vary significantly from that needed for risk management purposes. The building is shown "on the books" as worth $100,000. This is the original cost of the building. It is not clear from the entry in Exhibit 3-5 whether this includes the value of the land on which the building sits or whether the building alone cost $100,000 to construct. Many questions need to be asked about this one entry before it is known with certainty how large the exposure to loss is. If the building cost $100,000 to build in 1981, for instance, it should be clear that it is no longer a new building and that its value may have diminished because it is slowly deteriorating; or, because of current construction costs, the building replacement value could actually be double or triple that shown as book value.

The balance sheet shows inventory valued at $200,000. Inventory can be valued using one of several accounting alternatives for determining cost. FIFO stands for "first-in, first-out." This method assumes that inventory is sold in the order in which it is purchased or manufactured. LIFO stands for "last-in, first-out," which assumes the opposite—that inventory is sold with the newest items going first and working back to the oldest inven-

Exhibit 3-5
Balance Sheet—The Zepelin Company

Balance Sheet
The Zepelin Company
As of December 31, 19X6

Assets		
Cash	$ 3,000	
Accounts Receivable	50,000	
Inventory	200,000	
Total Current Assets		$253,000
Equipment	$ 10,000	
Building	100,000	
Depreciation on Building	(35,000)	
Total Fixed Assets		75,000
Total Assets		328,000
Liabilities and Owners' Equity		
Accounts Payable	$150,000	
Mortgage Payable	60,000	
Total Liabilities		$210,000
Owners Equity		118,000
Total Liabilities and Owners' Equity		$328,000

tory item. Neither of these accepted accounting methods tells what the inventory will cost to replace at current prices if the whole lot is damaged by a loss. Such a figure could be developed only by projecting what items will cost in the future, and this is clearly not possible with absolute certainty. Some businesses like to plan using estimates based on NIFO, "next-in, first-out," but this is a method not found in the accountants' books and must be developed by extending current costs into the future. NIFO is not an accepted accounting technique but merely a way to express the concerns of risk management to accountants who tend to think in terms of FIFO or LIFO. The balance sheet, then, only indicates that an exposure exists, so the risk manager or producer must quantify that exposure. The producer can also rely on expert advice in valuing assets. Property appraisers can estimate replacement costs, accountants can help with financial projections, and the business owner or the executive in charge of operations can often estimate the size of an exposure.

The balance sheet will rarely show any potential legal liabilities as liabilities. However, should the company lose a lawsuit for $150,000 because a product it manufactured injured a customer, this liability, if uninsured, would reduce the value of the firm.

The Income Statement This financial statement, which is sometimes referred to as the "profit and loss statement," shows revenues and expenses. It identifies exposures that could reduce income or increase expenses.

I. Selling and the Shift to Risk Management
II. The Risk Management Process
   A. Exposure Identification and Analysis
   B. Formulating Alternatives for Dealing With Each Exposure

Exhibit 3-6 shows two sources of revenue: sales, producing $450,000, and rental income, amounting to $12,000. Those figures indicate that exposures exist at the location where sales take place and at the location where some space is apparently rented to others. Certain expenses could increase following a loss, and each existing category of expense must be analyzed to see what effect certain losses would have on each other. Further, other categories of expense that could arise only following the loss should be identified. Such extra costs of staying in business on a temporary basis following a loss might include overtime payroll, equipment rental, and increased costs for materials and supplies.

Exhibit 3-6
Income Statement—The Zepelin Company

Income Statement
THE ZEPELIN COMPANY
Year Ending December 31, 19X6

Income		
Sale of Merchandise	$450,000	
Rental Income	12,000	
Total Income		$462,000
Expenses		
Cost of Merchandise	$225,000	
Payroll	50,000	
Other Expenses	60,000	
Total Expenses		$335,000
Net Income		$127,000

Statement of Cash Flows This financial statement, which is often labeled "Sources and Uses of Funds," tracks cash as it flows into the organization and as it flows out during the year.

Of course, the typical family would not have financial statements to be used for exposure identification in the same way a business does. By taking the information developed from a questionnaire, however, the producer can quickly prepare a rough financial statement. For instance, the producer should consider the answers to questions like, "Do you own your home or any other real estate? If so, what would it cost to rebuild each property if it were to be destroyed? What is the annual rental income from leased property? What would a comparable home cost to rent temporarily if you could not live at home? What would it cost to replace the contents of your home? Does that include items of special economic value like antiques, furs, jewelry, or coin collections? How about automobiles—how many and what kind do you own? What is their current value? Do you own any recreational vehicles, boats, or airplanes? What are the amounts of your investments and other financial holdings?" In a few short minutes, a producer who knows what to look for can develop all of the exposure identification information sufficient to formulate a personal risk management program.

Personal Inspections

No matter how many flowcharts, questionnaires, financial statements, or other records and documents are available, nothing substitutes for personal on-site inspections. Firsthand impressions are much more useful than secondhand information, and the producer should take every opportunity to observe and study different kinds of business operations to develop the exposure identification experience so important to risk management.

Loss Histories

An often important indicator of an organization's future accidental losses is its record of past losses. To the extent that history often repeats itself, the kinds of losses experienced in the past often reoccur in the future. The problem for the producer in relying on loss histories is that they could be incomplete or inaccurate. Further, changes in the organization such as growth or diversification might not be reflected in records of the past.

Marketing Tip

Many insurers have very qualified loss control departments. Exposure identification and analysis done by these experts will improve the service provided by the producer and should also help to improve sales. Producers should know the insurers that offer this service to their clients. Matching the right insurer (with the right services) to the client can be the difference in closing a new sale and retaining existing clients.

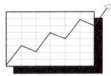

Analysis of Loss Exposures

Many resources are available to the risk manager or producer in loss exposure identification. The need to quantify identified exposures is of equal importance, but this is often quite difficult and requires assistance from experts in various areas. This section of this assignment introduces a framework for analyzing identified exposures.

The producer and risk manager need to know the following facts about each loss exposure:

1. The likelihood of a loss occurring (loss frequency)
2. The seriousness of losses that do occur (loss severity)
3. The potential total dollar losses in any given period of time (frequency times severity)
4. The reliability of the predictions of frequency and severity

Prouty Measures

Richard Prouty, risk manager for a large corporation, described measures of frequency and severity in these simple, nonmathematical terms:

I. Selling and the Shift to Risk Management
II. **The Risk Management Process**
   A. **Exposure Identification and Analysis**
   B. Formulating Alternatives for Dealing With Each Exposure

Categories for frequency of loss:

   Almost Nil—extremely unlikely to happen; virtually no possibility.

   Slight—it could happen, but it has not happened.

   Moderate—it happens once in a while.

   Definite—it happens regularly.

Categories for severity of loss:

   Maximum Possible Loss—the worst that could happen.

   Maximum Probable Loss—the worst that is likely to happen.

   Annual Expected Dollar Loss—the expected average severity times the expected frequency expressed in dollars.

Prouty's classifications are basic and easy to understand. In analyzing any exposure, risk management professionals can use these broad, general categories to estimate and explain the impact of the exposure without resorting to the use of statistical probability. Those categories represent subjective probabilities that can be estimated through reliance on judgment rather than on empirical data. Measuring loss probabilities statistically is also possible.

Statistical Probability

In order to fully understand the risk management process, one should know how statistics can assist in evaluating risk. A complete discussion of the application of statistics to risk management is beyond the scope of this text and is covered in the Associate in Risk Management (ARM) designation program of the Insurance Institute of America. It is crucial, however, that the producer who uses risk management as a sales technique have a general idea of what can be done with statistics. Very precise methods of analysis are available to assist risk management professionals in making reasonably accurate estimates of future losses. Although many of those methods are impractical for smaller entities, a general understanding of them will help the producer discuss risk management with smaller organizations in a meaningful way. The reason for using statistical probability in risk management is to forecast expected losses as accurately as possible.

The risk management professional uses past experiences to estimate future outcomes. Only the largest organizations have enough spread of risk and loss history to have credible statistics developed based on past experience. Most smaller entities, including many families and individuals, do not suffer losses often enough to make meaningful projections of future occurrences, and, in attempting to manage risks for those entities, the producer must rely on statistical averages rather than observed losses.

The chance or **probability** of an occurrence (or, in risk management terms, the "chance of loss") is expressed as a number ranging from 0.0 to 1.0. If an event cannot occur, it has a probability of 0.0; if an event is certain to occur, it has a probability of 1.0. Probability also may be expressed as a percentage ranging from 0 percent to 100 percent. Exhibit 3-7 shows the relationship between Prouty measures and probabilities.

Exhibit 3-7
Probability and Prouty Measures

Probability Alone				
Cannot Happen				Certain To Happen
0.0	.25	.50	.75	1.0 (Or 100%)
Probability Overlaying Prouty's Terms for Frequency				
Almost Nil	Slight	Moderate		Definite
0.0	.25	.50	.75	1.0 (Or 100%)

Probability projections are common in many activities. "The chance of rain is 60 percent today." "The chances of winning the game are 50-50." The formula for computing probability (P) is:

$$P = \frac{\text{Number of times an event takes place}}{\text{Number of times it could have taken place}}$$

Or,

$$P = \frac{\text{Number of events}}{\text{Number of trials}}$$

Or, in risk management terms,

$$P = \frac{\text{Number of losses}}{\text{Number of exposures}}$$

Consider the probabilities of tossing a coin and having it come up "heads." The chances of a coin coming up "heads" equals the number of times "heads" comes up divided by the number of times the coin is tossed. If the coin is tossed 100 times and "heads" comes up forty-five times, the probability of "heads" coming up would be:

$$P = \frac{\text{Number of events (heads)}}{\text{Number of trials (tosses)}}$$

$$P = \frac{45}{100} = 0.45 \text{ or } 45\%$$

The underlying probability of a tossed coin coming up "heads" is 50 percent. "Heads" should come up half the times the coin is tossed and "tails" the other half. What went wrong? The answer is that too few trials (tosses) were observed to develop statistical credibility and to compute the true underlying probabilities of the coin toss. The need for numerous trials is reflected in the law of large numbers. Simply stated, the law of large numbers says, in this case, the more times the coin is tossed, the more likely it is that the results will reflect underlying probabilities. In technical terms, the law of large numbers states:

I. Selling and the Shift to Risk Management

II. **The Risk Management Process**

   A. **Exposure Identification and Analysis**

   B. Formulating Alternatives for Dealing With Each Exposure

As the number of independent trials increases, it becomes more likely that the actual number of trials in which the event occurs will not differ from the expected number of occurrences by more than a specified amount.

In order to approach the 50-50 split expected in the toss of the coin, more trials are required. For example, 1,000 tosses might produce 495 "heads" and 505 "tails." The original experiment produced 45 percent "heads" in 100 tosses. In 1,000 tosses, the experiment produced 49.5 percent "heads." There is less deviation from the expected 50 percent when there are 1,000 tosses than when there are 100 tosses.

For the law of large numbers to work in risk management terms, each exposure to loss must exist independently from the others, which means it is unlikely that two or more units will be affected by a single occurrence. The exposures must also be similar and share the same major characteristics. If the exposures were dissimilar (heterogeneous), it would be like tossing dice and coins.

Additional laws of probability allow a statistician to calculate probabilities either when the exposures are not independent of each other or when they are dissimilar in nature. For instance, a supermarket chain with 3,000 stores might observe that on average three stores burn to the ground each year. This means the probability of future total losses is 3/3,000 per year, or 0.001. That represents 0.1 percent of all stores. If the chain expands to 5,000 stores, it would be reasonable to expect five stores per year to burn. The risk manager might like to know the probability of multiple stores being burned in one occurrence (that is, fires not independent of each other). Statisticians can make that calculation as well as predict the possibilities of stores and warehouses being burned simultaneously.

In sophisticated risk management planning, the goal is to predict with as much certainty as possible what the probabilities of future losses are (both frequency and severity) so as to better analyze the exposures to loss. Calculations based on the past can reliably predict the probabilities of future events *only if everything else remains unchanged*. Social or economic changes, for example, could greatly increase the number of supermarket fires—a slow economy could lead to lower sales, which could lead to reduced maintenance, which could lead to a fire. A change in the type of construction or size of the average store by the chain at new locations could reduce or increase potential fire losses in the future.

When the producer is working with large accounts, risk management support is often available from insurers and from outside consultants as well as from the risk management departments of larger agencies. In the case of smaller commercial accounts, or in the case of personal lines accounts, the producer must rely on common sense and attempt to locate sources for statistical data based on average exposures. For instance, if a producer were to ask Mr. Crown, owner of a local hardware store, what the chances of a fire in his store were, Mr. Crown might answer, "I have been in business for forty years, and I have never had a fire." What Mr. Crown means is if the future is like the past, the probability of loss is zero—a fire cannot happen to him. If the producer introduced Mr. Crown to the Prouty categories for estimating frequency of loss, Mr. Crown could say that chances of a fire at his store were almost nil. The producer could, however, use data from the insurance business or, better still, from a hardware dealers association (better because those statistics would reflect the losses of a similar type of business) to show Mr. Crown that every year *some* hardware stores do burn. Using the average figures for losses and knowing what is being studied, the producer could calculate Mr. Crown's estimated probability of fire *on the average*. Other factors—such as the type of fire protection available to Mr. Crown—would also need to be taken into account. In this example, the point is to get Mr. Crown to recognize that an exposure to loss exists.

The preceding discussion emphasized frequency of loss. If one uses the same techniques, however, it is possible to calculate average severity of loss for a past period. In fact, one can calculate the probabilities for specific ranges of possibilities—for instance—estimating the number of supermarket fires causing $10,000 or more but less than $100,000 in damage. In order for statistical findings to be useful, enough fires must occur for the law of large numbers to have its effect. Catastrophic occurrences are most difficult to predict simply because they happen infrequently. Even so, the producer can use probabilities in a risk management sales presentation. Knowing, for example, how many lawsuits result in judgments or are settled for over $1 million in a particular state could be used to illustrate the impact of a lawsuit being brought against the producer's prospect. The producer could use questions like the following to introduce an important exposure into the sales presentation: "Did you know, Mrs. Rossi, that in this state during the past five years manufacturers like yourself have lost or settled thirty lawsuits of $1 million or more resulting from product-related injuries? That does not sound like many, but suppose one of them had been you?"

Marketing Tip

Statistics can be important in selling insurance. Each producer has a different comfort level with mathematics and should use whatever statistical measures he or she is comfortable with. Prouty measures can be substituted for equations in many cases for those who are uncomfortable with mathematics. High-frequency, low-severity loss exposures might be best treated through noninsurance risk management techniques or through insurance combined with the use of a relatively high deductible. If a prospect can be convinced to use noninsurance techniques and deductibles, it is possible to free more premium dollars for purchasing insurance to treat previously neglected low-frequency, high-severity exposures. In that way, the producer could provide better service while making sales and possibly offering risk management services on a fee basis.

Check your understanding of the *Key Words and Phrases* found in the first part of this assignment.

Risk management (p. 1)

Insurance management (p. 3)

Pre-loss goals (p. 5)

Post-loss goals (p. 5)

Elements of a loss exposure (p. 8)

Exposure identification methods (p. 12)

Flowchart (p. 15)

Probability (p. 20)

Review the concepts presented in the first part of this assignment by answering the following questions. **Note: Acceptable answers to all questions appear at the end of this segment.**

1. How does risk management differ from insurance management? (pp. 3-4)

2. What are the goals of risk management? (pp. 5-7)

Assignment 3—Risk Management and the Producer / 3-25

3. Illustrate the elements of a loss exposure using:

    (a) the commercial auto exposure (p. 9)

    (b) the premature death exposure (p. 9)

4. What are the steps in the risk management process? (p. 10)

5. There are several useful methods for identifying loss exposures, each with its own strengths and weaknesses.

    (a) What are the principal methods for identifying loss exposures? (p. 12)

    (b) What are the advantages and disadvantages of each of the methods described in (a)? (pp. 12-19)

6. (a) Explain the three methods for valuing inventories (LIFO, FIFO, and NIFO). (pp. 16-17)

   (b) How are the valuation methods explained in your answer to (a) relevant, if at all, to the insurable value of business personal property? (p. 17)

7. What information is required to analyze a loss exposure? (p. 19)

8. How do the Prouty measures categorize the following?
   (a) frequency of loss (p. 20)

   (b) severity of loss (p. 20)

> **Applying** the concepts you have learned can be done at the end of the second part of this assignment with a case.

Assignment 3—Risk Management and the Producer

Read the definitions of the *Key Words and Phrases* that follow. Being familiar with these important words will help you better understand the second part of this assignment.

Risk control techniques	Used to reduce the frequency and severity of losses as much as possible with the resources available
Avoidance	A risk control technique that eliminates the chance of a particular loss by either disposing of an existing exposure or by not assuming a new exposure
Loss prevention	A risk control technique that attempts to stop losses from happening
Loss reduction	A risk control technique that attempts to reduce the severity of losses that do occur
Heinrich's "domino theory"	A theory that states an unsafe act began the chain of events that ultimately led to the injury
Haddon's energy release theory	A theory that considers accidents as resulting from mechanical failures
Segregation of loss exposures	A risk control technique to reduce concentrations of value subject to a single accident and make aggregate losses more predictable
Risk financing techniques	When losses cannot be avoided, they must be paid for by either retention or transfer methods
Retention	Absorbing all or part of a loss
Unfunded reserve	Financing technique whereby an account is set up on the balance sheet allocating funds for a retained loss
Funded reserve	Financing technique whereby money is actually on hand in an account to pay for the losses
Affiliated captive insurer	Financing technique to fund losses from a combination of premiums paid by the parent to the captive for an insurance policy, from investment income on those funds, and from reinsurance purchased from other insurers
Hold harmless agreements	An agreement that transfers the financial consequences of a loss from one party to another
Indemnitor	The party receiving the transfer of loss responsibilities
Indemnitee	The party transferring loss responsibilities

Study the second part of this assignment, which includes the following sections:

II. The Risk Management Process (continued)

- I. Selling and the Shift to Risk Management
- II. The Risk Management Process
    - A. Exposure Identification and Analysis
    - B. Formulating Alternatives for Dealing With Each Exposure
    - C. Selecting the Apparently Best Technique or Techniques

Formulating Alternatives for Dealing With Each Exposure

The second step in the risk management process is to formulate the best combination of techniques for dealing with each exposure. The alternatives should be designed to meet the goals of the risk management program. The alternatives available fall into two major categories. The first set of alternatives—risk control techniques—attempts to change this probability of loss for the better. The second set of alternatives—risk financing techniques—provides ways of paying for those losses that inevitably will occur.

Risk Control Techniques

Risk control techniques used to be referred to as "engineering" and were limited in scope. Most insurers and some producers had "loss control" or "risk control" departments staffed by fire protection and/or safety specialists. Fire protection engineers limited their activities to improving physical structures to minimize the possibility of loss. Safety consultants concentrated primarily on the safety of workers to prevent industrial accidents.

Today, insurance companies still employ loss control specialists, but they fill many different roles. Some are generalists who visit insureds' locations and evaluate property, liability, auto, workers compensation, and other exposures. Others are specialists—they focus on only one type of exposure. The size and complexity of the client and the marketing preferences of the insurer often determine which of these two loss control representatives visits the client. In either case, those representatives frequently make recommendations to prevent or minimize losses.

As risk management has developed, the concept of controlling losses has expanded to include a number of alternative techniques for treating losses. The goal of the **risk control techniques** is to reduce the frequency and severity of losses as much as possible with the resources available. The risk control techniques include exposure avoidance, loss prevention, loss reduction, segregation of loss exposures, and certain noninsurance transfers.

Exposure Avoidance

Avoidance eliminates the chance of a particular loss by either disposing of an existing exposure or by not assuming a new exposure. The advantage of avoidance as a risk management technique is that the probability of loss equals zero—there is no doubt or uncertainty. Exposure avoidance, however, has the disadvantage of sometimes being impractical and is often impossible to accomplish. Further, avoiding one exposure often means creating another. For example, a family might decide not to face the exposures inherent in automobile ownership. The family has reached this decision because it believes the chance of damage to the asset (the car itself) is too great for it to take. It also recognizes that the loss of use of the car, should it be damaged, would mean additional costs. Further, the family is unwilling to assume the chance of liability imposed by law, or it cannot afford to comply with the compulsory automobile insurance law in its state. Quite obviously, for this family, automobile ownership should be avoided: the family should sell its car, or if it does not currently own a car, it should not purchase one.

Avoidance of this exposure might pose problems for the family, however. Is there a need for a car for commuting or for other activities? If so, the exposure of automobile ownership will have to be exchanged for the exposures inherent in automobile rental, automobile leasing, or the use of public transportation. The rental or leasing alternatives might be substantially more expensive than automobile ownership. Doing totally without a car would mean traveling by public transportation, hitchhiking, or getting around by bicycle or on foot, and any of these alternatives could prove more hazardous to the family than riding in its own car. In short, exposure avoidance is a desirable technique but often is not a viable alternative.

Loss Prevention

As the name implies, **loss prevention** is an attempt to stop losses from happening. An example of this risk management technique is inspection of elevators to be certain they are in good operating condition. Such routine inspections conducted at regular intervals have been so effective in preventing losses that the probability of elevator mishaps approaches zero. Loss prevention is a frequently used risk management technique because it is very effective. Other examples of loss prevention activities include safety guards on machines, safety apparel, driver safety training programs, and rigid control procedures for the handling of cash or other valuables.

Loss Reduction

The risk control technique of **loss reduction** seeks to lessen the severity of those losses that do occur. Examples of loss reduction devices include automatic sprinklers or other fire suppression devices designed to slow or stop the spread of fire once one starts. Although the probability of a loss occurring is not altered by such equipment, the fire that does occur can be expected to be less severe than would have been the case in the absence of the loss reduction devices.

A second type of loss reduction is "expediting expenses," which are any expenses that speed the repair of damaged property and hence reduce the loss of income an entity might otherwise suffer.

A third example of loss reduction is the rehabilitation of a seriously injured worker. Clearly, the more serious the injury, the more costly the loss to the employer either directly (if the workers compensation exposure is self-insured) or indirectly in the form of increased insurance costs. The loss can be reduced by returning the worker to a productive role in society through vocational rehabilitation. Perhaps the injury was such that the worker could not return to his or her former occupation. Rehabilitation in that case would encompass retraining for another job suited to the disabled worker.

I. Selling and the Shift to Risk Management
II. **The Risk Management Process**
   A. Exposure Identification and Analysis
   B. **Formulating Alternatives for Dealing With Each Exposure**
   C. Selecting the Apparently Best Technique or Techniques

Loss Prevention and Reduction Activities

When loss prevention and reduction activities are undertaken, the risk manager must make several choices. First, the risk manager must decide which approach to loss control is appropriate. Second, the timing of the loss prevention and reduction measures must be determined. Finally, the risk manager must decide how to fund the selected loss control techniques.

Approaches to Loss Prevention and Loss Reduction Two basic approaches to loss control measures formed the foundation of loss control and have been supported over the years. The first theory was conceived by H. W. Heinrich, a safety engineer and a pioneer in the field of industrial safety. After studying industrial accidents, Heinrich concluded that all such losses were the result of unsafe acts of persons: accidents were the fault of people. Heinrich's so-called "**domino theory**" stated that an unsafe act began the chain of events that ultimately led to the injury. It was also Heinrich who first attempted to estimate indirect costs of industrial accidents. His conclusion was that the indirect costs were about four times greater than direct costs. For instance, if a worker were injured, the medical bills resulting from the injury might amount to $1,000, but the indirect costs to the employer resulting from the injury would be about $4,000. Those costs include time taken to care for the injured worker, the time of that person and someone else to visit the doctor or hospital, management time to investigate the accident, lost production time, and so on.

A second and somewhat contradictory theory was developed by Dr. William Haddon, Jr., president of the Insurance Institute for Highway Safety and a safety expert. While Heinrich's theory addresses human behavior, Haddon approaches accidents from the engineering perspective. Haddon's **energy release theory** considers accidents as resulting from mechanical failures. If the driver were unable to avoid an accident by stopping the car, the car was at fault because it released too much energy to be controlled as required. By comparison, Heinrich would attribute such an accident to the driver's unsafe handling of the car.

Those two approaches have been combined effectively by many loss control experts. Not only are machines guarded to prevent excessive releases of energy, but operators are also instructed in their use and are constantly reminded of the need for safety to prevent the domino effect.

Heinrich's and Haddon's traditional theories have more recently been eclipsed by loss control efforts that focus on modifying systems and processes. Scientific progress in ergonometrics coupled with greater management involvement in process safety is further helping loss control efforts to evolve into a more effective science. The Associate in Loss Control Management (ALCM) designation program developed by the Insurance Institute of America has significantly more detailed information about this important segment of the insurance profession. ALCM is recommended for loss control material beyond the scope of the Accredited Adviser in Insurance program.

Timing of Loss Prevention and Loss Reduction Measures   Loss prevention measures must be taken before the loss. Loss reduction measures can be taken before the loss (such as a driver education program), during the loss (such as firefighting), or following the loss (such as worker rehabilitation).

Funding Loss Prevention and Reduction Measures   Most loss prevention and reduction techniques require the expenditure of money. Risk management professionals and producers might meet resistance to loss control programs from top management because of costs. The problem of expense is difficult to resolve, and the cost of each loss control technique must be measured against future benefits. A risk manager with adequate statistical data can project changes in loss costs as a result of a given loss control device and can relate the value of those reduced costs to the expense of the program. Such a quantitative analysis is difficult for smaller organizations, and the decision is generally based on such immediate considerations as reductions in the cost of insurance. The producer can get help from specialists (insurers, larger agencies, or on a consulting basis from independent firms) who can help weigh the factors involved in deciding which loss control measures can be adopted economically.

Segregation of Loss Exposures

Segregation of loss exposures is another loss control alternative that has academic credibility but is difficult to apply in most day-to-day situations. The point of this alternative is to reduce concentrations of value subject to a single accident and hence to make aggregate losses more predictable. Segregation of loss exposures can take one of two forms: separation or duplication. Separation entails the dispersal of a particular activity or asset over several locations, while duplication implies reliance on backups—spares or duplicates used only if primary assets or activities suffer loss. An example of segregation would be to take the contents of one large distribution center and separate them into two or more smaller warehouses not subject to a single loss. In that way, the maximum possible loss is reduced and, if this could be done enough times, the spread of risk would be great enough to develop credible probabilities of future losses. An example of duplication would be the daily backing up of computer data and storing the second copy at a secure location.

Control-Type Contractual Transfers

This risk control alternative attempts to rid the organization of any financial responsibility for a loss. It is different from exposure avoidance, which reduces the probability of loss to zero. In this case, the probability of loss remains the same, but the activity that generates the loss is transferred to another party. An example of this technique would be for a manufacturer to have a particularly hazardous process performed by an outside contractor rather than to perform the process on the premises. Rather than shifting financial responsibility for losses that might result from the process, this alternative allows control of the process itself to actually be transferred to the outside contractor.

- I. Selling and the Shift to Risk Management
- II. **The Risk Management Process**
  - A. Exposure Identification and Analysis
  - B. **Formulating Alternatives for Dealing With Each Exposure**
  - C. Selecting the Apparently Best Technique or Techniques

Risk Financing Techniques

If losses cannot be avoided, they could occur; and if they do occur, they must be paid for. The two major **risk financing techniques** are retention and transfer.

Retention

Retention is absorbing all or part of a loss. Retention is often a last resort, a residual method that must be used when no other option is available. War, for instance, causes losses that often fall into this category. There simply is not another adequate risk management technique for this peril.

Retention works best when losses are not too serious and are fairly predictable (low severity and high frequency). The producer must remember that "too serious" for one organization could be "trivial" for another, and each entity needs to determine when losses can safely be retained. Retention should also be achieved by an active decision—the exposure is retained consciously. Passive retention occurs when an exposure to loss is retained because it was never identified—a very dangerous situation because no plan will exist to deal with the loss should it occur.

Financing Retained Losses The risk management professional has five alternative sources of funds to meet the costs of retained losses: current expenses, unfunded reserves, funded reserves, borrowing, and affiliated captive insurers.

- Current Expensing of Losses   Losses can be paid, just like maintenance expenses, from current income. Many small losses are paid in this way, and it is a simple way to deal with retained losses: pay the bills when they come in. This method has the advantage of requiring no segregated funds or any borrowing. The family or organization must, of course, have the money available for this method to be effective. When an appliance breaks down at home, the owner usually has it repaired and pays the bill. This is an example of a retained loss that has been financed from current income.

- Unfunded Reserve   With the **unfunded reserve** financing technique, an account is set up on the balance sheet of the organization. This account allocates funds for retained losses. A company would actually show a reserve for losses in its financial statements, but no cash or other asset is specifically earmarked for retained losses. In the case of a family, the existence of the unfunded reserve might be recognized but not actually called such. For instance, a family knows it could face a loss if an appliance breaks down, but it also knows it has resources that could be used to pay such a bill—the savings account at the local bank. This technique is not as effective for families as it is for businesses.

- Funded Reserve   This method of paying for retained losses is more certain than either paying out of current income or hoping resources are available to pay for the loss. With a **funded reserve**, money is actually on hand in an account to pay for the losses. The cash has been segregated and is available as needed by withdrawing it from the account. This method requires a great deal of discipline to accumulate the fund and to refrain from spending it on other things if no losses occur. A family with a $500 deductible on its home might set up a savings account and put money into that account each month so that if a loss occurs within its deductible, the cash would be ready. A problem can arise if the loss occurs before adequate funds have been accumulated or if there are multiple losses.

- Borrowing   Retained losses can be paid by borrowing. If current income is insufficient to pay for repairs, and if there is no reserve (funded or unfunded) with which to pay for the loss, cash will have to be raised through borrowing. The problem with this method is that the family or firm that needs to borrow as the result of a loss might be unable to do so because of inadequate credit.

- Affiliated Captive Insurer   One additional method is available to finance retained losses, but it is used only by the largest organizations because of the method's complexity and cost. The technique is to establish an **affiliated captive insurer** to fund retained losses. For the purposes of this assignment, it is sufficient to define this kind of captive as an insurer that is owned entirely by its parent, which is either the only policyholder of the captive or one of a very few policyholders insured by the captive. Numerous business and tax considerations are involved in establishing a captive insurer. The purpose of an affiliated captive is to fund losses, so it is considered a financing technique rather than a transfer technique. That is especially true when the captive's only policyholder is the parent company. The captive funds the losses from a combination of premiums paid by the parent to the captive for an insurance policy, from investment income on those funds, and from reinsurance purchased from other insurers. Setting up an affiliated captive for a client requires special knowledge, and producers unfamiliar with this form of loss financing should seek the help of experts.

Advantages and Disadvantages of Loss Retention   The advantage of retention in risk management is that the ultimate cost to the organization is often reduced. If a windstorm damages a building, the owner can repair it at a cost lower than the cost to transfer the exposure to an insurer or another party. That is true because those assuming the loss (the insurer) must add overhead and profit to the estimated loss costs to establish a price for transfer. For instance, on the average, of every dollar paid to a property and liability insurer, about $0.65 to $0.80 is paid out in losses. The remainder is for expenses and profit for the insurer.

If losses occur as anticipated and are not too severe, retention should reduce the cost of the risk management program. If, however, losses exceed what was thought probable, retention could be more expensive than insurance in the short run. If events go according to plans, the organization should get better cash flow with the use of retention than with the use of transfer because losses are paid for only when they occur, not in advance. However, if losses are excessive and occur early, retention could prove to be more of a drain on cash flow than transfer.

There are also income tax considerations in selecting retention. Other methods of dealing with losses, like loss control or insurance, offer

I. Selling and the Shift to Risk Management
II. **The Risk Management Process**
   A. Exposure Identification and Analysis
   B. **Formulating Alternatives for Dealing With Each Exposure**
   C. Selecting the Apparently Best Technique or Techniques

deductions that reduce the amount of tax that must be paid. Those deductions can often be taken at the time expenses are incurred. With loss retention, however, the deduction can be taken only when losses actually occur. Depending on the timing and severity of losses, retention could increase an organization's taxes.

Another factor that must be weighed when considering retention as an alternative to insurance is that such a decision might mean the loss of insurer services offered in conjunction with insurance protection. Lost services could include loss control support, claims administration, exposure identification, and, in the case of liability losses, the cost of a legal defense.

Risk Transfers

Two kinds of transfers are used to pay for losses. The first is transfer of loss to other entities by a business contract. The second is transfer of loss to an insurer by an insurance contract.

Financing-Type Contractual Transfers Transfers to parties other than insurers are made by a legal contract and are often called **hold harmless agreements**. Hold harmless agreements are also referred to as "indemnity agreements." Those agreements transfer the *financial consequences* of a loss from one party to another. The **indemnitor** (the one receiving the transfer) agrees to hold harmless the **indemnitee** (the one transferring loss responsibilities). As opposed to the control-type transfer discussed earlier, only the financial consequences of the loss are transferred using a written contract wherein another party assumes financial responsibility. For instance, in some premises leases, responsibility for bodily injury and property damage occurring on premises is assumed by the tenant in a hold harmless provision. In such a case, the tenant is the indemnitor, and the landlord is the indemnitee.

Varying degrees of responsibility can be transferred by contract. In some cases, the indemnitor assumes responsibility for only its own negligence. Sometimes the indemnitor will go further and agree to assume responsibility for the negligence of the indemnitee. In even more extreme cases, the indemnitor might assume responsibility for all loss regardless of negligence. In some states, transfer of sole negligence is prohibited in specific situations, such as at construction sites.

E&O Alert!

Producers should exercise extreme caution in reading contractual transfer agreements. Reading an entire contract is important because the responsibilities of concern to the producer or the risk manager might not be clearly labeled and might be found in different sections of the document. The advice of an attorney should always be sought in drafting and interpreting legal contracts.

A hold harmless agreement is *not* avoidance. Avoidance eliminates loss exposures and reduces frequency to zero. The hold harmless agreement merely shifts financial responsibility for a loss exposure. It is also unlike loss control because it does not alter the potential frequency or severity of the exposure.

Advantages and Disadvantages of Contractual Transfer The advantages of a contractual transfer include the ability to shift responsibility for exposures that may not be insurable. This approach can also be less expensive than insurance, and each agreement is tailored to meet individual needs. A very important advantage of this kind of transfer is that it can be used to place responsibility on the party that is in the best position to control the exposure—the tenant, for instance, who occupies the premises, rather than the owner who might not even be located in the same city or state as the leased property.

The disadvantage of a contractual transfer is that the transfer might not be as effective as intended. Because the transfer is made by a legal contract, the agreement is always subject to litigation and to reinterpretation by a court of law. Even if the transfer is complete, the indemnitor might be financially unable to comply with the terms of the agreement and be unable to pay for the loss, in which case financial responsibility would revert to the indemnitee. Because of that possibility, the indemnitee usually maintains insurance, and therefore the transfer might not reduce its insurance costs. Additionally, the transfer might shift loss control to an indemnitor who is unable to exert control over the exposure.

Insurance The final risk management alternative to be considered here is transfer by insurance. An insurance contract differs from a hold harmless agreement because the former deals exclusively with the transfer of risk, and a premium paid is for that purpose, while the latter is usually a part of a contract primarily covering some other topic. Insurance is available to cover many kinds of exposures whether they arise from damage to physical assets; the loss of use of physical assets; obligations externally imposed; or the human asset exposures of sickness, disability, and death.

Insurance provides indemnification for uncertain losses in exchange for a fixed sum—the premium. The insurer sets the premium based on expected loss costs, the costs to settle those losses, a component for other expenses, and an allowance for profit and for contingencies. The cost to the buyer includes more, however, than just the premium because the purchase of insurance is a time-consuming activity. Further, the mere existence of insurance can sometimes increase costs in other areas of the risk management program, since insurance can reduce the incentive for loss control and can lead to the exaggeration or falsification of claims. On the other hand, for some exposures, insurance might be the only or the most economical risk management technique available.

The selection of an insurer and intermediary agent or broker should be based on four criteria. First, the financial strength of the insurer (and of the producer if independent of the insurer) must be considered. A second consideration is the willingness of the insurer to provide the protection sought. Third, the risk management professional must consider the additional services various insurers provide to clients in return for their premium dollars. Finally, the cost of coverage should be considered.

Marketing Tip

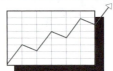

The question could be asked, "Isn't the producer who earns a living from insurance commissions in a conflict of interest with the client when implementing a risk management program?" The answer is that there can be a conflict of interest, but the existence of that conflict is not enough to invalidate the risk management approach for the producer. The producer must be conscious of that potential problem and discuss it with prospective clients before they undertake the risk management process. The producer who is dedicated to the risk management philosophy can use it without apology. The producer who competently assists a client through the various risk management decisions will usually find enough insurance has been sold to adequately remunerate the producer. Even when other risk management alternatives are used instead of the purchase of insurance, the producer usually has earned the respect of the client and will get referral leads, which in turn will produce commission income. In those states that allow it, producers may offer clients risk management advice and services on a fee basis so that the producer's income is generated whether or not any insurance is sold. For most individuals and organizations, however, insurance remains a significant part of the risk management program because alternative risk management techniques are impractical, too expensive, or too risky.

Selecting the Apparently Best Technique or Techniques

Once the exposures have been identified and analyzed and alternative risk management techniques formulated for minimizing the effects of these exposures, the risk management professional must select the apparently best technique or combination of techniques for dealing with each exposure. The picture is rarely black and white so that one technique seems to be clearly the best. Rather, the future is uncertain; therefore, the producer or risk manager must select what appears to be the best technique.

The risk management professional in possession of a large statistical database of loss experience, built up over the years, is in a better position to plan than the individual without reliable data to aid in the projection of probable losses. Almost always, the risk management plan will include a mix of alternative techniques. Exposures will be avoided, if possible, but those that must be faced will be subjected to loss control to attempt to prevent them or to reduce their severity. Contractual transfers of losses might be accomplished. Some exposures will be retained when they are not too serious and are predictable, and exposures that cannot be managed in any other way will also be retained. Insurance will be arranged to cover some exposures. Two different methods for selecting among the available risk management alternatives are possible: the insurance method and the minimum expected cost method.

The Insurance Method

One approach to technique selection, which was once very widely used, is the insurance method. In this approach, the prospect would ask the producer or the insurer to price all possible insurance coverages and to assist the prospect in placing the various kinds of insurance into three categories: essential, desirable, and available. The buyer would then start with the essential coverages and see how far down the list the insurance budget would allow the buyer to get.

This method only relates cost to insurable exposures, and it ignores risk management techniques other than insurance. Yet it is the approach many individuals and small business owners continue to use today because it is understandable and they feel comfortable with it. The producer using a risk management sales approach will find it necessary to make the prospect aware of the other risk management alternatives and the potential for saving premium dollars through their use.

The Minimum Expected Cost Method

A better approach to the selection of the apparently best combination of risk management techniques than the insurance method is called the minimum expected cost method. The minimum expected cost method compares the cost of each possible risk management technique and estimates the results of applying each technique to potential losses. The program with the lowest overall cost is the one that is selected if it also best meets the pre-loss and post-loss objectives of the organization. An example of the minimum expected cost method is presented below. The major problem in using this approach is that loss costs are often difficult to predict with any certainty. A producer attempting such an analysis might need to project the future value of current capital expenditures and could benefit from the help of an accountant, an actuary, or an economist.

The Department Store Case

Department Store is attempting to select the proper risk management techniques. Until now, Department Store has purchased building and personal property insurance for the full value of its physical assets and for loss of the use of those assets. Department Store's risk manager has suggested that Department Store install automatic sprinklers at a cost of $100,000 in the building and retain some of the exposure by taking a $10,000 deductible on its building and personal property insurance policy. The sprinklers alone will reduce the premium on the policy from $40,000 to $15,000 per year. The $10,000 deductible will reduce insurance costs, with or without sprinklers, by 20 percent. Experts from the local fire department have told Department Store that, without sprinklers, the average amount of damage to be expected from any fire would be $25,000. Sprinklers would cut the estimated damage to $10,000 for an average loss. Department Store, from its own experience, can predict that it will have approximately one fire in each ten-year period. No exposure avoidance or contractual transfer of exposures appears possible with regard to this exposure to loss.

I. Selling and the Shift to Risk Management
II. The Risk Management Process
   B. Formulating Alternatives for Dealing With Each Exposure
   C. Selecting the Apparently Best Technique or Techniques
   D. Implementing the Chosen Techniques
   E. Monitoring Results and Modifying the Program

The minimum expected "cost" as developed in this simplified example is installing the sprinklers and taking the higher deductible. (See Exhibit 3-8.) This result could be seen as even more desirable by the risk management professional for Department Store if major pre-loss and post-loss goals of the Department Store risk management program were social responsibility. Before a loss, the store would be more socially responsible if sprinklers were installed because, should a loss occur, the sprinklers would no doubt reduce the possibility of injury or death to the occupants of the store. If the costs had worked out differently, and the cost of installing the sprinklers were more expensive, the Department Store risk manager might have persuaded top management—in spite of the additional expense—that sprinklers were important because of the organization's concern for human safety. The final decision to install the sprinklers and accept the higher insurance deductible combines the techniques of control (loss reduction), retention (in the form of the deductible), and an insurance transfer.

Exhibit 3-8
Department Store—Ten-Year Projection

	Department Store 10-Year Projection [1]			
	No Sprinklers		Sprinklers	
	$100 Insurance Deductible	$10,000 Insurance Deductible	$100 Insurance Deductible	$10,000 Insurance Deductible
Exposure Avoidance	N/A	N/A	N/A[2]	N/A
Risk Control	$0	$0	$10,000	$10,000[2]
Contractual Transfer	N/A	N/A	N/A	N/A
Retention	$ 10[3]	$ 1,000[4]	$ 10	$ 1,000
Insurance	$40,000	$32,000	$15,000	$12,000
Expected Annual Cost	$40,010	$33,000	$25,010	$23,000

(1) Maintenance costs and the time value of money are ignored.
(2) 1/10 of capital expenditure used arbitrarily to illustrate that full capital cost must be amortized over time of use.
(3) One loss over ten years averages $10 per year in retained losses per year.
(4) One loss over ten years averages $1,000 per year in retained losses per year.

Marketing Tip

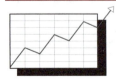

Some producers reading this example would be quick to point out that by practicing risk management, Department Store reduced its insurance costs by $17,000 and that the producer on the Department Store account presumably lost approximately 15 percent of that amount in commission. Both observations are correct, but the producer who assisted Department Store in reaching the conclusion to install the sprinklers and retain $10,000 per loss has helped the client to greatly reduce its costs, and *this will not go unnoticed.*

> Further, it is possible that if Department Store's premium savings resulted from a producer's recommendation, that producer could then suggest that the insured use some or all of the premium dollars saved to treat previously neglected loss exposures—the directors' and officers' liability exposure or earthquake insurance, for example.

Implementing the Chosen Techniques

Implementing selected risk management techniques requires that the risk management professional make technical decisions as to what should be done and managerial decisions about who should be responsible for accomplishing each phase of the program. In addition to arranging for implementation of the program, a communications system must be set up along with a method to allocate the costs of the program.

Deciding What Should Be Done

Once the general outlines of the program of risk management have been agreed upon, the risk management professional must work out the details. For instance, the risk manager at Department Store must decide what kind of sprinkler system is to be installed and which contractors should be asked to bid on the job. There may be questions about the water supply and building permits, and the top management of Department Store will certainly want to see that customer disruption at the store is minimized. Aesthetics will be involved, too, since the store must be pleasing to the eye, even with sprinklers. The producer or risk manager must also negotiate the terms of the insurance policy and must make certain the coverage fits the new risk management program. Those considerations, and many others like them, must be taken into account in deciding exactly how a particular risk management technique is to be implemented.

When a risk management professional is deciding what needs to be done, the other members of the organization are usually available to assist. Smaller organizations and families, however, must seek professional help from outside to assist with the details of implementing risk management techniques. One of the major resources for organizations without risk managers is the producer. The producer might not be skilled in a particular area (sprinkler installation, for instance) but will be counted on to gather together a team of experts to assist with the risk management program.

Deciding Who Should Be Responsible

The risk manager is usually a staff officer (without line managerial authority to direct operations) and therefore must depend upon others to implement the program based on the advice and assistance of the risk management department. The authority for the risk management program is sought from senior management, and in larger organizations it is codified into a risk management policy statement and a risk management

I. Selling and the Shift to Risk Management
II. **The Risk Management Process**
   C. Selecting the Apparently Best Technique or Techniques
   D. Implementing the Chosen Techniques
   E. Monitoring Results and Modifying the Program
III. The Wilson Case

manual. Nevertheless, the risk manager is often without the ability to command action, so he or she must possess a good sense of diplomacy to guide the program into being. In smaller organizations, the person making risk management decisions is often the person implementing the program because that person is the owner or manager.

Communications and Allocation of Costs

Any risk management program must include a communications network. Risk management departments of large organizations generally rely on a risk management manual to inform others of what risk management techniques are being employed, how to report claims, how to identify new exposures, and other important information. The communications process must be two-way. The resources of the risk manager are limited, and information must be funneled to the risk manager so that the program can be adjusted for new exposures, claims can be reported, and an evaluation can be made of the effectiveness of the techniques employed.

Of equal importance is the allocation of risk management costs. When there are numerous operating divisions or various locations, the costs of control, insurance, retained losses, and even the overhead of the risk management department must be spread equitably. In fact, one of the strongest holds the risk management department may have on a manager is the allocation of loss and other costs to that manager. If losses are excessive at a location, if loss control expenses are higher than expected, or if insurance premiums for that exposure increase greatly, the financial results of the manager's department will be adversely affected. The manager then becomes very interested in risk management to be certain the costs allocated to the department are relatively low and its profit is as large as possible.

In smaller organizations, or within a family, assessing cost is obviously less important, although, for example, an employee of a small business might be required to pay the deductible arising from damage to a company car, or "Junior" might have to pay to fix a neighbor's window that he had inadvertently broken.

Monitoring Results and Modifying the Program

This last step in the risk management process is really a return to the first step. The risk management process is constant and requires regular reevaluation and change. New exposures develop, and existing exposures change or disappear. The alternatives available for dealing with particular exposures might change or might be found to be ineffective. Changes must be detected and the risk management program adapted to them. In larger firms, the risk manager might be able to establish standards of performance by which to judge the program. For example, the number of automobile collisions to be expected from a given fleet of vehicles during the year might be estimated by statistical probability. Measurement of actual performance would then be made to determine how many accidents did occur. If there was significant variance between the standard set and the performance achieved, reasons would be sought. It is possible the standard was not appropriate and, if not, could itself be modified. It could also be that performance was substandard and in need of improvement. Perhaps driver training refresher sessions should be held. Further monitoring might determine how best to improve performance and result in modifying the risk management techniques used.

One standard that is used to evaluate the performance of an organization's risk management program is its cost of risk. Cost of risk includes the total of the values lost to actual accidents and the cost of the resources devoted to risk management. A good risk management program will minimize the cost of risk of an organization's current activities and will enable the organization to cost effectively undertake activities it once considered not worth the cost of risk.

In smaller organizations and with families, the producer's role as a risk management professional requires constant contact to determine whether clients' needs have been changed by changing exposures. The risk management review process (before insurance policy renewal dates) allows the producer to assist in identifying new exposures and to recommend appropriate risk management techniques to treat those exposures.

> **Check** your understanding of the *Key Words and Phrases* found in the second part of this assignment.

Risk control techniques (p. 28)

Avoidance (p. 28)

Loss prevention (p. 29)

Loss reduction (p. 29)

Heinrich's "domino theory" (p. 30)

Haddon's energy release theory (p. 30)

Segregation of loss exposures (p. 31)

3-42 / Foundations of Insurance Production: Principles of Insurance

Risk financing techniques (p. 32)

Retention (p. 32)

Unfunded reserve (p. 32)

Funded reserve (p. 32)

Affiliated captive insurer (p. 33)

Hold harmless agreements (p. 34)

Indemnitor (p. 34)

Indemnitee (p. 34)

Review the concepts presented in the second part of this assignment by answering the following questions.

9. Explain the principal alternative techniques for dealing with loss exposures. (pp. 28-34)

10. The term "loss control" is sometimes used to include both loss prevention and loss reduction.

    (a) How do loss prevention and loss reduction differ with regard to (1) effect and (2) timing? (p. 29)

    (b) Give two examples of loss prevention and loss reduction techniques that illustrate the timing differences mentioned in your answer to (a). (p. 31)

11. What is the difference between active retention and passive retention? (p. 32)

12. Explain the various methods of financing retained losses. (pp. 32-33)

13. What are the characteristics of a loss exposure that determine the desirability (or lack of desirability) of retaining it? (pp. 32-34)

14. What are the (a) advantages and (b) disadvantages of retention as compared with transfer? (p. 34)

15. Does a hold harmless agreement constitute avoidance of a loss exposure? Explain why or why not. (p. 34)

16. What are the (a) advantages and (b) disadvantages of risk transfer by a hold harmless agreement? (p. 35)

17. The risk management process is rapidly replacing the older methods of selling insurance.
    (a) How can a producer use the risk management process to increase sales? (p. 36)

    (b) How might compensation by commission place producers in a conflict-of-interest situation? (p. 36)

18. Explain two methods used to select appropriate risk management techniques for the treatment of loss exposures. (pp. 36-37)

Apply the concepts presented in this assignment by reading the following case and answering the questions. This case study has no specific right answer. It should be used to practice case study analysis that can later be used in analyzing actual clients' needs.

The Wilson Family Case

Sam Wilson and his wife, Zelda, are in their mid-forties. They live in an upper-middle-class neighborhood of San Francisco. Sam is a business executive with a large corporation involved in the manufacture and distribution of electronic equipment. Zelda works part time on a consulting basis as an economist for a law firm, having recently earned a master's degree.

The Wilsons have two children. The elder, Sam, Jr., is a student away at college while the younger, Sally, lives at home and attends a local high school. Zelda and Sally have a business on the side to provide party catering and gourmet cooking lessons. The kitchen of the Wilson home has been remodeled into a commercial cooking facility. Lessons can be given there, and the kitchen can be used for preparing the food to be catered. Generally, Zelda does the cooking and the teaching, and Sally delivers the food to the customers, often staying to help serve and clean up. Sam has been known to help out for large parties by either cooking or acting as bartender/butler.

The Wilsons like to ski and own a condominium in the mountains about three hours from their home. They use the mountain home year-round and have access to a swimming pool and sauna near their unit.

Sam Jr. is interested in restoring automobiles, and he is currently working on a 1957 Thunderbird coupe. From time to time he earns extra money by working on his friends' cars in his family's garage.

Sam Jr. and Sally jointly collect stamps and coins. They have been collecting since they were small children and now have a valuable collection of American stamps and coins. The coins are kept in a safe-deposit box at a bank near the Wilson home. The stamps are kept in a file cabinet in the family room of the home.

Over the years, Sam and Zelda have accumulated a good deal of antique furniture, some fine paintings, and more silverware than they really need. Zelda does not care for jewelry, but she does have some expensive pieces, including family heirlooms inherited from her mother and grandmother. Zelda has a fur coat.

The Wilsons own three cars—not counting Sam Jr.'s Thunderbird, which does not run. They have a snowmobile at their mountain condominium and belong to a cooperative that owns a sailboat. The expenses of maintaining the thirty-six-foot sloop are shared with the three other families in the cooperative, and a person has been hired to care for the boat eight hours per week.

One of the major family projects each year is a garage sale. The Wilsons are well-known in their neighborhood for this annual activity, which has become so popular that the Wilsons secretly buy merchandise to resell at the event. Because of the availability of their commercial-type kitchen, this year Zelda and Sally plan to sell food at the time of the garage sale.

Sam is active in the community on a number of boards of directors for charitable organizations. Zelda belongs to a stock investment club that meets monthly and invests as a group based upon research the group does under the leadership of a member stockbroker. Zelda is the treasurer for the group and has authority to buy and sell securities as well as to sign checks.

Sam and Zelda like other sports in addition to skiing and sailing and have recently taken up racquetball. Zelda's CPR (cardiopulmonary resuscitation) training and her background as a registered nurse were recently put to practical use following an accident on the racquetball court in which another player was seriously hurt in a fall.

A housekeeper comes to the Wilson home three times per week to clean.

Questions

Like most case studies, the Wilson family case provides inadequate data to conclusively develop a risk management program. It would be important to talk to the family members to determine their risk management objectives and to see where they place their priorities. Substantial additional information could also be gathered on the exposures to attempt to better analyze them. In the absence of a personal interview or of additional data, the following questions illustrate the risk management process applied to a personal lines situation.

1. What specific physical assets of the Wilsons create exposures in the following categories:

    (a) Buildings

    (b) Personal property

2. What loss of use exposures exist because of physical assets?

3. What obligations do the Wilsons have imposed on them externally?

4. What human asset exposures exist for the Wilson family?

5. What liability exposures exist for the Wilson family?

6. With regard to all of the exposures identified, what are the
   (a) methods of exposure measurement that may be used?

   (b) avoidance alternatives?

   (c) loss control alternatives?

   (d) suggested retentions?

   (e) noninsurance transfer alternatives?

   (f) suggested insurance transfers?

7. What additional questions would you ask the Wilsons in order to complete your risk management program for them?

8. What underwriting information, not presented in the case, would you need to complete an application for recommended insurance?

9. Why is the risk management approach to this case advantageous to the Wilsons?

10. How can the risk management approach increase your income even though you might often recommend a noninsurance technique to treat an exposure?

11. How can statistical probability be used to estimate losses for the Wilsons?

12. What other persons might you need to contact for assistance in designing the Wilsons' risk management plan?

Summary

The process of risk management need not be complex. A simple example of a broken shoelace is used here to summarize the fundamentals of the risk management process and to keep it in perspective.

1. Identify and analyze loss exposure.
   a. Exposure: Shoelace breakage identified by personal observation.
   b. Frequency of Loss: Difficult to predict, although past loss statistics could be reviewed. In Prouty's terminology, the frequency is moderate.
   c. Severity of Loss: Maximum probable loss is the cost of laces and possible loss of use of the shoes.
   d. Item(s) Subject to Loss: Laces and loss of use of the shoes.
   e. Causal Force: Breakage from strain or wear and tear.
   f. Financial Impact: $1.25 plus indeterminate costs, depending on the value of the shoes.
2. Formulate alternatives for treating the exposure.
   a. Exposure avoidance: Sell laced shoes. Buy loafers, cowboy boots, or sandals, or go barefoot.
   b. Loss Prevention: Use stainless steel laces.
   c. Loss Reduction: Carry an extra lace (will not reduce breakage cost of asset but will minimize loss of use of shoes).
   d. Segregation of Exposures: Rotate laces daily from large supply.
   e. Contractual Transfer: Have shoe store that supplies shoes and laces agree to replace laces immediately and free of charge if broken.
   f. Retention:
      (1) Current Expensing of Losses: Pay for laces when broken from small change in pocket.
      (2) Unfunded Reserve: Be aware of bank balance and equity in home and car to be certain there are always enough funds to buy laces.
      (3) Funded Reserve: Toss a penny daily into a beer mug on dresser.
      (4) Borrowing: Get a loan from a friend to buy laces.
      (5) Captive Insurer: Not applicable unless hundreds of thousands of shoes owned.
   g. Transfer to Insurer: Buy a policy from Shoelace Fire and Marine.
3. Select the apparently best technique. Combination of loss control (stronger laces) and retention using funded reserve (beer mug on dresser @ $0.01 per day).
4. Implement the selected combination of techniques. Purchase stronger laces, and fund the reserve.
5. Monitor the results. Next time the laces break, does the owner have enough money to replace them? If not, was loss control at fault, or was the funding scheme inadequate?

Insurance Sales and Account Development

Assignment 4

Assignment Objectives

After completing this assignment, you should be able to:

1. Contrast the following selling techniques, using illustrations of each:
   a. order processing
   b. creative selling
   c. missionary selling
2. Given a sales situation, illustrate how a producer might use selling skills to close a sale.

   In support of the assignment objective listed above, you should be able to do the following:
   a. Explain the importance of developing selling skills.
   b. Distinguish among the various selling skills.
   c. Identify the five prospect reactions that might be encountered in a sales call.
   d. Describe a method the producer would use in response to each of the reactions in c. above.
   e. Illustrate closing techniques used in insurance sales.
3. Given an insurance agency case, design an account development program that will improve the agency's sales performance.

   In support of the assignment objective listed above, you should be able to do the following:
   a. Explain why an agency should balance its sales activities between account development and account acquisition.
   b. Explain why the producer should concentrate on developing stable sources of premium dollars rather than just increasing the number of clients.
   c. Illustrate the sources of new premium dollars for a producer.
   d. Explain the nature of and procedures for the account review process.
   e. Differentiate between minimum agency standards and minimum account standards.
   f. Describe various types of agency support activities that will enhance the account upgrading and total account selling process.
   g. Justify the "Automatic Add-On" and "Personal Contact" selling approaches in account development.
   h. Compare the sales process for basic accounts and technical coverage accounts.
   i. Explain the benefits of account upgrading and total account selling to:
      (i) the agency and the producer.
      (ii) the client.
4. Define or describe each of the Key Words and Phrases for this assignment.

Assignment Outline

I. Sales Management
   A. Agency Sales Planning
   B. Personal Sales Planning
II. Selling
   A. Selling and the Producer
   B. Individual Selling Skills
III. The Sources of Business in an Agency
   A. Account Acquisition Versus Account Development Approach
   B. Product-Customer Marketing Matrix
IV. The Account Review Process
   A. Establish Priority Accounts
   B. Segregate Accounts by Coverage
   C. Organize Client Files
   D. Account Information Summary Sheets
   E. Methods of Organizing Files and Completing the Account Review Summary Sheets
V. Agency Procedures for Complete Account Development
   A. Putting the Account Review to Use
   B. Sales Activities Supporting Account Development
   C. Specific Sales Activities for Basic Accounts
   D. Technical Coverage Accounts
VI. The Benefits of Account Development
   A. Agency and Producer Benefits
   B. Client Benefits
VII. Summary

Assignment 4

Insurance Sales and Account Development

Orient yourself to this assignment by reading the following introduction.

An insurance agency's primary activity is marketing. That process includes finding, selling to, and providing service to insureds. A producer's primary activity, however, is selling. This assignment presents material on several areas of selling. The first section describes the sales planning process for both the agency and the producer. Planning, one part of the management process, is an essential step in the selling process. (A detailed discussion of agency management principles can be found in AAI 83, *Agency Operations and Sales Management*.)

The second section of this assignment presents the selling techniques and skills that a producer needs to become effective in closing sales presentations. Those techniques and skills can only be introduced in a textbook—they must be learned through constant on-the-job practice and courses specifically designed for sales training.

The rest of this assignment focuses on what happens after the sale has been made. Every agency should adopt the marketing concept of account development, that is, selling upgraded coverages and total account selling. With decreases in commission levels and increases in agency expenses, monoline policy clients are unprofitable. Selling the entire account makes clients profitable for both the agency and the producer.

The importance of marketing that focuses on finding new clients or selling new products cannot be underestimated. However, marketing efforts should also be concentrated on account selling to retain and upgrade current clients. The advantages of account selling apply to the agency, the producer, and the client, whether the client is commercial or personal. The concepts presented in this assignment should be applied to all AAI assignments and to all sales opportunities.

This assignment concludes with appendixes that include samples of checklists and other forms that can be used to evaluate client needs and summarize client file information. Those forms are provided as examples of what some agencies use, not necessarily as the best or only way to develop client information. An agency that wants to organize its files can use those forms as a guide and can adapt them to meet its specific needs.

4-2 / Foundations of Insurance Production: Principles of Insurance

> **Read** the definitions of the *Key Words and Phrases* that follow. Being familiar with these important words will help you better understand the first part of this assignment. *Key Words and Phrases* appear in bold in the text when they are defined.

Market	Collection of potential clients that can be subdivided into distinct groups on the basis of criteria established by the producer
Market segment	Specifically defined portion of a market
Market segmentation	Process of dividing a market into smaller groups of similar prospects
Product targeting	Designing a specific product for a market, a specific approach to a market, or both
Suspect	Member of a market
Prospect	A suspect the producer intends to approach
Sales strategy	A way to achieve the producer's goal
Order processing	The producer identifies a need, points out the need, and takes the order
Missionary selling	Indirect selling that establishes the goodwill and competence of an organization through technical services to clients and potential clients
Creative selling	Persuasion—bringing the needs to the customer's attention in a logical way
Cold calling	A call on a prospect without an appointment
Joint calls	Sending a new producer with a successful, experienced producer as part of the training process
Product feature	When a product known to satisfy the customer's need is pointed out by the salesperson
Product benefit	When the product feature can be applied to the customer's need
Nonleading question	Allows the prospect to respond in any manner, encouraging the prospect to talk
Leading question	Calls for a specific, limited response from the customer
Agreement	When the prospect agrees that the features presented are suitable for the needs
Disbelief	The prospect doubts that the policy can perform as indicated
Indifference	The prospect does not see the need or is satisfied with the current producer
Objections	The prospect's reaction caused by misunderstandings or a real disadvantage of products or services
Delay	Expression of undisclosed underlying attitude

Closing	When the objective of the sales call has been met
Controllable sources of additional premium	Three sources: (1) account development, (2) account acquisition, and (3) merger
Account development	Making additional sales to existing accounts
Account acquisition	Making sales to new customers
Product-customer marketing matrix	A chart showing two types of clients—current and those new to the agency—and two types of products—those that exist in the client's account and those that are new to the client's account
Account upgrading	Sales activities such as increasing an account's limits or adding coverage to existing policies to better cover the client's needs
Account selling	Selling new types of insurance products to existing clients
Temporary monopoly	A situation in which an agency is currently the exclusive provider of a product/service that clients want/need. It is temporary because other agencies/companies will copy the idea, restoring competition to the market

Study the first part of this assignment, which includes the following sections:

I. Sales Management
II. Selling
III. The Sources of Business in an Agency

Sales Management

Sales management—the application of the management process to selling—is considered part of a broader field, marketing management. Marketing management has been defined as follows:

> ... the analysis, planning, implementation, and control of programs designed to bring about desired exchanges with target markets for the purpose of achieving organizational objectives. It relies heavily on designing the organization's offering in terms of the target market's needs and desires and using effective pricing, communications, and distribution to inform, motivate, and service the market.[1]

Producers are frequently and heavily involved with many aspects of marketing management. The nature and extent of that involvement will vary widely depending on the size and the kind of marketing organization with which the producer is associated. Distribution is a primary and constant marketing management function performed by producers. Product design, on the other hand, has been traditionally viewed as an insurer function—though producers can and do have influence. In addition, producers can do much to customize insurance products through the imaginative use of deductibles and endorsements or, in some cases, through the preparation of manuscript policies.

I. **Sales Management**
   A. Agency Sales Planning
   B. Personal Sales Planning
II. **Selling**

Producers are affected by two types of sales planning: agency planning and personal planning. The planning usually performed annually for an entire agency includes agency-wide goals and objectives intended to contribute to the achievement of the plan. The sales planning an individual producer performs should be a coordinated part of the agency-wide plan. In a small, one-producer agency, agency planning and personal planning are basically the same.

Agency Sales Planning

An example will clarify the relationship between agency planning and personal planning. A relatively large agency might set a sales goal of $1 million in commission income. One objective aimed at achieving that goal might possibly be the installation of a computer and the automation of much of the agency's billing and other clerical systems so that the office could profitably handle the paper flow from this volume of business. The agency manager might devote much time and energy to the achievement of that objective. The sales manager, however, would be given the $1 million commission income figure as the agency-wide sales goal. It would be up to the sales manager to work with the agency's individual producers to ensure that the sum of the producers' personal sales goals will result in achievement of the agency's sales goals. *How* the sales manager achieves the overall goal will vary from agency to agency. Some sales managers might not inform producers of the agency-wide goal and will encourage producers to set personal goals on a "bottom-up" basis, whereby the personal sales goal was set by the producer and approved by the agency's management. Other sales managers might meet with all the producers in the agency as a group, announce the agency-wide goal, and assign a personal sales goal to each producer on a "top-down" basis, whereby the producer's goal was set by the agency's management. In either case, responsibility for achievement of the personal sales goal rests with the individual producer. For that reason, personal sales planning is an important part of each producer's job.

Personal Sales Planning

The personal sales planning an individual producer performs should include the functions of all management planning: establishing a personal mission statement; developing strategies, goals, and objectives; preparing budgets; developing sales policies; and setting procedures. Much of this may be accomplished in a very flexible, informal way. In this assignment, the material will focus on the producer's goals and some of the tools available to achieve those goals.

Whether the producer or the agency's management sets the producer's overall sales goal for the year, establishing specific objectives that will contribute to the achievement of the overall goal is necessary. Those objectives should be expressed in terms of amount and kind of business to be sold and should be periodically reviewed throughout the annual planning period—either monthly or quarterly. Those specific sales goals and objectives should be directly tied to and coordinated with market analysis, segmentation, and targeting.

A **market** is a collection of potential clients that can be subdivided into distinct groups on the basis of criteria established by the producer.

A **market segment** is a specifically defined portion of a market. **Market segmentation** is the process of dividing a market into smaller groups of similar prospects. **Product targeting** is designing a special product for a market, taking a special approach to a market, or both. For instance, a producer's auto insurance market might include everyone who drives a car and lives within a pre-defined geographical territory. Each individual in that group would be a suspect for auto insurance. In marketing, a **suspect** is defined as a member of a market. The producer, however, might intend to sell auto insurance only as part of a complete personal lines insurance program. If so, it would be necessary to further subdivide the auto insurance market in order to target those members who are also homeowners or tenants. In addition, if a personal umbrella policy is to be part of the personal lines program offered by the producer, a minimum annual income of $50,000, for instance, might be an additional market criterion established by the producer. Ultimately, the producer will have targeted a relatively narrow group of **prospects**, those suspects whom the producer intends to approach.

The flexibility and informality inherent in personal sales planning can also be seen through consideration of another example. A producer has set as part of a personal sales plan the goal of generating 40 percent of the producer's annual commission income through personal lines sales. The producer might have set this personal lines goal because of a **sales strategy**, a way of achieving the goal the producer wishes to use. It could be that one of the producer's commercial lines accounts is a large manufacturing firm that recently moved into the producer's marketing area. Because of the producer's relationship with the management of that firm, the producer plans to achieve part of the new personal lines goal by offering the agency's personal lines insurance program to the executives and managers of the manufacturing firm. If so, the producer's prospects would be clearly and narrowly targeted as the members of the managerial staff of one of the producer's commercial lines accounts.

Should the producer fail to meet the goal through those prospects, it would be necessary to formulate a new strategy that would result in a new kind of market segmentation, transforming an additional number of suspects (those homeowners and tenants in the area who drive cars and earn $50,000 or more per year) into prospects.

Exhibit 4-1 illustrates another example of market segmentation and targeting. The outer circle in Exhibit 4-1 represents a segmented market—in this case, individuals with a residence exposure. That market is further segmented into (1) residences that qualify for homeowners insurance; (2) residences valued at more than $100,000; and (3) the target market, residences valued at more than $100,000 whose owners need catastrophe (umbrella) liability coverage and can afford a high deductible.

I. Sales Management
   A. Agency Sales Planning
   B. **Personal Sales Planning**
II. Selling
   A. Selling and the Producer
   B. Individual Selling Skills

Exhibit 4-1
Residence Insurance Market

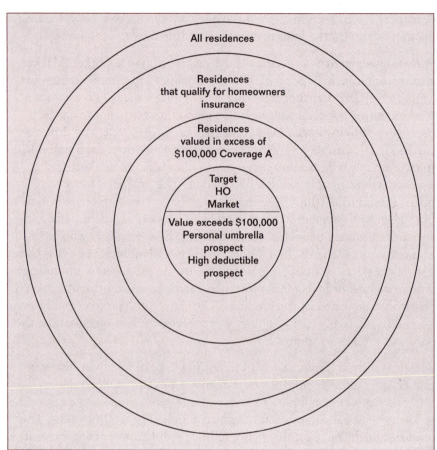

Personal sales planning should coordinate strategies, goals, objectives, budgets, policies, and procedures with market analysis, segmentation, and targeting. Sales strategies, goals, and objectives should guide market segmentation to targeting prospects. Once prospects are identified, a sales approach must be devised. The producer might decide to approach some prospects with a cold call, dropping in unannounced. The producer might, instead, choose to approach prospects with a letter. There are literally dozens of ways producers can introduce themselves, their organizations, and their products and services to prospects. The agency's and the producer's sales procedures and policies help shape the way the producer approaches prospects.

Selling

Selling requires product knowledge, market knowledge, and knowledge of selling techniques (the "sales trilogy" discussed in Assignment 1). Much of the AAI 81 and 82 texts are devoted to product knowledge. The discussion of sales management in this chapter, however, should assist producers in developing market knowledge as well as their selling techniques. Those techniques must be practiced and evaluated to be useful, and producers are encouraged to invest in a course that concentrates solely on the development of sales skills.

Selling and the Producer

Salespeople add an important dimension to the products and services they sell. In many cases, when consumers see all products as similar or undifferentiated (substitutes for each other), the salesperson can make the difference. Similarly, a producer who uses a professional approach to solving client problems can make seemingly undifferentiated insurance policies actually different through the service performed. In general, a professional approach to sales is one that shows how the product satisfies customer needs.

Selling Techniques

There are three different selling techniques. Each can be found in insurance selling. No one technique is necessarily better than another. Although the planning and goals of any one producer might indicate a particular selling technique that should be used, no one technique should be used to the exclusion of all others.

Order Processing

When a customer immediately recognizes his or her needs, order processing is an excellent technique. It can be successfully used in the insurance business at renewal. It should be used with caution, however, for it might lead producers to miss potential sales opportunities. In **order processing**, the producer identifies a need (renewal of automobile insurance), points out the need (calls the client or sends a bill), and takes the order (renews the policy).

E&O Alert!

Order processing is simple—the client tells the producer what coverages are desired, and the producer fills the order. **But beware!** The client does not know as much about insurance as the producer and might order improper or inadequate coverage. In addition, the producer should provide the client with professional advice in selecting among various risk management alternatives. E&O claims can easily arise when a producer does no more than process the client's order.

Missionary Selling

Missionary selling is indirect selling that establishes the goodwill and competence of an organization through technical services to clients and potential clients. Its most frequent use in insurance is through consulting or risk management services, often provided on a fee basis. The goodwill of the agency is established when customers are provided with high-quality technical or operational assistance, raising the probability that the client will purchase needed insurance products from the agency.

Creative Selling

Persuasion is paramount in **creative selling**. Needs that are not obvious to the customer must be brought to the customer's attention in a logical

I. Sales Management
II. Selling
    A. **Selling and the Producer**
    B. Individual Selling Skills

way. The producer then shows how the suggested policy meets those needs. Creative selling is used most frequently in an exposure-based sale. A customer's needs are highlighted, and a package is designed for those needs. Creative selling is the kind of selling that will be analyzed and discussed in the next section.

Calling on Prospects

The producer can make face-to-face contact with a prospect in two ways. The first method involves initial contact by letter, telephone, fax, or E-mail. An appointment is then made with the prospect. The producer might make this face-to-face contact alone or with another representative of the agency. Joint calls might be used in training new producers, to add technical backup, or to introduce office personnel to a client with whom they might deal in the future.

The second method is to call on a prospect without an appointment, or "**cold calling**." Cold calls might seem difficult to make, but they provide the producer an opportunity to practice selling and can generate business. Successful producers recognize both methods as effective when used properly—to fit the plans and meet the goals of the producer.

Joint Calls

For the new producer, making **joint calls** is a good idea. The joint call allows a new producer to see how a successful producer sells and allows the successful producer to guide, coach, and constructively criticize the sales techniques of the new producer. It also has other potential benefits. Staff members who will service the account can go along for introduction. The adage "two heads are better than one" serves as the impetus for a team call. One successful agency principal reports:

> We rely heavily on the joint call approach. The joint call can be of one or two types. The first is one in which two partners from our agency make a call on a prospect or insured to take full advantage of the "two heads are better than one" philosophy. This type of call is made purely for effect and to add a second party to back up the producer in any area in which he may not feel totally adequate. The other type of joint call is one in which, again, two people are present, but one of the two is a person who will be making the call—the other is there simply as an observer. This is most often done with the producer and the sales manager but quite frequently may be done with a senior producer and a relatively new producer. The second party's function on these calls is to make mental notes of the primary producer's actions and approach so as to give him a reading on those things that he did well and those things that he, in the opinion of the second party, did not do well. This exercise is effective in terms of sales success. It is also valuable for the two people involved in the sense that it does give them an opportunity to see someone else in action. Often, both the observed and the observer benefit from the experience.

Cold Calls

That same agency principal also reports that the majority of his agency's joint calls are cold calls. He believes that cold calls are the least effective method of approaching customers but that "they do work occasionally and, more important, give the salesperson and sales manager an opportunity to develop confidence and experience in selling the insurance service in the most difficult sales situation."

For an individual producer, the cold call provides an opportunity to practice sales techniques, but it can also be a "time filler." It is a technique that can be used effectively by either the new or experienced producer. Another example of cold calling is from an experienced producer from Georgia. He moved to Florida and joined an agency in the central part of the state. As he did not need to spend a substantial amount of time learning coverages, he chose to fill his time by making cold calls in the area. He had no personal contacts in the town, so he spent his first two months with a tape recorder in his car exploring the cities in the area. He dictated names and addresses of businesses into the tape recorder, later extracting them and arranging them not only in alphabetical order but also cross-referencing them with a particular part of town. He reports:

> My pride and joy was my "black book" that all this information ended up in ultimately. Each prospective business account was listed in its appropriate section with pertinent information such as owners' names, addresses, telephone numbers, and a brief summary of the business itself. Keep in mind that I had seen each prospect and could summarize as far as housekeeping and so on. If I happened to be in the northeast section of town with a spare hour or so of time, I could look into the northeast geographic section of my manual, select one or two prospects that were nearby, turn over to the alphabetical information on the prospective business, and then make the call with the necessary confidence to achieve an expected level of success.

He then entered the date of the call, the results, and the name of one person with whom he spoke into his "black book." His goals were to obtain expiration dates of current policies and the names of the present agent and company. Within twenty-four hours after the call, he sent a personal follow-up letter, thanking the prospect for the visit. He then would give a proposal on the business. He found the cold call method successful and recounts:

> During the first four months, I made slightly over 500 calls and secured approximately 150 expiration dates. The surprising thing I found was that contractors, small manufacturing plants, etc., were much more receptive to accepting quotes on their insurance program than the small retail stores. In retrospect, I feel that any person can make cold calls if he prepares himself psychologically for the possibility of rejection. If he realizes beforehand that out of every ten calls made, he will pick up between three and four expiration dates, the unpleasantness of rejection is greatly diminished.

I. Sales Management
II. Selling
   A. **Selling and the Producer**
   B. **Individual Selling Skills**
III. The Sources of Business in an Agency

This producer knew that his reward would be the generation of sales. But he also realized that generating a sale would take a relatively large number of cold calls. For new producers with time available, deciding to make five cold calls each week can be a worthwhile goal. But combining goal setting with a personal system of motivational rewards might also be useful. That is, a producer might establish a reward in advance—an afternoon off or dinner at a special restaurant, for example—if the goal of making five cold calls within one week is achieved. Some producers find personal motivational reward systems useful in many of their activities.

Needs-Based Selling

The premise of a face-to-face sales call is that the customer has a need that the salesperson's product can fill. The customer does not necessarily know a need exists. It is up to the salesperson to uncover the need and be certain the total sale satisfies the customer's need. To satisfy the need, the salesperson points out an applicable feature of the product. When a **product feature** can be applied to the customer need, the feature becomes a **product benefit** for the customer—the need is satisfied, and the customer is motivated to buy. Selling techniques, discussed later in this assignment, should be designed to uncover as many needs of the customer as possible so that the salesperson can satisfy them and close the sale.

To illustrate the difference between a product feature and a product benefit, consider a standard porcelain-covered metal cooking container suitable for home canning of fruits and vegetables. This device has the following features: (1) constructed principally of metal for use on any cooking surface, (2) covered with porcelain for heat distribution and reduction of oxidation, (3) containing a wire basket to separate glass canning containers from the heating surface, and (4) sufficient size to handle up to seven one-half gallon glass containers. Each of these traits is a physical attribute, or feature, of the product.

In order to make a needs-based sale, the salesperson must use these inherent features of the product to satisfy a need of the customer considering such a purchase. A customer looking for a pot large enough to make homemade soup, for instance, would not be interested in the capacity of the container as it relates to canning but more as it relates to the volume of soup that could be made at any one time. Therefore, the feature of holding up to seven one-half gallon containers would not be a benefit for this particular customer. However, a customer whose pot just rusted through after two years of use would see the porcelain covering as a benefit. The customer canning principally in half-gallon sizes would be very interested in the large capacity. When a product feature suits an individual's need, the feature is a benefit.

Motivation theory suggests that one cannot motivate by appealing to a satisfied need. For instance, all people have a need for food, but it would be difficult, if not impossible, to motivate someone to eat by offering a seven-course dinner immediately after he or she completes an excellent meal. A satisfied need cannot be used to motivate; only unsatisfied needs are motivational.

Individual Selling Skills

Any face-to-face sales call involves certain steps. First, the salesperson must present benefits, work with the prospect's reactions to the benefits, and, finally, close the sale. Each part of the sales call requires a separate skill.

Good training helps the producer develop the skills needed to become and remain successful. Although all of us "sell" at one time or another in our lives, selling is not easy. Exhibit 4-2 lists eight major causes of failure. It is clear from the list that this program can deal with some of those causes of failure—particularly the third most common cause, inadequate product knowledge. Courses in applied sales techniques can deal with others. Some of those causes of failure, however, can be handled only by a producer who makes the commitment to overcome them. The techniques discussed below are good places to begin.

Exhibit 4-2
Why Sales Personnel Fail

Causes of Failure
Lack of initiative
Poor planning and organization
Inadequate product knowledge
Lack of enthusiasm
Salesperson not customer-oriented
Lack of proper training
Inability to get along with buyers
Lack of personal goals

Presentation of Benefits

It would be ideal for the producer to have some knowledge of the prospect's insurance needs before calling. That knowledge might have come from the producer's study of the prospect or from some other source. Unless the prospect has a need and the producer's product can satisfy the need, the producer has no reason to make the call.

Prospect Mentions a Need

In the purchase of insurance, the prospect must feel comfortable with and trust the producer and the services offered. If a prospect mentions a need, the producer can assume that some level of trust exists. When the prospect mentions a need the producer can satisfy, it makes sense for the producer to agree that the need is important and then mention how the insurance policy will meet that need.

By agreeing with the prospect's need, the producer is "tied" to the service offered. The producer is showing concern and consideration for the prospect's point of view. The agreement shows the prospect that the producer is listening and understanding the needs. It also reinforces the producer's role as the need satisfier and shows the prospect that the insurance producer and service offered are needed.

I. Sales Management
II. **Selling**
   A. Selling and the Producer
   B. **Individual Selling Skills**
III. The Sources of Business in an Agency

For illustrative purposes, assume a producer is trying to sell a personal umbrella liability policy to Ms. Jones, a corporate vice president who earns $80,000 a year. In the sales call, Ms. Jones might say, "I do a substantial amount of traveling to our plant in Mexico. As you know, American auto insurance is not valid there, but I still need protection." The producer introduces a benefit by saying, "You are smart to recognize that your auto policy does not cover you while driving in Mexico and that a claim in Mexico can be as destructive to your financial health as one here in the United States. That is why the umbrella we offer has worldwide coverage. We would respond to a claim in Mexico as we would to one in Texas."

As another example, the producer might be trying to sell an office package to an accountant. The accountant might be less specific in his statement: "Creating worksheets and audit trails takes a long time. Yet, their existence is vital to my work with my clients." The producer can respond to the implied need: "The expense to reconstruct detailed financial records can be enormous if they were destroyed. Crowley Fire and Marine has both an accounts receivable policy and a valuable papers policy that would help you by paying for the costs of recreating those documents." Those statements illustrate how serving the prospect, showing empathy, and building trust between the producer and the prospect can help to make the sale.

Prospect Does Not Mention a Need

On a cold call or at any other time when a producer is before the customer for the first time, having customers state their needs might not be possible. But even on a cold call, an assumed need can be stated. Perhaps the salesperson is familiar with problems that people in the prospect's business have. That knowledge could come from information obtained during the market segmentation activities of a producer, prior research on the company or person, a newspaper article, a conversation at a party, or from any one of a number of sources. The more accurate the assumption of need is, the more likely that the customer or prospect will be receptive to it.

When the producer must assume a need in order to present a benefit, it is best not to refer directly to the prospect, because if the assumption is incorrect, the relationship between the prospect and producer is diminished. For the vice president above, the producer might say:

> Ms. Jones, many successful executives have worked hard to build up an estate. An accident caused by a successful person can bring on a very large lawsuit and a judgment in an amount exceeding basic insurance limits. The personal umbrella policy of Crowley Fire and Marine is designed to protect these people for an amount of $1 million dollars in excess of their basic policy limits.

That statement is related to executives in general. Ms. Jones is not referred to personally. The insurer (it could have been the agency) is introduced, and a feature of the umbrella is introduced. The producer does not list all provisions (features) of the policy. The statement is a specific approach to an assumed need. The same technique might also be used with the accountant:

> Mr. Smith, many CPAs would rather spend their valuable time serving their clients than watching over the details of their own operations. My agency, along with Crowley Fire and Marine, has designed an insurance plan for the offices of professionals that is so complete that CPAs can concentrate on their profession and know that their own operations are protected.

Again, details are not mentioned at this point. Mr. Smith is given the feature of time savings—time to concentrate on what he does best.

One other time when this type of statement can be used in a sales call is when the prospect becomes reluctant to talk. In such a situation, the producer must introduce new features of the product. Generally, a good sales presentation allows prospects to bring up *their* problems and *their* needs. The salesperson then responds with corresponding benefits.

Asking Questions

Another vital skill a producer must learn is when and how to ask questions. The producer can ask nonleading and leading questions.

Nonleading Questions

A **nonleading question** allows the prospect to respond in any manner on any subject. The purpose of the nonleading question is to urge the customer to talk.

Needs-based selling requires that needs be identified so that the producer can respond to them. When a prospect is talking freely or when the producer thinks that the prospect is about to reveal an important bit of information, the nonleading question is appropriate. For instance, Ms. Jones says, "Well, it sounds good, but one thing bothers me." It appears Ms. Jones has some unsatisfied need and is willing to talk about it. The producer could respond with a nonleading question such as, "Oh?" or "What would that be?" Those questions show that the response is open for the prospect. It encourages the prospect to talk and reveal his or her concern.

Leading Questions

A **leading question** calls for a specific, limited response. In some cases, a prospect might be reluctant or unwilling to talk. In other cases, based on prior knowledge or an assumption of need, the producer wants to guide the prospect to a specific topic. In those situations, the leading question is ideal. The best questions are based on clues to subjects the prospect is interested in. The clues might be picked up in conversation, by observation, or they might come from pre-call research. The leading question must be based on an intelligent guess at what interests the prospect. For instance, the accountant has become reluctant to talk, but the producer knows that a client of the CPA has recently had a large uninsured business interruption loss. Based on that knowledge, the producer can construct a leading question designed to open a conversation about the prospect's business interruption exposures:

I. Sales Management
II. **Selling**
   A. Selling and the Producer
   B. **Individual Selling Skills**
III. The Sources of Business in an Agency

Have you ever encountered problems in which a successful business goes out of operation because a fire (tornado, ice storm, or whatever) makes it impossible to continue vital day-to-day operations?

Responses to leading questions are usually short, in many cases limited to a simple "yes" or "no." The producer has selected the topic of discussion and guided the prospect to that subject. The area of discussion should be one that the producer's policy or service can handle. If the prospect responds:

> You know, I just had a situation in which a client of mine had a fire. Fire insurance could replace the building, but the client was a dairy, and it could not deliver milk for three months. It had to go out of business because its customers needed milk and went to another dairy. My client could not get that business back in time to save the company.

At this point, the producer can respond by agreeing and illustrating how business interruption insurance could protect the CPA's business.

As a general rule, initial questions should be nonleading. The producer should try to get the prospect to reveal needs and talk openly. If the prospect is not talking, questions should become leading; but when the prospect begins to open up again, the producer should go back to asking nonleading questions.

Rarely does a producer find a prospect who responds favorably to being "led by the nose" with questions. Agility in moving from leading to nonleading questions and back again is an essential skill in selling. The need for that skill and good oral communication skills in general supports the need for the producer to take a sales course and not to rely solely on the description of skills presented here.

A final comment on questioning relates to the universality of the skill. Psychologists, social workers, family counselors, and marriage counselors all agree that communication is the most vital aspect of living and growing together. Knowing how and when to ask an appropriate question is a universal skill that can improve office, family, and community relations. If it is properly learned and executed, it is an efficient way to learn about the problems and needs of any person or any organization. Producers must also learn when to stop talking and start listening, especially after the prospect has begun answering nonleading questions.

Prospect's Reactions

Asking the right question means that the producer must be constantly aware of the reactions of the prospect. If the reaction is one of cooperation, a nonleading question can be used. If the reaction is reluctance to talk, the leading question is more appropriate. A flexible set of sales skills also allows producers to make a sales call without having to rely on a "canned" sales presentation. In order to be flexible, the ability to identify customer reaction is vital. Five reactions typically occur in a sales call:

1. Agreement
2. Disbelief

3. Indifference
4. Objections
5. Delay

Agreement

When the prospect agrees that features presented are suited to his or her situation and has no questions, the reaction appears to be one of **agreement**. At that point, the producer should attempt to close, or complete, the sale. Closing the sale (discussed later) assumes that some benefits have been mentioned and accepted as relevant by the prospect. There is no need to attempt to relate each feature of the policy or service being sold to the prospect. Just enough benefits should be presented so that the producer feels comfortable. Exactly what constitutes "enough benefits" varies from producer to producer and from situation to situation. When the salesperson thinks there is agreement, closing should occur.

Disbelief

Disbelief is doubt—doubt that the policy can or will perform as indicated. When a prospect reacts with disbelief, the producer must offer some form of proof to convince the prospect. A simple, "I will show you it is true" will not suffice. Psychologically, it is best to first rephrase the feature under discussion. This shows that the producer is listening carefully, considering the prospect's needs and problems, and understanding that the prospect's needs are paramount.

After rephrasing the feature, the producer can offer proof. The producer should include any facts, figures, testimonials, or other objective information that shows the prospect the policy will perform in the manner indicated. The producer should not use personal experience as proof, such as "My experience has been. . ." or "In my case. . . ," as this approach tends to personalize the doubt and make the situation potentially argumentative.

If a proof is rejected, the producer must use a nonleading question to determine why. Proof can be rejected for a number of reasons. The prospect simply might not like or approve of the proof source cited. A prudent producer would, in that case, cite some other form of proof.

In the previous example, Ms. Jones might have indicated she heard that no American insurance is valid in Mexico. A proof statement handling that disbelief could be:

> Ms. Jones, if you are considering catastrophe liability insurance, it is important to know if the coverage is truly worldwide. Here is a copy of the policy. You can read here in the contract that there are no territorial limitations as there are in the auto policy. What that means to you is that if the limits of your auto policy purchased in Mexico prove to be inadequate, this policy will respond up to an additional one million dollars.

Perhaps the accountant does not believe he can obtain business interruption coverage without having to reveal what he considers proprietary income information. The producer might respond:

- I. Sales Management
- II. Selling
  - A. Selling and the Producer
  - **B. Individual Selling Skills**
- III. The Sources of Business in an Agency

I can understand why, in a competitive business like yours, you would not want to reveal billing information. Here is an article from the *Journal of Information* that describes the type of policy I am offering—one in which you select your monthly business income amount. The article goes on to say that the selected amount is the policy limit at time of loss. You can see then that your privacy is protected and your profits insured.

Appropriate proof is the best response to doubt.

Indifference

The attitude of **indifference** or "who cares?" is the most difficult reaction to deal with. When a prospect is not interested, it means either that the prospect does not see a need for the policy or service or that the prospect is happy with his or her current producer. In both cases, the producer must use leading questions to uncover areas of need or areas of dissatisfaction with the current product. If the prospect does not perceive any needs, the prospect will believe there is nothing to discuss. If the prospect is happy, nonleading questions will reveal the happiness and not disclose areas of dissatisfaction.

Posing leading questions that are based on educated guesses about the needs or possible areas of dissatisfaction is essential. Pre-call research is helpful in determining the types of needs or areas of dissatisfaction that might exist with current insurance. The producer should remember that no prospect wants to admit a mistake in a past purchase. Therefore, leading questions must be asked tactfully.

Objections

When salespeople meet, one universal topic of conversation is how to handle **objections**. When objections arise in a sales call, they must be dealt with immediately. Ignoring objections allows the prospect to concentrate on the objection and ignore other comments the producer might be making. Objections fall into two classifications, each requiring a different technique. Objections might arise because of a *misunderstanding* or because of a *real disadvantage* of the producer's products or services. In either case, the first step is to rephrase the objection in the form of a question. The rephrasing shows attention but not agreement.

If an objection is the result of a misunderstanding, it should be addressed immediately after rephrasing the objection. If the objection is the result of a real disadvantage, it should be restated in the form of a question in which the positive benefits of the product or service are stressed. In other words, an objection based on a real disadvantage is a reason for the prospect not to buy. Stressing benefits takes the prospect through the policy and, in effect, shows that strong advantages exist for the prospect and outweigh a single disadvantage. In stressing benefits, the producer should focus on the ones that are important to the prospect.

The same objection could be the result of either a misunderstanding or a real disadvantage. Assume that both Ms. Jones and Mr. Smith respond in the following manner: "I don't like your policy because it costs too much!" Assume also that the cost objection is a misunderstanding for Ms.

Jones and a real disadvantage for Mr. Smith. To handle Ms. Jones's objection, the producer might say:

> If I understand you correctly, you think the price is too high. Well, I am happy to tell you that this million-dollar umbrella policy will have an annual premium of only $150.

The misunderstanding was treated by rephrasing the objection and giving a direct answer. Mr. Smith could be handled this way:

Producer: "You think the premium will be excessive, is that correct? Mr. Smith, do you agree that the value of "all-risks" type coverage as provided by a risks of physical loss policy is better than a specified causes of loss policy?"

Smith: "Well, yes."

Producer: "And having all of your coverages in one package policy not only provides a rate credit but also simplifies your handling of the insurance?"

Smith: "Yes...."

Producer: "Wouldn't it be more expensive to go out of business because of no business interruption insurance—like the dairy?"

Smith: "Well, sure...."

Producer: "And Mr. Smith, isn't there a real value to you in the coverages I am recommending?"

That technique could be continued until the producer is satisfied that the prospect sees that the premium is reasonable for the total package of protection offered. However, if the prospect does not budge, it is better not to belabor the point. Producers should not run the risk of offending prospects.

Delay

Many times a prospect's comments do not help a producer identify the prospect's reaction. Maybe the prospect says, "Well, I don't know. Let me think it over." Or, "I'll run this by a friend of mine. Call me next week." Obviously there is not agreement. But should this attitude be classified as disbelief, indifference, or objection? In cases like this, or whenever the producer is not really sure of the prospect's attitude, the producer should realize that the prospect is delaying. Whether the producer uses leading or nonleading questions depends on the situation. The producer must uncover the reason for the **delay** and then handle the reaction. If the producer does not determine and handle the underlying attitude, there will be no opportunity to close.

Closing

Closing is what the sales call is all about. **Closing** does not necessarily mean the sale is made, but it means that the objective of the sales call has been met. The objective of each call is based on the producer's marketing

II. Selling
   A. Selling and the Producer
   B. Individual Selling Skills
III. The Sources of Business in an Agency
   A. Account Acquisition Versus Account Development Approach
   B. Product-Customer Marketing Matrix

plan. It is not unusual in the property-liability business to make two or more calls on a prospect, each with a different objective. The first call could be to introduce the producer and to get expiration dates of current policies. The second call could be designed to obtain copies of current policies. The third call could be the actual sales call. Having an objective for each call in advance is important. The techniques and words used in the closing depend on the objective.

Many successful salespersons say that if a producer can get the prospect to agree throughout the call, the sale will be made. Begin to close by summarizing those features of the policy or service that have been accepted by the prospect (start the head nodding "yes"), and then request a commitment. Only the features that have been accepted by the prospect are summarized, not all of the features of the policy. Using the closing to introduce new features is inappropriate as it gives the prospect the opportunity to direct the conversation away from making a commitment. Closing properly can be powerful. Ms. Jones, for instance, has expressed no further needs. The producer might close by saying:

> Ms. Jones, we have discussed the personal umbrella liability policy—how it adds a million-dollar layer of protection on your existing coverage. It covers you worldwide—even in Mexico. It even provides you a million dollars of coverage where you do not now have coverage. All of this costs only $150 a year! Ms. Jones, what is the name of your automobile insurer?

Notice that both the summary and the requested policy application information flowed into each other. Some think that using one of the benefits as part of the commitment request is a good idea. Others think that giving the prospect a choice between two actions, both of which would mean the prospect will buy, is better. Both of those ideas are evident in the closing statement for the accountant:

> The protection of your office facilities can be ensured with the coverage I've described, Mr. Smith. Risks of physical loss coverage will mean they will be replaced for almost any cause of loss. The office package is simple in design and contains cost-saving features for you. With the valuable papers endorsement, your clients' records can be reconstructed. And if your office is destroyed, your payroll and profits are covered while you are spending time getting back into full operation. Do you want a $50,000 or $60,000 limit on your business income coverage?

Concluding Comment

The types of sales techniques described here will be found in almost any selling course available to producers. Every sales call will not result in a sale. However, the important aspect of any sales approach is that it should increase the "batting average" of the producer by making the policy or service appear to fit the needs of the prospect. Taking a more complete course in the application of sales techniques would be well worth the investment of time and money.

The Sources of Business in an Agency

Three **controllable sources of additional premium** for an insurance agency are: (1) additional sales to existing customers, called "account development"; (2) sales to new customers, called "account acquisition"; and (3) merger, or acquiring customers by purchasing another agency. (Agency mergers, because of their diversity, are beyond the scope of the AAI Program.) The product-customer marketing matrix (Exhibit 4-3) graphically depicts both the account development and account acquisition methods of generating additional premium. **Account development** activities include upgrading insurance coverages on existing policies and total account selling. **Account acquisition** activities include target marketing and developing temporary monopolies.

Marketing Tip

Account development is presented early in AAI because it is one of the best marketing techniques a producer can use. For less time, and definitely less expense, a producer can earn significantly higher commissions by selling fully developed accounts. Throughout the AAI courses, producers will find suggestions for developing accounts—new policies, broadening endorsements, and adequate limits of coverage—all of which provide better protection for a producer's clients as well as more income for the producer. Use the ideas in this assignment as the foundation, and build on that foundation with the material covered in future assignments.

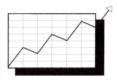

Exhibit 4-3
Product-Customer Marketing Matrix

	Products — Existing	Products — New
Account Development —Current Clients	1 Account Upgrading	2 Account Selling
Account Acquisition —New Clients	3 Target Marketing	4 Temporary Monopoly

Account Acquisition Versus Account Development Approach

Agencies that attempt only to acquire accounts deal with each customer as representing a new but limited amount of business. Those agencies want to have as many clients as possible. On the other hand, an agency that practices account development activities sees that each client represents an account and that time must be spent developing that account. In other words, account acquisition activities are designed

II. Selling
III. The Sources of Business in an Agency
   A. Account Acquisition Versus Account Development Approach
   B. Product-Customer Marketing Matrix
IV. The Account Review Process

primarily to bring new customers into the agency, while account development activities are designed to increase the value of each client's account to the agency.

Product-Customer Marketing Matrix

The **product-customer marketing matrix** shows that there are two types of clients: those to whom the agency is currently selling (current clients) and those customers who are new to the agency. The matrix also shows two types of insurance products: products that already exist in the client's account and products that are new to the client's account.

Account Upgrading

Quadrant 1 in the product-customer marketing matrix represents account upgrading. **Account upgrading** consists of sales activities such as raising limits on existing coverages and adding coverages to existing policies, such as replacement cost coverage on contents for homeowners. That opportunity is often overlooked in account development.

Account Selling

Quadrant 2 of the product-customer marketing matrix represents selling new types of insurance products to existing clients and is called "account selling." **Account selling** allows a producer to (1) develop the existing relationship with the client, (2) ask to write all the business for a particular client, and (3) help to lock out the competition. The ultimate goal of total account selling is for clients to never buy insurance from any other producer.

E&O Alert!

Having one producer selling all of a client's insurance also serves to minimize uninsured and overlooked exposures that could arise when multiple producers are involved. Total account selling, therefore, offers greater security for the client and decreases the E&O concerns of the producer.

Target Marketing

Quadrant 3 of the matrix represents selling new clients products with which the producer is familiar. This account acquisition activity can be rewarding for a producer as it allows the producer to choose a particular insurance product, such as umbrella coverages, homeowners, or service station package programs, and also to choose a group of prospects to approach. Those sales activities might also involve market segmentation—for instance, targeting a particular ZIP Code with a mailing. Highly valued homes within a certain geographic territory, for example, might be selected for a preferred personal lines program currently offered by an agency. That type of marketing activity is covered in detail in AAI 83.

Temporary Monopoly

A **temporary monopoly** is a situation in which an agency is currently the exclusive provider of a product or service that clients want or need. This situation is usually temporary because other agencies or insurance companies will copy the original idea and restore competition to the market.

An example of a temporary monopoly is an insurer offering a new package policy to an agency on an exclusive basis within its marketing territory. This type of marketing activity is also covered in detail in AAI 83.

Quadrant 4 of the product-customer marketing matrix represents selling a new customer a new type of insurance product. It is the area of the matrix that brings out the entrepreneurial spirit in a producer because this activity allows a producer to take on a totally new insurance product. With this new product in hand, the producer can develop a new customer base.

The product-customer marketing matrix makes clear that a careful balance of account acquisition and account development activities needs to be established so that:

1. The producer and agency are attracting a potentially loyal book of business through account acquisition activities.
2. Existing accounts are retained and developed.
3. The agency's insurance companies can have a chance to grow through a book of business that is expanding consistently with the insurer's underwriting standards.
4. The book of business is profitable for the insurer and agency over the long term.

> **Check** your understanding of the *Key Words and Phrases* found in the first part of this assignment.

Market (p. 5)

Market segment (p. 5)

Market segmentation (p. 5)

Product targeting (p. 5)

Suspect (p. 5)

Prospect (p. 5)

Sales strategy (p. 5)

Order processing (p. 7)

Missionary selling (p. 7)

Creative selling (p. 7)

Cold calling (p. 8)

Joint calls (p. 8)

Product feature (p. 10)

Product benefit (p. 10)

Nonleading question (p. 13)

Leading question (p. 13)

Agreement (p. 15)

Disbelief (p. 15)

Indifference (p. 16)

Objections (p. 16)

Delay (p. 17)

Closing (p. 17)

Controllable sources of additional premium (p. 19)

Account development (p. 19)

Account acquisition (p. 19)

Product-customer marketing matrix (p. 20)

Account upgrading (p. 20)

Account selling (p. 20)

Temporary monopoly (p. 21)

Review the concepts presented in the first part of this assignment by answering the following questions. **Note: Acceptable answers to all questions appear at the end of this segment.**

1. How are agency sales planning and personal sales planning (a) similar and (b) different? (p. 4)

2. What is the difference between top-down planning and bottom-up planning? (p. 4)

3. In sales terminology, how do a suspect and a prospect differ? (p. 5)

4. How can a producer's sales strategies improve sales performance? (pp. 5-6)

5. How are the following three selling techniques used in insurance sales? (pp. 7-8)
   (a) order processing

   (b) missionary selling

   (c) creative selling

6. What are the advantages of joint calls in sales training and sales management? (p. 8)

7. When does a product feature become a product benefit? (p. 10)

8. What are the selling skills a producer needs for a successful sales call? (pp. 11-14)

Assignment 4—Insurance Sales and Account Development / 4-25

9. Illustrate the following: (pp. 12-13)
   (a) a nonleading question

   (b) a leading question

10. When should a producer use (a) leading questions and (b) nonleading questions in a sales presentation? (pp. 13-14)

11. What are the five prospect reactions a producer might encounter in a sales call? (pp. 14-15)

12. How should a producer handle both types of objections from a prospect? (p. 16)

13. Illustrate a closing statement. (pp. 17-18)

Apply the concepts presented in the first part of this assignment by answering the following questions.

1. Joan Sellers, who has been a commercial lines producer for a large agency, has decided to move to a different city and start her own agency. She does not know many people in the new city and does not have any personal knowledge of any of the potential commercial accounts there. Outline a strategy Ms. Sellers might use in (a) segmenting the market, (b) targeting products, and (c) making a sales approach to the prospects.

2. An agent recently stated that "property and liability insurance is bought, but life insurance must be sold." He believes that consumers are aware of their need for property and liability insurance but must be shown that they need life insurance.

   (a) Identify and explain the three selling techniques discussed in the assignment.

   (b) If the agent's statement is correct, which one of the three selling techniques would be used most frequently for (1) property and liability insurance and (2) life insurance?

3. Tom, the newest producer at the agency, isn't doing well. You've just overheard him telling a CSR, "This is hopeless. I know there must be hundreds of people out there who might need my products, but where do I start? And insurance policies are so technical that explaining them to a prospect is difficult. I wish I knew how the more experienced agents handle it." As a "more experienced agent," you invite Tom to lunch the next day to discuss his statements.

   (a) Explain to Tom how market segmentation could help him.

   (b) Explain to him why you don't sell technicalities but you do sell benefits.

   (c) How could your offer to make joint calls with Tom help him?

4. Your sales manager has reminded you that "No money is made until the sale is closed." Although your prospecting activity has been good and you have presented numerous proposals to prospects, you have not succeeded in closing the sales. The sales manager suggests that your problem might stem from not properly understanding and responding to the prospects' reactions. Suggest one way in which you could respond or react to each of these prospect reactions:

   (a) agreement

(b) disbelief

(c) indifference

(d) objections

(e) delay

> **Read** the definitions of the *Key Words and Phrases* that follow. Being familiar with these important words will help you better understand the second part of this assignment.

Account review process	The process to review the account by prioritizing and organizing in order to develop any sales action
Priority accounts	Determining which accounts have the greatest need for use of agency resources
Basic accounts	Personal lines and small commercial accounts
Technical coverage accounts	Accounts with larger and more complex commercial-type exposures
Minimum agency standards	Statements of broad conditions an account must meet to receive the best service from the agency
Minimum account standards	Statements of minimum coverages an account must have to receive the best service from the agency
X-dating	A process to obtain expiration dates of policies not currently written by the agency
Automatic "add-on"	Automatic coverage changes made to an account at renewal to bring it up to minimum standards
Contact sales	Selling additional insurance to meet agency standards by telephone or mail contact with the client
Value-added service	The increase in the worth of a product because of an enhancement added to that product

> **Study** the second part of this assignment, which includes the following sections:

IV. The Account Review Process
V. Agency Procedures for Complete Account Development
VI. The Benefits of Account Development

The Account Review Process

The **account review process** involves five elements. First, priority accounts must be established. Second, all accounts in the agency are grouped based on the technical expertise required to handle each account. Third, every client file is organized so that information can be efficiently extracted from it. Fourth, information from the file is transferred to an account information summary sheet or computer file. Finally, the information in the summary is translated into some sales action.

Establish Priority Accounts

Establishing **priority accounts** allows the agency or producer to ascertain which agency resources will be needed during the sales process and concentrates sales efforts on accounts with the greatest need. The resources needed could be for mailing letters, keeping the office open at night for telephone calls, assistance in placing coverage, and so forth. The accounts with the greatest need are identified when the boundaries for each priority are set. Some accounts deserve or require attention before others. Account development requires that all accounts be analyzed for coverage, and the placement of each account into its priority category can take place during this step.

Agencies using account development prioritize accounts in different ways. Two examples will be given here. The first example is a set of priority accounts from an agency just beginning the account development process. The second example is from an agency that has had account development as part of its marketing plan for ten years.

New Account Development Priorities

To gain the maximum benefits for all parties, an agency new to account development could establish four priority levels for its accounts:

1. Accounts with the greatest need for insurance changes
2. Accounts with the greatest errors and omissions potential
3. Accounts with the greatest premium potential
4. Accounts with adequate coverages and limits

Established in that manner, the priorities direct subsequent sales efforts where they will do both the client and the agency the most initial good.

Established Account Development Priorities

One agency with over $15 million in commission income uses what it calls the "80-20 Rule" to establish its account priorities. The account development adaptation of the rule is that 20 percent of the agency's accounts develop 80 percent of its revenues. The agency concentrates its account development work on that 20 percent of its accounts. The commercial lines division categories are priority commercial and other commercial. The personal lines division has also established two categories, priority personal and other personal lines. Exceptions to the categorization by revenue are made only for sources of influence. Therefore, if an otherwise non-priority account is a good source of influence for referrals, it will be placed in the priority category.

Segregate Accounts by Coverage

The account review process continues by dividing accounts within the agency by the expertise required to handle the account. The traditional agency processing split, as indicated in the previous example of account priorities, has been between personal and commercial lines. Personal lines are usually handled by customer service representatives (CSRs) or new producers; commercial lines are usually serviced by more experienced CSRs, account executives, or experienced producers. Every account is then identified as one of two secondary categories: one category reflects accounts that do not require much technical expertise to understand or service; the other category, at a minimum, reflects accounts that require technical expertise to service. One name used in agencies for those accounts that do not require much technical expertise is "**basic accounts**." Other names include "family and small business accounts" or "personal and light commercial accounts." Those accounts include all personal lines and small commercial accounts, including businessowners policies and small commercial packages. Names used for the other category are "**technical coverage accounts**," "complex commercial accounts," or "business accounts." Technical coverage accounts include accounts with larger and more complex commercial exposures. The exact definition of which accounts qualify as technical coverage accounts varies by agency.

Basic Accounts

Because basic accounts have personal lines policies such as auto, homeowners, flood, umbrella, and commercial lines policies such as businessowners, these accounts will require less expertise than large complex commercial accounts. Basic accounts give inside support staff and less experienced producers the opportunity to display their talent.

An efficient and financially rewarding innovation in the sale of insurance has been the implementation of sales centers for personal lines and small commercial accounts. In such an operation, a group of individuals, often CSRs licensed to sell property and liability insurance, work as a team under the direction of a sales center manager. In addition to their responsibility for developing new business, sales center personnel are also involved in account development. The sales center is the perfect model to be used in handling the account development process for basic accounts because a routine sales procedure is vital to account development.

Technical Coverage Accounts

Technical coverage accounts require the technical expertise of more experienced producers and customer service representatives. In many cases, those accounts also require the application of advanced risk management techniques. The large or complicated accounts most likely fall into the priority selling account category. They generally represent higher amounts of premium for the agency as well as additional opportunities to obtain the complete account. Even if the review of those accounts can be done mechanically or by clerical personnel, the actual account development selling activities should be handled by an experienced CSR or producer.

> ### E&O Alert!
>
>
>
> The preceding discussion about experienced and inexperienced personnel is important in preventing E&O claims. Since large premium accounts generally involve many policies and a wide variety of exposures, these accounts require the more experienced personnel in the agency to properly advise and service them. Relatively new producers are often successful in soliciting and closing large accounts, but some of these successful sales might be due to a low premium that does not include all of the policies or coverages proposed by a more knowledgeable and experienced producer. Big E&O claims caused by improper coverage are not worth the commission dollars generated by this sales situation.

Organize Client Files

The third step in the account review process is to organize the information within client files in a manner that will allow relevant coverage information to be extracted quickly and systematically. For the agency that has not yet established a standard automation file procedure, this step in the account review process can be overwhelming. What is required is simple but not necessarily easy to accomplish. In essence, all personal and commercial accounts within the agency must be individually organized so that they can be reviewed to determine the existing coverages and those that are needed. This organizing part of the account review process accomplishes two goals. First, it allows the producer to become familiar again with individual clients and the nature of their accounts. Second, it generates prospect lists that will serve as the "selling source" for account development selling.

In some instances, this portion of the account review process reveals the need for reorganizing the hard copy client files of the agency. If that is so, several sources, such as Master Agency Manager developed jointly by the Independent Insurance Agents of America (IIAA) and the Florida

Association of Insurance Agents, can provide information for the design and construction of standard agency files. Organizing can be as simple as placing policies on the right-hand side of the file, endorsements on the left-hand side of the file, and stapling bills and messages in separate corners. The purpose is to make sure that, during the review of an account, all items of a similar nature appear in the same place in each client file.

In an automated system, file consistency is equally important. It is also important that the data entry be completed with editing safeguards. Those safeguards should not allow information to be entered into or deleted from the system unless certain data fields have been either entered or overwritten by deliberate choices on the operator's part. The safeguards ensure that the file contains the information relative to coverages, endorsements, and limits provided necessary for the account review process.

Account Information Summary Sheets

A document that must be produced by the account review process is some form of customer profile or data summary sheet. Different profile or data summary sheets are used for personal accounts and for commercial coverage accounts. Although the following sections of this assignment refer to "sheets," the processes and information also apply to computer summary files.

Personal Account Review Sheets

Agency personnel need to pay close attention to the format of the account review or profile summary sheet. The sheet should indicate:

1. The exposures of the insured
2. The coverages the insured has purchased from the agency
3. The coverages the insured has declined to purchase in the past
4. The coverages the insured has purchased elsewhere
5. The expiration dates for coverages purchased elsewhere
6. The suggested sales action for the immediate future
7. The results of account development sales activities

Every attempt should be made to provide backup information in the customer file when a suggested coverage has been declined. This should include the coverage offered, date declined, and the customer's initials or signature, if possible.

The checklists shown in Appendix A of this assignment do not provide for all of this information. They do, however, provide a sampling of the information needed for a review summary sheet. Every agency should design its own account review summary sheets to reflect the way the information they contain will be used in the account development process. Some will be able to use profile sheets for purposes other than account development. The most important consideration is to determine what the agency wants from the account review process and then to design, adopt, or modify an account review summary sheet that will capture the information necessary to accomplish the goal. Although basic coverage accounts are less complicated than technical coverage accounts, the proper amount of time and effort must be spent in reviewing all client files.

Marketing Tip

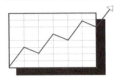

Most agencies are now automated, so they will probably use the personal or commercial account summary forms provided by their software vendor rather than create new hard copy forms. After the account summaries are entered, the automated data can be sorted fairly easily to provide a wide variety of marketing opportunities. Personal lines clients, for instance, can be sorted by those clients who insure their auto but not their homeowners through the agency. CSRs, sales center personnel, or less experienced producers can then contact these clients to sell homeowners policies.

E&O Alert!

Published national statistics indicate that more than 30 percent of all agency errors and omissions claims result from personal lines, and most of these arise from auto and homeowners coverage.[2] Don't underestimate the E&O exposures of "basic accounts" simply because the premium is small or the exposures are not as extensive as technical coverage accounts.

Commercial Account Summary Sheets

The process required to comprehensively service the more complex or larger commercial accounts, both in review and in prospecting, is more complicated than for personal accounts. Checklist 2 in Appendix A helps identify major areas of exposures commonly encountered in commercial insurance. Use of this or similar forms assists in identifying potential loss exposures and noting whether or not the client has that coverage with the agency. This will lead to the natural step of suggesting to the client that he or she purchase any coverage that is not currently placed through the agency. The form used should have a place to indicate whether a suggested coverage is rejected and the date when the recommendation was made. The coverages and exposures listed on this or similar exposure identification forms are not exhaustive. The producer or CSR cannot rely on these forms to completely analyze all of an account's exposures. These forms are guidelines that direct the producer or the CSR to inquire and examine other areas to which the client might be exposed.

E&O Alert!

Account files can be organized by support personnel. However, only those who possess the necessary technical expertise should be involved in the account development sales process for large and technically complex commercial accounts. A team approach works particularly well for these accounts since an agency can bring a great deal of talent to bear in solving coverage issues.

Methods of Organizing Files and Completing the Account Review Summary Sheets

The initial account review process might appear to be overwhelming. It need not be. Its benefits should more than compensate for the necessary hard work. Organizing files and completing account review summary sheets can be (1) part of an agency project, (2) part of the annual renewal process, or (3) performed with temporary employees.

Agency Project

The best and most thorough way to complete the initial account review process is to have agency personnel organize the files and complete the reviews for the business for which they are responsible. This could be a one-time agency project, accomplished at the rate of a few hours a day until all accounts are reviewed. Some regular day-to-day activities of the agency will be necessarily, but temporarily, hampered or curtailed. However, as an agency project, the files are quickly put in order, the review sheets are completed, and the priority accounts can be contacted immediately for additional sales. The account review process in subsequent years will become part of the routine renewal procedure and will prove much less onerous and disruptive once this project approach is completed.

Completing Summaries as Account Renewal Activity

The second way to implement the account review process is to organize the files and review the accounts as an additional activity during the normal renewal process. This will require the time spent by agency personnel at renewal to be increased so that all accounts receive adequate attention. One drawback to this approach is that it will take at least a full year before all accounts are reviewed and even longer before the sales to these accounts can be dealt with. Also, because this review process will take place for a full year, it may lead to decreased enthusiasm among the participants. Finally, some of the errors and omissions exposures faced by the agency remain unidentified and untreated for twelve months or longer. The positive side of account review as a part of the renewal process is that the disruption to other agency business is minimized.

Completing Account Review Summaries With Temporary Employees

A final method used by agencies to complete the initial account review process is to use temporary employees. Temporary employees can, for example, establish an order for the contents of a file so that declaration pages, endorsements, and so forth appear in the same place in every file. This way, when regular agency employees complete the account review summary sheets, the process will be faster and simpler for them. Temporary employees could also attach the client summary sheet to the file or load the information into the computer. Students from local colleges or universities who are pursuing business degrees can sometimes be used in the account review process.

IV. The Account Review Process

V. Agency Procedures for Complete Account Development
   A. Putting the Account Review to Use
   B. Sales Activities Supporting Account Development

Agency Procedures for Complete Account Development

The purpose of the account review is to translate exposure identification into sales. This section of the assignment addresses the broad types of sales that should be made from the information generated. It discusses sales activities that support account development and gives two specific sales procedures that can be used for personal and commercial accounts.

Putting the Account Review to Use

As a result of the account review, sales can be made through account upgrading and total account selling.

Account Upgrading

The client data sheets completed for both personal and commercial accounts should help to identify those coverages the agency should recommend for upgrading. Those upgrades should be automatic because they will raise the coverage for the account either to minimum agency standards or minimum account standards.

Minimum Agency Standards

Agencies write many types of accounts. Some of them might be excellent accounts that deserve attention, and some might be accounts that never have been and never will be developed (such as those that insist on buying minimum limits only). The purpose of minimum agency standards is to communicate to all agency personnel the nature of the accounts that should receive the highest attention and service. Those that do not meet the standard are still treated courteously but do not receive the same attention and level of service. Some agencies, in fact, actively "invite" these clients to seek insurance from another agency that is prepared to give them greater attention and service. This invitation to leave could have an added benefit of reducing E&O exposures. Many E&O claims arise from the inadequate coverages or limits carried by this type of client.

The **minimum agency standards** are statements of the broad conditions an account must meet to receive the best service from the agency. For example, for personal lines, the minimum agency standards could be:

1. Annual premium potential of $2,000 or more within three years
2. Three-policy minimum
3. Direct bill only

Similar standards would be established for basic commercial accounts and for technical coverage accounts.

Minimum Account Standards

The **minimum account standards** are more specific than the minimum agency standards. Those standards are statements of the minimum coverages an account must have to receive the best service. For example, in the case of personal lines accounts:

Required Coverage
- HO-3 only
- Section II HO limits of $300,000 minimum
- PAP liability limits and UM/UIM of $300,000 minimum

Recommended Coverage
- Personal umbrella
- Floater coverage for personal property (furs, jewels, coins, etc.)
- Life insurance with the death benefit no less than the mortgage on the main dwelling

Once the standards are established, any account that currently does not meet agency standards or account standards would be a priority account for automatic account upgrading. This could be as simple as raising every personal auto policy with limits of less than $300,000 for bodily injury and property damage liability up to $300,000.

If an account and all of its policies meet both minimum standards, "add-on" sales could occur through coverage enhancements. Many insurers offer, with few underwriting restrictions, such enhancements as inflation guard for dwellings, replacement cost on contents, and so forth. Those coverage enhancements provide opportunities to improve coverage for clients as well as to generate additional commission income for the agency. All that is necessary is to establish procedures to regularly add such coverages at renewal to accounts without them. Such "add-on" coverage sales activities are most applicable to personal accounts.

Marketing Tip

Frequently, the agency can arrange to have both minimum limits and coverage enhancements "rolled on" by the insurance company at policy renewal. This eliminates the need to request endorsements on every policy individually and. . .

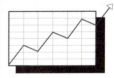

E&O Alert!

. . . reduces the possibility that coverage standards will be overlooked. Clients should be asked to provide a written request to have coverage deleted.

Total Account Selling

The second intended sales result of an account review is total account selling activity. Major loss exposures are identified as a result of each

IV. The Account Review Process

V. Agency Procedures for Complete Account Development

A. Putting the Account Review to Use

B. Sales Activities Supporting Account Development

C. Specific Sales Activities for Basic Accounts

account reviewed. If no insurance is currently written to cover the exposure, or if it is written by another agency, some initial sales activity must begin. In the first situation, the client must be contacted and information obtained so that coverage can be discussed. However, if coverage is written through another agency, X-dating activities are undertaken so that a proposal can be submitted to the client at renewal. In either event, the account review should highlight those lines of insurance not currently written by the agency so that they can be clearly marked on the client review sheet and sales activities can be initiated.

It is critical that renewal upgrades and enhancements become a permanent procedure in the agency because after the novelty of this new project wears thin, the enthusiasm for it might wane. Once implemented, however, the process must be incorporated as a normal agency function and included in the job descriptions of all personnel involved.

Further, not every producer or CSR is going to achieve a 99 percent closing rate. Many insureds are going to decline to purchase additional coverages and enhancements or increased limits for various reasons. However, through the contact with the insured, the "seed has been planted," and the insured has six months or a year for this suggestion to grow. The producer is likely to encounter less resistance to suggested account improvements in the future.

Sales Activities Supporting Account Development

Mailing sales letters and obtaining X-dates are two specific activities that can be undertaken by agency personnel to support the development of accounts.

Sales Letters

One good method for addressing account development sales is through the use of an individually addressed sales letter. Such a letter begins by stating the purpose of the communication, usually identified from the client profile sheet attached to the account file. The letter discusses any exposures that have been identified for coverage upgrades, enhancements, or additional lines of insurance. The letter asks the client to consider the implications of the uninsured loss exposure. Finally, the client is asked to take some action on the suggestion.

On accounts of all types, reviews clearly identify those loss exposures that need to be treated. Consequently, sales letters can be systematically generated and sent to clients at least ninety days prior to renewal. All involved staff, managers, producers, and CSRs must be keyed into this activity.

With basic accounts, the letter should state the needed upgrades or enhancements to be added to existing coverage at renewal. If the insured does not wish to purchase them, he or she should return the letter and indicate the rejection of the upgrade or enhancement. A release form should be part of the letter, as shown in Exhibit 4-4. Any such client rejection should become a permanent part of the client file to protect the agency in case of errors and omissions claims.

Exhibit 4-4
Sample Automatic Add-on Letter to a Client With a
Release Statement

Mr. Steven O'Toole
1234 South Oahu Drive
Honolulu, Hawaii 96813

Dear Mr. O'Toole:

We are pleased to report that your automobile insurance will be renewed on May 17th. Because of your excellent driving record, your premiums will be approximately the same as they were last year. The slight increase in your premium is due to the increase in your liability, uninsured, and underinsured limits from $50,000 to $300,000, effective May 17.

In the last few years, judgments here in Hawaii have been increasing. A successful businessman like yourself is a greater target for a lawsuit. That is why we have raised your liability insurance limit. We are happy to tell you that this 600 percent increase in protection will only add about $80 to your annual premium. If you would like more information or higher limits, please call me at 555-6590.

In the event you do not want this important increase in coverage for your automobile insurance, please sign the release at the bottom of this letter and return it to us. We will delete the increase and bill you only for the renewal of coverage at your current limits. In any event, it is our pleasure to serve you, and we hope that you will think of us for all of your insurance needs. (We also sell life insurance.)

Cordially,

George Akai, AAI

I understand the importance of the increased limits recommended to me but have decided not to purchase the increased limits at this time.

_____   _____
Insured (Steven O'Toole)   Date

For the more complex technical coverage accounts, the insured is alerted to gaps in coverage by the letter and told that he or she will receive a call from the producer within the next few days. At that time, the producer will review the account coverages and deal with any add-on or enhanced coverages that need to be discussed. Here, too, the client should be asked to sign or initial any recommended coverage he or she declines. Coverage that has been declined should be recommended at each renewal. The account review sheets are vital in order to ensure that this procedure is followed in subsequent years.

X-Dating

For personal lines accounts, no single activity produces more opportunities for a sale than an organized, well-managed X-dating program. As an account development tool, **X-dating** is geared toward obtaining the expiration dates of policies not currently written by the agency. In this

IV. The Account Review Process
V. Agency Procedures for Complete Account Development
    B. Sales Activities Supporting Account Development
    C. Specific Sales Activities for Basic Accounts
    D. Technical Coverage Accounts
VI. The Benefits of Account Development
    A. Agency and Producer Benefits

process, a CSR or an inside sales representative would call a client and identify the reason for the telephone call. For example, "Mr. Smith, I notice we do not handle your homeowners insurance. Would you please tell me when your homeowners policy expires so that we can provide you with a proposal at renewal?" Once the expiration date has been obtained, the caller obtains the information necessary to quote prior to renewal. Actual delivery of the proposal must be early enough so that a sale is possible.

This X-dating system has long been the backbone of success for members of the direct writing and exclusive agency systems, such as Allstate, State Farm, and Nationwide. In the account development context, X-dating allows the agency to use its positive image with current clients to develop each account as a natural source for continuing sales.

Specific Sales Activities for Basic Accounts

Basic accounts can be developed by the automatic "add-on" coverage technique or by a personal contact made for the sale.

Automatic Add-Ons

For every personal lines account (and some small commercial accounts that fit in the basic category), coverage changes to meet the agency or account standards should be handled as **automatic add-ons** at renewal (whenever state law allows). In such instances, personal lines liability limits could be automatically raised to the account minimum or, for property coverages, replacement cost on contents could be added.

Contact Sales

For accounts that require additional lines of coverage, such as adding auto insurance when the agency already writes the homeowners, it is recommended that such coverages be sold by **contact sales**. Because the commission on personal lines often does not support an outside sales call, the sale can be handled over the telephone, using licensed CSRs or sales center personnel.

For example, in one agency the account review process showed that an insured who was teaching piano lessons in the home did not have the permitted business occupancy endorsement on the homeowners. This need was addressed by an automatic add-on using a letter to inform the insured of the need and the price. During the review, it was also discovered that the insured did not have any excess liability coverage. For this second sale, a flyer on umbrella liability coverage was included with the letter.

Four days after the letter was mailed, a CSR called the insured. The add-on was no problem and was readily agreed to. However, the insured did not see the need for the umbrella. A few months later, when the insured's auto insurance came up for renewal, an umbrella quote along with a copy of a newspaper article on a recent large judgment in the community was mailed with the auto renewal notice. A second telephone call to the insured resulted in the sale of the umbrella policy.

Technical Coverage Accounts

Technical coverage accounts require a contact sale that is benefit oriented and individually tailored for any coverage upgrades, add-ons, or new lines to be sold. The producer, armed with the knowledge that certain coverages need upgrading or enhancement and that additional coverages are needed, approaches the insured from a risk management standpoint. Each sales presentation is individually tailored and geared to that client's commercial insurance needs (exposures).

Appendix B to this assignment is a form called "Client General Information" that is used by one large agency for all of its large commercial coverage accounts. The first page identifies the insured, and the subsequent pages develop general information on the business of the insured. The file of the insured also contains a risk management exposure identification survey used to identify specific exposures, a portion of which is shown in Appendix C.

The Client General Information form is used to brief the producer, CSRs, and account executives on the nature of the account. The Information Checklist is developed prior to the personal call on the client. Exhibit 4-5 is an illustrative section from the Information Checklist used to examine an insured's umbrella liability coverage. Ninety days prior to renewal, the producer, account executive, and CSRs involved meet to complete the entire form. In this umbrella portion, the group would determine (1) if coverage is a true umbrella or straight excess, (2) whether the insured is indemnified or the insurer pays on behalf of the insured, (3) whether broad-named insureds are covered, (4) the level of the self-insured retention (SIR), (5) the nature of the defense coverage, and so forth. For each item on the form, the group notes whether the relevant coverage applies and is in force. If a coverage upgrade or enhancement is applicable, a note is made on the right-hand column of the sheet.

When this form is completed, the producer and perhaps others call on the client. The Client General Information sheet is updated first, and then a general discussion of current coverage is held. All upgrades or enhancements are discussed. Any rejected ideas are noted on the information checklist by the insured, who initials the rejected coverage and writes "no." From this meeting, the renewal policies are generated.

If the producer had attempted to discuss some of the technical enhancements available or to explain, for example, the different type of defense provisions that can be found in an umbrella in a letter, he or she would be less likely to make the additional sale. The technical nature of the account requires a personal call on the insured.

The Benefits of Account Development

Any marketing activity of an agency should ultimately work for the benefit of the agency and its producers, clients, and represented insurance companies. Account upgrading and account selling can provide real benefits for these groups.

Exhibit 4-5
Information Checklist

	Coverage in Force				Available Improvement (or) Uninsured Exposed
	Yes	No	Unknown	Not Applicable	
IX. Umbrella Liability—Limits _____					
(1) True umbrella	___	___	___	___	___
(2) Essentially excess liability	___	___	___	___	___
(3) Indemnifies insured	___	___	___	___	___
(4) Pays on behalf of insured	___	___	___	___	___
(5) Broadened named insured endorsement	___	___	___	___	___
(6) Retention—Amount _____	___	___	___	___	___
(7) Defense within retention amount	___	___	___	___	___
(8) Following form endorsement	___	___	___	___	___
(9) Employers liability	___	___	___	___	___
(10) Covers Mandolidis, Blankenship, etc.	___	___	___	___	___
(11) Covers care, custody, control	___	___	___	___	___
(12) Covers personal injury	___	___	___	___	___
(13) Covers worldwide operations	___	___	___	___	___
(14) Covers worldwide products	___	___	___	___	___
(15) Non-owned aircraft	___	___	___	___	___
(16) Non-owned watercraft	___	___	___	___	___
(17) Warranted underlying coverage is in force	___	___	___	___	___
(18) Underlying limits required					
CGL _____	___	___	___	___	___
Auto _____	___	___	___	___	___
Empl. Liab. _____	___	___	___	___	___
Other (identify and describe)	___	___	___	___	___

Agency and Producer Benefits

Account development can be successful because both the agency and the producer immediately receive its benefits. The agency should enjoy increased profit and better insurer relations through increased commission income, decreased expenses, increased retention, lessened errors and omissions exposures, improved producer training, increased professionalism, and the opportunity to show clients the value added by the agency.

Increased Commission Income

Increases in commission income from both account upgrading and account selling activities are in part achieved because of the higher closing ratio for sales to existing clients. The closing ratio is higher because the existing book of business is a qualified customer base. If clients have had a positive experience with the agency, they are likely to be in a receptive frame of mind to discuss the proposal with the producer. The credibility gap that exists when producers face new prospects is reduced or eliminated.

Because sales are easier to obtain in account development, the rate of commission income growth can be accelerated by concentrating on account upgrading and account selling.

Decreased Expenses

Selling activities create expenses. Selling expenses are either direct or indirect. Direct expenses to the agency include travel, entertainment, commissions payable to producers, and other expenditures that could be tied directly to a specific sale. Indirect expenses include those costs that are allocated to a sale but are not directly chargeable, such as a portion of a producer's automobile allowance, clerical salaries and benefits, and so forth. Selling expenses are greater for new account production because the necessary activities related to prospecting, proposing, and selling are high and do not result in sales with each proposal made. The costs of those sales activities are borne by the income produced from new accounts. In actuality, new business production is the most expensive selling activity in agency operations. It is even more expensive when the producer is not careful to relate controllable expenses to potential sales.

Conversely, account development selling is relatively less expensive. Most of the activities relating to account review, client discussions, ordering the renewal, and processing the renewal are a part of the normal account renewal activity. Many of these same activities create the opportunity to upgrade the account through increased or new coverages. Hence, the additional costs are directly related to the existing account, and the costs are met through increased commission income. Account development sales activities can cause an immediate increase in agency profit through lower selling expenses, increased revenue, and a high closing ratio.

Increased Retention

Accounts that are fully developed are less likely to be lost to the competition. A slogan that every producer might consider adopting is, "The best business you have is the business you have." Studies by agency management consultants, insurance companies, and the Independent Insurance Agents of America (IIAA) have indicated that when the number of policies or coverages written for an account are increased, the retention rate for that account increases. This is important because, as noted previously, account retention has a major effect on the profitability of an agency.

Exhibit 4-6 shows the results of a survey conducted by the Presidential Commission to Enhance Agency Values of the IIAA. The Commission was formed to identify "new ways for agencies to grow, increase profitability and stability, and perpetuate their ownership and operations."[3] This survey showed that the account retention rate was consistently higher for agencies in the top 25 percent most profitable agencies of those responding.

Exhibit 4-6
Retention Rates of Independent Insurance Agents

*Retention Rate		Revenues less than $250,000	$250,000- $500,000	$500,000- $1,250,000	$1,250,000- $2,500,000	$2,500,000- $5,000,000	more than $5,000,000
Personal Property and Casualty	Average	90.8%	90.9%	89.6%	90.4%	89.6%	88.9%
	Top 25%	96.8	96.8	93.7	95.2	94.7	94.8
Small Commercial Lines**	Average	93.0	94.5	91.8	91.1	89.6	88.5
	Top 25%	97.3	97.2	95.7	95.9	96.1	95.7
Medium to Large Commercial Lines	Average	95.4	96.3	91.6	93.1	92.2	92.5
	Top 25%	100.0	99.0	98.0	97.4	97.7	96.3

* Retention rate is the measurement of number of accounts renewing coverage.

**The accounts classified as "small" differ by agency size from a premium of less than $3,800 for the smallest agencies to nearly $14,000 for the largest agencies.

Source: *The Best Practices Study*, © 1995 Independent Insurance Agents Association, Inc., and Reagan & Associates, Inc.

Marketing Tip

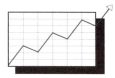

Account development has a series of benefits. First, the more policies written for an account, the greater the likelihood that the account will be retained. This improved retention then leads to the agency's enhanced profitability. Agencies that have solid profit performance offer additional positive features such as greater job security and the ability to provide employees with higher income and better employee benefits. Every agency and producer should look for opportunities to sell the entire account to every client.

Lessened Errors and Omissions Exposure

In today's lawsuit-conscious society, agencies are being sued more frequently for errors and omissions. Whenever an insured suffers a loss and insurance does not respond sufficiently to make the client whole, or nearly whole, the likelihood exists that the client will blame the agent and then sue.

E&O Alert!

Approximately one in eight agents faces an errors and omissions claim each year.[4] This trend will most likely increase the number of suits filed in the future. The account development process lessens the errors and omissions exposure.

Improved Producer Training

Many agencies are reluctant to hire inexperienced producers because agency principals often believe they do not have the time or ability to develop these producers. Account development provides training and allows the new producer to immediately begin to practice what he or she learns. Not only can an agency hire new and inexperienced producers, but those producers should also become productive within a very short period of time.

Training Track

Account development uses many of the ideas of the risk management exposure identification process. Any good exposure identification tool can provide a training track for new producers. One of the best and easiest exposure identification tools is an exposure checklist that reveals the most common exposures of clients. Checklists 1 and 2 in Appendix A are checklists that also serve as account development summary sheets. A producer's training could begin with the Personal Insurance Needs checklist (Checklist 1) that analyzes dwelling, personal property (in its many forms), liability, auto, boats, aircraft, accident and health, life, and retirement exposures. Checklist 2 could be used to train a producer who is ready to learn commercial exposures and commercial insurance products.

Becoming Productive

As the producer becomes comfortable discussing certain coverages, he or she can be assigned files that have or need those coverages. The new producer can be the one who initiates or is asked to make contact with the client. In this way, the new producer is doing the selling job, but with little exposure to rejection since this type of sale has a high close ratio. The producer gets sales experience working from a logical training track, while the agency gets organized productivity from an otherwise inexperienced producer.

Professionalism

Perhaps no area is more important for the producer than the professional status he or she attains within the community and with clients. Producers, by earning professional designations (such as CPCU, AAI, ARM, or CLU), demonstrate their commitment to professionalism in their business dealings. In part, professionalism is based on a body of technical knowledge including risk management and how certain coverages are best applied to a particular client's exposures. Producers are able to demonstrate this aspect of their professionalism through account development. By logically determining the client's exposures and explaining the coverages required, producers demonstrate knowledge of the risk management process. Those professional activities generally result in client satisfaction.

Value-Added Service

The term **value-added service** refers to the increase in the worth of a product because of an enhancement added to that product. For example,

V. Agency Procedures for Complete Account Development

VI. The Benefits of Account Development
   A. Agency and Producer Benefits
   B. Client Benefits

VII. Summary

part of the value added by a steel mill is the conversion of iron ore into steel. The value added by an airline is through moving passengers and cargo efficiently and safely from one location to another. For years, some people have questioned whether or not the producer and the agency have added any value to the insurance product. Their belief is that a producer and agency should do more than merely distribute a product. If, the argument goes, mere distribution is all a producer does, the producer and agency are not necessary.

That argument ignores the real value added by those who place products in specific locations, such as wholesalers, marketing representatives, transportation companies, and so forth. But even if one ignores the so-called "place utility" value added by the insurance distribution force, agencies and their producers do add real value to the insurance product, and account development makes this added value clear to clients.

The insurance product consists of (1) the policies and endorsements that constitute the coverage provided and (2) the services of the producer and agency delivering the policies and endorsements. Standard coverage forms are used for the majority of insureds. However, it is the individual most familiar with the account, the producer or CSR, who recognizes a special need and orders the appropriate endorsement(s) or modifications of coverage. This demonstrates value added. In some cases, a manuscripted policy or endorsement is drafted as a result of a special exposure identified by the producer. This is a real value added. Finally, all activities of the staff of an agency that help provide the insurance requirements of the client add value to the insurance product.

Throughout account development, value added is principally from suggestions for coverage on uninsured exposures or suggestions to modify coverage based on underinsured exposures. In those cases, the concern for the client and the application of risk management are part of the value added. This can be as simple as pointing out to a family that jewelry is limited to $1,000 for loss by theft in the standard homeowners policy. It could be as complicated as a total risk management survey for a large commercial client.

The cost to the insured for the value added by account development is usually minimal compared to both the benefit gained and the outlay for the original policy. For example, Exhibit 4-7 shows the increased limits factors for one state on a personal auto policy. The mandatory minimum liability limits for this state are $35,000 combined single limit (CSL). A glance at the table indicates the nominal cost of increasing coverage limits, and most insureds will need limits significantly higher than the minimum of $35,000. Increasing limits from $35,000 to $1,000,000, an increase of 2,757 percent, increases the liability premium by only 64 percent. This is a classic example of providing a value-added service.

Client Benefits

Benefits of the account development process that accrue to the client are better service, comprehensive exposure treatment, and increased efficiency.

Exhibit 4-7
Increased Limits Factors—Personal Auto Policy—Liability*

Limits	Factors
$ 35,000	1.00
50,000	1.09
75,000	1.14
100,000	1.19
200,000	1.32
300,000	1.39
500,000	1.48
1,000,000	1.64
2,000,000	1.83
3,000,000	1.94
4,000,000	2.05
5,000,000	2.12
10,000,000	2.33

*Reprinted with permission from Insurance Services Office, New York.

Better Service

One advantage for a client from an agency's account development process is that service to that client is enhanced. For example, the producer who handles all lines of insurance for a client is more likely to make sure that all activities, such as the annual review of the account, are accomplished. Also, a client with all coverages written by one agency is an important client and receives priority treatment. When the client has a single source and a single individual with whom to work, he or she is more likely to obtain the kind of service that results in higher satisfaction.

Comprehensive Exposure Treatment

Perhaps the greatest benefit to the client is having all loss exposures identified and dealt with. From the client's perspective, coverage gaps or inadequate limits create potentially nightmarish loss situations. When insurance settlements are not sufficient to indemnify a commercial client, the client might be forced out of business and, on a personal level, have his or her standard of living substantially reduced. The knowledge that the exposures have been systematically and comprehensively identified and treatment explored with the producer generates a real value of account development for the client's peace of mind.

Increased Efficiencies

Clients have the same need for increased business efficiency as do the agency and the producer. With the necessity of dealing with an ever more complex insurance environment, clients can be secure in knowing that exposures are comprehensively identified and treated. That knowledge can reduce the time a client needs to spend on such management activity. This savings of time and money arises from the increased efficiencies of dealing with one agency. Even the client with the least complex personal lines exposures can have the knowledge that the time spent with the producer has been invested wisely. If a client must deal with several producers from several agencies, he or she will find that (1) additional time is required to communicate with each, (2) activities will overlap, and (3) there will be constant pressure for sales presentations for the insurance lines not insured by each.

Check your understanding of the *Key Words and Phrases* found in the second part of this assignment.

Account review process (p. 28)

Priority accounts (p. 28)

Basic accounts (p. 29)

Technical coverage accounts (p. 29)

Minimum agency standards (p. 34)

Minimum account standards (p. 35)

X-dating (p. 37)

Automatic "add-on" (p. 38)

Contact sales (p. 38)

Value-added service (p. 43)

Assignment 4—Insurance Sales and Account Development

Review the concepts presented in the second part of this assignment by answering the following questions.

14. What is the purpose of an account review? (pp. 28-36)

15. What type of sales should result from an account review? (pp. 34-36)

16. Illustrate a minimum agency standard. (p. 34)

17. Illustrate a minimum account standard. (p. 35)

18. Why are sales letters appropriate for account development sales to basic accounts? (p. 36)

19. Why is X-dating appropriate for account development sales to technical coverage accounts? (pp. 37-38)

20. How does an automatic "add-on" sales process work? (p. 38)

21. How would a contact sale work for:
    (a) a basic account? (p. 38)

(b) a technical coverage account? (p. 39)

22. What are the benefits of account development for (a) the agency and (b) its producers? (pp. 40-44)

23. How can account development reduce the errors and omissions exposures of an agency? (p. 42)

24. What is value-added service? How does this phrase apply to a producer? (pp. 43-44)

25. What are the benefits of account development for the client? (pp. 44-46)

Apply the concepts presented in the second part of this assignment by answering the following questions.

5. A relatively new producer comments, "The hardest thing is to get the customer. Once you have the account, it's only a matter of renewing it."
   (a) Does this producer consider account acquisition or account development as more important?

   (b) Why, sooner or later, will this producer have to become concerned with renewals?

(c) What are the differences between looking at accounts as a source of premium and looking at clients as a source of premium?

(d) How does value-added service affect the following?
   (i) new account acquisitions

   (ii) account retention

6. An agency principal and an owner of another business are talking at a cocktail party. The owner of the other business is intrigued by the insurance agency business and asks questions about the business.
   (a) Explain to the businessperson (i) two sources of sales (premium) from existing customers and (ii) two sources of business from potential customers using the product-customer marketing matrix as an illustration.

   (b) How do the adoption of minimum agency standards and minimum account standards help ensure that the business written by an agency is profitable?

7. The assignment describes two categories to be used when splitting accounts by coverage for the account review process. These are basic accounts and technical coverage accounts. Do you believe this is a good division of accounts for your agency? Why? If not, what division would you establish?

8. The principals of the Johansen, O'Toole, Topoleski, and Turner Agency, Inc. have agreed to begin to develop their accounts. You have been called in as a consultant.

   (a) What are three ways the account information summary (profile) sheets can be completed? Which one is best and why?

   (b) Explain the types of sales activities that should take place as a result of the account development process.

   (c) What are two sales activities that can be used to support account development?

9. (a) Why are account development activities necessary for the accounts you handle?

   (b) How would you proceed if you believe that more premium dollars are available in these accounts?

   (c) What are the potential benefits to you and your clients from this process?

10. One source of additional premium for an agency is merger or acquisition. How would you proceed with the files of an agency that your agency recently purchased relative to each of the following?

    (a) one-policy files

(b) low liability limits

(c) minimum coverages

(d) low premiums per account

Summary

Sales management is important for the producer whether the producer's goals are developed by the producer or by agency management. Personal sales planning helps establish the producer's goals and provides some of the tools the producer can use to achieve those goals.

Successful producers must know about the product, the market, and selling techniques. Although selling techniques can be introduced in a textbook, producers are encouraged to take courses that analyze and critique the producers' applications of these techniques. The fundamental aims of face-to-face selling are to uncover and identify client needs and to satisfy those needs through specific features of the products and services being offered. This is often achieved through the careful use of leading and nonleading questions.

Agencies should actively seek to acquire new customers to increase their premium. An agency may acquire new customers through account acquisition sales activities or by merging with or acquiring other agencies. An agency can also increase its premium by selling more insurance to its current customers. Account development activities include (1) account upgrading, selling existing customers upgraded and enhanced coverage in lines they have already purchased; and (2) account selling, selling existing customers new lines of insurance.

The account review process begins by establishing priority accounts and then splitting accounts by the nature of their coverage. Each account file is organized so that relevant information for the account review can be extracted easily and systematically. Account or customer information summary sheets are then used to take information from the file so that the account can be developed. The account summary sheets are completed before selling activities begin. From the summary sheets, each account is targeted for automatic "add-on" coverage, coverage enhancements, or new lines of insurance.

Account development activities benefit the agency, its producers, and its clients. The agency benefits through increased profits, better relations with insurers, and reduced errors and omissions exposures. Producers benefit through increased commission income. Clients benefit by receiving better service, more comprehensive treatment of their insurable exposures, and increased efficiency.

Chapter Notes

1. Philip Kotler, *Marketing Management*, 4th ed. (Englewood Cliffs, NJ: Prentice-Hall, 1980), p. 22.

2. *Errors and Omissions Claim Prevention Student Manual*, a joint project of the IIAA and Employers Reinsurance Corporation, 1995, p. 5.

3. "The Best Practices of the Leading Independent Insurance Agencies in the United States," Independent Insurance Agents of America and Reagan & Associates, 1995, p. 3

4. "How Agents Can Escape Disaster," © A.M. Best Company. Used with permission, *Best's Review*®—Property/Casualty Edition, February 1993, p. 34.

Appendix A

1: A Checklist of Personal Insurance Needs

	Needs	Has	Recommended	Accepted	Rejected
Dwelling and Garage					
Increased valuation	☐	☐	☐	☐	☐
Upgrade form perils	☐	☐	☐	☐	☐
Earthquake coverage	☐	☐	☐	☐	☐
Flood	☐	☐	☐	☐	☐
Personal Property					
Increased valuation	☐	☐	☐	☐	☐
Increased off-premises coverage	☐	☐	☐	☐	☐
Coverage at secondary location	☐	☐	☐	☐	☐
Increased coverage on money/securities	☐	☐	☐	☐	☐
Scheduled coverage on furs	☐	☐	☐	☐	☐
Scheduled coverage on jewelry	☐	☐	☐	☐	☐
Scheduled coverage on cameras	☐	☐	☐	☐	☐
Scheduled coverage on musical instruments	☐	☐	☐	☐	☐
Scheduled coverage on antiques, fine arts	☐	☐	☐	☐	☐
Scheduled coverage on silverware	☐	☐	☐	☐	☐
Scheduled coverage on stamps and coins	☐	☐	☐	☐	☐
Scheduled coverage on guns	☐	☐	☐	☐	☐
Scheduled coverage on golf equipment	☐	☐	☐	☐	☐
Business personal property off-premises	☐	☐	☐	☐	☐
Liability Coverage					
Professional equipment off-premises	☐	☐	☐	☐	☐
Increased liability limits	☐	☐	☐	☐	☐
Increased medical payments	☐	☐	☐	☐	☐
Additional owned premises	☐	☐	☐	☐	☐
Premises rented to others	☐	☐	☐	☐	☐
Business pursuits endorsement	☐	☐	☐	☐	☐
Farming operation	☐	☐	☐	☐	☐
Incidental occupancy	☐	☐	☐	☐	☐
Professional liability coverage	☐	☐	☐	☐	☐
Watercraft over 25, 50 horsepower	☐	☐	☐	☐	☐

	Needs	Has	Recom-mended	Accepted	Rejected
Automobile Coverage					
Increased liability limits	☐	☐	☐	☐	☐
Increased medical payments	☐	☐	☐	☐	☐
Uninsured/underinsured motorists coverage	☐	☐	☐	☐	☐
Comprehensive	☐	☐	☐	☐	☐
Collision	☐	☐	☐	☐	☐
Accidental death/dismemberment/disability	☐	☐	☐	☐	☐
Extended non-owned auto coverage	☐	☐	☐	☐	☐
Motorcycles—motorscooters	☐	☐	☐	☐	☐
Snowmobiles—golf carts	☐	☐	☐	☐	☐
Trailers	☐	☐	☐	☐	☐
Boats					
Liability	☐	☐	☐	☐	☐
Medical	☐	☐	☐	☐	☐
Hull	☐	☐	☐	☐	☐
Equipment	☐	☐	☐	☐	☐
Aircraft					
Liability	☐	☐	☐	☐	☐
Passenger liability	☐	☐	☐	☐	☐
Medical payments	☐	☐	☐	☐	☐
Hull	☐	☐	☐	☐	☐
Accident and Health					
Disability income	☐	☐	☐	☐	☐
Major medical	☐	☐	☐	☐	☐
Hospitalization and surgical expense	☐	☐	☐	☐	☐
Life Insurance					
Programming family income needs	☐	☐	☐	☐	☐
Retirement Income					
Cash value life insurance	☐	☐	☐	☐	☐
Variable annuity	☐	☐	☐	☐	☐
Mutual funds	☐	☐	☐	☐	☐
IRAs	☐	☐	☐	☐	☐

_____

(Insured)   (Date)

2: A Checklist of Commercial Insurance Needs

	Needs	Has	Recommended	Accepted	Rejected
Liability					
Workers compensation	☐	☐	☐	☐	☐
Commercial general	☐	☐	☐	☐	☐
Products and completed operations	☐	☐	☐	☐	☐
Independent contractors	☐	☐	☐	☐	☐
Contractual-specific	☐	☐	☐	☐	☐
Contractual-blanket	☐	☐	☐	☐	☐
Personal injury	☐	☐	☐	☐	☐
Fire legal liability	☐	☐	☐	☐	☐
Premises medical	☐	☐	☐	☐	☐
Aircraft	☐	☐	☐	☐	☐
Watercraft	☐	☐	☐	☐	☐
Owned automobiles	☐	☐	☐	☐	☐
Leased or hired automobiles	☐	☐	☐	☐	☐
Employers non-ownership	☐	☐	☐	☐	☐
Drive other car, limited-broad	☐	☐	☐	☐	☐
Auto medical payments	☐	☐	☐	☐	☐
Bailee liability	☐	☐	☐	☐	☐
Umbrella liability	☐	☐	☐	☐	☐
Fiduciary/employee benefits	☐	☐	☐	☐	☐
Directors and officers	☐	☐	☐	☐	☐
Professional/errors and omissions	☐	☐	☐	☐	☐
Employment practices	☐	☐	☐	☐	☐
Other _____	☐	☐	☐	☐	☐
Buildings					
Special perils	☐	☐	☐	☐	☐
Earthquake	☐	☐	☐	☐	☐
Flood	☐	☐	☐	☐	☐
Sprinkler leakage	☐	☐	☐	☐	☐
Water damage	☐	☐	☐	☐	☐
Difference in conditions	☐	☐	☐	☐	☐
Sinkhole	☐	☐	☐	☐	☐

	Needs	Has	Recommended	Accepted	Rejected
Agreed amount	❐	❐	❐	❐	❐
Replacement cost	❐	❐	❐	❐	❐
Increased cost of construction	❐	❐	❐	❐	❐
Contingent liability—building code	❐	❐	❐	❐	❐
Demolition	❐	❐	❐	❐	❐
Signs	❐	❐	❐	❐	❐
Plate glass	❐	❐	❐	❐	❐

Loss to Business Personal Property

	Needs	Has	Recommended	Accepted	Rejected
Special perils	❐	❐	❐	❐	❐
Earthquake	❐	❐	❐	❐	❐
Flood	❐	❐	❐	❐	❐
Sprinkler leakage	❐	❐	❐	❐	❐
Water damage	❐	❐	❐	❐	❐
Agreed amount	❐	❐	❐	❐	❐
Replacement cost	❐	❐	❐	❐	❐
Manufacturers output	❐	❐	❐	❐	❐
Reporting form/peak season	❐	❐	❐	❐	❐
Improvements and betterments	❐	❐	❐	❐	❐
Auto physical damage	❐	❐	❐	❐	❐
Marine hull	❐	❐	❐	❐	❐
Transportation floater	❐	❐	❐	❐	❐
Equipment floater	❐	❐	❐	❐	❐
Salesman's samples	❐	❐	❐	❐	❐
Installation floater	❐	❐	❐	❐	❐
Processing floater	❐	❐	❐	❐	❐
Parcel post	❐	❐	❐	❐	❐

Loss of income

	Needs	Has	Recommended	Accepted	Rejected
Business income	❐	❐	❐	❐	❐
Extra expense	❐	❐	❐	❐	❐
Rent and leasehold	❐	❐	❐	❐	❐
Accounts receivable	❐	❐	❐	❐	❐
Valuable papers	❐	❐	❐	❐	❐
Contingent business interruption	❐	❐	❐	❐	❐

	Needs	Has	Recommended	Accepted	Rejected
Boiler and Machinery Loss					
Boiler and machinery	☐	☐	☐	☐	☐
Business interruption (use and occupancy)	☐	☐	☐	☐	☐
Outage	☐	☐	☐	☐	☐
Human Failure					
Employee dishonesty—Coverage A	☐	☐	☐	☐	☐
Blanket	☐	☐	☐	☐	☐
Specific	☐	☐	☐	☐	☐
Forgery or alteration—Coverage B	☐	☐	☐	☐	☐
Theft, disappearance, and destruction—Coverage C	☐	☐	☐	☐	☐
Robbery and safe burglary—Coverage D	☐	☐	☐	☐	☐
Premises burglary—Coverage E	☐	☐	☐	☐	☐
Computer fraud—Coverage F	☐	☐	☐	☐	☐
Extortion—Coverage G	☐	☐	☐	☐	☐
Premises theft and robbery outside—Coverage H	☐	☐	☐	☐	☐
Employee Protection					
Group life	☐	☐	☐	☐	☐
Group disability	☐	☐	☐	☐	☐
Major medical	☐	☐	☐	☐	☐
Accidental death and dismemberment	☐	☐	☐	☐	☐
Hospitalization—surgical	☐	☐	☐	☐	☐
Pension	☐	☐	☐	☐	☐
Management Protection					
Life-keyperson, proprietor, partnership, corporation	☐	☐	☐	☐	☐
Business continuation	☐	☐	☐	☐	☐
Retirement benefits	☐	☐	☐	☐	☐

Customer Name _____

Address _____

Date _____

3: Insured's Data Sheet

Name _____

Address _____

Contact _____ Time _____ Res. Phone _____

Occupation _____ Place _____ Bus. Phone _____

Coverages

Policy Type	We have	They have	Interested in	"X" Date	"X" Made	Annual Premium	Offered Date	Declined Date
Auto								
Homeowners								
Life								
Mutual Fund								
Boat								
Disability Income								
Hospitalization								
Fire								
Floater								
Commercial								

Approximate yearly premium _____

Loss Record

Loss Date	Type of Loss	Amount Paid	Loss Date	Type of Loss	Amount Paid	Loss •Date	Type of Loss	Amount Paid

Remarks and Recommendations

Source _____

_____

_____

Reprinted and used with permission from the Independent Insurance Agents of America.

4: Customer Profile Sheet

Name _____ Birthdate _____ SS Number _____
Spouse _____ Birthdate _____ SS Number _____
Child _____ Birthdate _____ SS Number _____
Child _____ Birthdate _____ SS Number _____
Child _____ Birthdate _____ SS Number _____
Address _____ Phone _____
Husband's occupation _____ Employer _____ Bus. Phone _____
Wife's occupation _____ Employer _____ Bus. Phone _____
Own home _____ Construction _____ Year built _____
Mortgagee _____ Amount _____ Maturity _____
Replacement cost _____ Date calculated _____ Insurance _____
Other owned premises _____ Rented to others? ____
Office in home? _____ Type of incidental occupancy _____
Value of contents _____ Date inventoried _____ Insurance _____
Jewelry _____ Furs _____ Cameras _____
Musical instruments _____ Antiques _____ Fine arts _____
Silverware _____ Stamps _____ Coins _____
Guns _____ Golf equipment _____ Professional _____
Boat _____ Snowmobile _____ Golf cart _____
Year/model car _____ _____ Youthful drivers _____
Serial number _____ _____ Drivers education? ____
Horsepower _____ _____ Good student? _____
Use of auto _____ _____ At school 100 miles?? __
Loss payee _____
Recreational vehicles _____
How long claim free? _____
Company car or other automobile furnished for regular use? _____

Coverage	Agency	Expiration	Premium		Loss Date	Type of Loss	Amount Paid
Homeowners							
Automobile							
Floater							
Boat							
Umbrella							
Hospitalization							
Disability Income							
Life Insurance							

Remarks and Recommendations _____
_____
_____

Reprinted and used with permission from the Independent Insurance Agents of America.

5: Commercial Lines Policy Review

Name _____ Indiv _____ Corp _____ Part _____
Contact and Telephone # _____
P.O. Address _____
Brief description of risk _____
Sales/receipts _____ # Emp _____ Area _____ Parking area _____
Compensation _____
Classification   Payroll   Pension plan Yes __ No ___   Group plan Yes __ No __

Property Values
Building:
Amount	Address	Type Bldg	Const	ACV/Repl	Co-Ins
1. _____	_____	_____	_____	_____	_____
2. _____	_____	_____	_____	_____	_____

Contents
1. _____	_____	_____	_____	_____	_____
2. _____	_____	_____	_____	_____	_____

Deductible _____ ; BLANKET;   Perils _____
Mortgagee _____
Loss Payable _____
Earnings _____ Type _____ Form _____ Co-Ins _____ Excl Ord. P/R _____
Rents _____ Sprinkler _____ Glass _____
Alarm? _____ Name _____ Grade _____ Cert. # _____ Exp. Date _____
Hold-Up In _____ Out _____ Hoc _____ Safe Burg _____
Boiler __ Pressure Vessels _____ A/C? _____ Misc. Elec _____ R&R _____ U&O _____
Limits of Liability: $300,000; $500,000; $1,000,000   Med Pay _____
Umbrella Limits: $1,000,000; $2,000,000 _____
  Inds. Contractors;   Owner's Protective;   Products;   Completed Operat.;
Fidelity;   Fiduciary;   Additional Insured _____
PI _____ DEL C _____ EMP/ADD/INSD _____ Auto Non-own _____ Hired Car _____
WDLL _____ FLL _____ Liq Law LL _____ Vendors _____ Contractual _____
Transit _____
    VEHICLES:

Year/Make/Model	Trucks GVW	Cost New	Serial #	Ded Comp	Ded Coll
1. _____	_____	_____	_____	_____	_____
2. _____	_____	_____	_____	_____	_____
3. _____	_____	_____	_____	_____	_____

Limits _____ Towing _____ PIP _____

Loss Payee _____ Vehicle # _____

Drivers   D.O.B.   License #   Acc/Violations

1. _____   _____   _____   _____

2. _____   _____   _____   _____

3. _____   _____   _____   _____

Officers, Partners, Management

Name   Title   Activities

1. _____   _____   _____

2. _____   _____   _____

3. _____   _____   _____

Newsletter Y ____   N _____   New Acct Letter _____

                                                  Dear _____

Submitted By _____   Date _____

Use space below for comments and details. **IMPORTANT:** Attach pictures; leases; literature; brochures; loss history; purchase orders; and present coverage

Reproduced and used with permission from the Independent Insurance Agents of America.

Appendix B
Client General Information

_____
(Firm Name)

_____ _____
(Mailing Address)   (Telephone)

_____
(Information Received From)

_____
(Information Taken By)

_____ _____
(Interview Date)   (Action Date)

Date business established

Legal Status: Proprietorship, partners, or corporation

Number of potential entities

Ownership (public or private)

Description of business operations, trade, or industry

Trade area definition

Number of locations

Number of persons employed

Size of automotive fleet

The approximate annual property/casualty budget

The approximate annual group life/health insurance budget

The name of the persons responsible for insurance and risk management, risk manager/insurance buyer

History of any large or unique claims, either insured or uninsured

Client's perception of unresolved problem areas with current insurance risk management programs (safety-loss control-loss adjustment-price-coverage, etc.)

Operations outside the U.S.

Client's commitment to safety and loss control—(actual, not conceptual)

The worst loss potential—property damage risk (cite locations, values, perils, etc.)

The worst loss potential—liability risk (describe activity or source of loss and possible consequences)

Client's attitude or experience toward large deductibles and self-insurance

The availability of formal property records to adequately support a property damage claim

Operating locations that can accumulate more than $1,000 of cash or negotiable securities

Accounts receivable records risk

Description—raw, in-process, finished inventories

Mode of shipment: incoming inventories and outgoing shipments to customers

Leased machinery or equipment

Leased buildings

Utilization of aircraft or watercraft either owned or non-owned

Special values—records, patterns, other proprietary data

The client's commitment and dependency on data processing

Attitude toward insuring real and personal property on a replacement cost basis vs. ACV

Possibility of off-site or temporary locations exposures for personal property

Consequential effects of property damage—shutdown and loss of earnings or continuous and extra expense or both

Contingent impact on operations if a major supplier or customer should be shut down

Property of others in care, custody, and control of client

Incident of contracts and other written agreements

Employment of independent contractors

Employees aboard ship or alongside navigable waters

Employees working in other states or out of the country

Appendix C
New/Renewal Information Checklist

Area Summary		Page
I.	General	1
II.	Buildings	2
III.	Furniture/Fixtures/Equipment/Inventory	4
IV.	Time Element	6
V.	Boiler and Machinery	7
VI.	General Liability	9
VII.	Auto Liability	11
VIII.	Auto Physical Damage	12
IX.	Umbrella Liability	13
X.	Crime Insurance	15
XI.	Inland Marine	17
XII.	Workers Compensation	19
XIII.	Employee Benefits	20
XIV.	Miscellaneous Coverages	21
XV.	Miscellaneous	23

INSTRUCTIONS

To be completed:

a) On all new commercial accounts;

b) Annually at renewal on all commercial accounts equal or over $1500 commission; and

c) At least once every three (3) years on all commercial accounts under $1500 commission.

Account Name _____ Date: _____

Interview With _____

Producer/Account Executive _____

CSR/AS

Assignment 4—Insurance Sales and Account Development / 4-65

	Yes	No	Unknown	Not Applicable
I. General				
(1) Named insured(s) and addresses correct				
(2) Broadened named insured definition				
(3) Policies countersigned				
(4) Written binders in hand for unissued policies				
(5) Financial rating of carriers acceptable				
(6) Expanded cancellation terms				
(7) Loss reporting conditions modified				
(8) Package employed where eligible and appropriate				
(9) Lease analyzed				
(10) Appraisals/rate analysis				
(11) Builders risk exposure				
(12) Business structure—				
corporation				
partnership				
individual				
(13) Good payment history				
(14) Financing needed				
(15) Credit policy explained				

	Coverage in Force				Available Improvement (or) Uninsured Exposure
	Yes	No	Unknown	Not Applicable	

II. Buildings
   (1) Limit—_____
       Date of last increase—_____
   (2) Values include building service equipment
   (3) Coinsurance applies—____%
   (4) Agreed amount or equivalent
   (5) Inflation guard
   (6) Valuation: ACV _____;
       Repl. Cost _____
   (7) Other than standard wording for deductible?
       Amount? $_____
       Increase?
   (8) Written blanket
   (9) Perils
       a) Basic
       b) Broad
       c) Special

Assignment 4—Insurance Sales and Account Development

	Coverage in Force				Available Improvement (or) Uninsured Exposure
	Yes	No	Unknown	Not Applicable	
(10) DIC					—
Includes flood—amount _____ deductible _____					
Includes earthquake _____ —amount _____ deductible _____					
(11) Separate flood coverage	—	—	—	—	—
(12) Automatic coverage—new exposures (other than in standard form)	—	—	—	—	—
(13) Eligible for HPR rating	—	—	—	—	—
(14) Demolition/increased cost of construction/operation of building laws	—	—	—	—	—
(15) Outside structures/exposures	—	—	—	—	—
(16) Towers	—	—	—	—	—
Glass	—	—	—	—	—
Signs	—	—	—	—	—
Improvements and betterments	—	—	—	—	—
Fences	—	—	—	—	—
(17) Waiver of subrogation executed	—	—	—	—	—
(18) Vacancy	—	—	—	—	—
(19) Builders risk form used? _____	—	—	—	—	—

This checklist is intended as an illustration and might have to be modified for use today.

Answers to Review and Application Questions

Assignment 1
Answers to Review Questions

1. The sales trilogy represents the elements necessary to the sale of any product:
   (1) Product knowledge (understanding the technical details of the product being sold)
   (2) Market knowledge (knowing where to find customers and how to identify their needs)
   (3) Selling skills (bringing the sale to a successful close)

2. An insurance agent is the authorized representative of an insurance company, whereas an insurance broker is the authorized representative of an insured.

3. A fundamental risk is a risk of loss that affects a large portion of society (an economic depression). A particular risk is a risk of loss to which relatively few members of society are exposed in a single occurrence (the failure of a joint venture).

4. A pure risk is a chance of financial loss that does not also offer a chance of financial gain. A speculative risk offers not only the chance of financial loss but also the opportunity for gain.

5. Particular risks—those with limited exposure—and pure risks—those which are accidental in nature and present no opportunity for financial gain—are insurable. Fundamental risks are not because they may be too catastrophic in scope. Speculative risks are not because the insurance contract cannot allow for material betterment or financial gain.

6. Losses with high frequency and low severity, such as small collision losses, are best treated by the firm retaining the risk or using a very high insurance deductible. Losses with low frequency and high severity in terms of the resultant financial loss, such as a tornado wiping out an entire fleet of vehicles, are best treated with insurance.

7. A peril is a cause of loss. A hazard is anything that increases the frequency or severity of a loss.

8. (1) Physical hazards, those which are tangible characteristics of property, persons, or operations, are largely insurable.
   (2) Moral hazards are the insured's character traits that tend to increase the probability or severity of loss and are difficult to detect. Therefore, moral hazards are not insurable.
   (3) Morale hazards stem from the insured's attitude, and can be easily detected if they are physically manifested, such as with poor housekeeping. They may be more difficult to detect if the insured's attitude is not reflected in his or her surroundings or practices. Thus, they may be more difficult to insure against.
   (4) Legal hazards are those hazards affected by the involvement of the legal system and its associated costs. Both the cost of dealing with the loss and the ultimate settlement amount are difficult to insure against.

9. Insurable interest enforces the concept of indemnity by requiring that a financial interest be at stake before an insurable loss may be covered.

10. (a) At the time the policy is purchased.
    (b) At the time of loss.

11. (1) Many persons must be independently exposed to the loss to allow the law of large numbers to operate.

(2) The exposures should be similar.
(3) The losses should be definite as to cause, time, place, and amount.
(4) The expected loss for each insured during the policy period should be calculable in order to produce a reasonable premium rate for the exposure.
(5) The loss should be accidental from the insured's viewpoint to prevent the insured from profiting from the existence of insurance.

12. (1) Floods—many insureds are subject to the same loss
    (2) Personal injury coverage—the loss is not definite
    (3) Business interruption losses—the amount of the loss is far from definite

13. (1) Identifying and analyzing the loss exposures faced by a business or family
    (2) Evaluating techniques for dealing with loss exposures
    (3) Selecting the best technique or combination of techniques to treat the exposures
    (4) Implementing the technique or combination of techniques for treating exposures
    (5) Monitoring the effectiveness of those techniques

14. There are six measurable economic benefits to insurance that together exceed the cost of producing those benefits:
    (1) Indemnification for losses
    (2) Reduction of uncertainty for society
    (3) An equitable assessment of the cost of uncertainty
    (4) A source of long-term funds
    (5) A reduction of losses
    (6) Promotion of business competition

15. • The human and material resources expended to operate the insurance business—resources that could have been used in other businesses
    • Morale and moral hazard losses—the true costs of the insurance business

16. A stock insurance company is owned by stockholders who have invested their money, formed a corporation, and seek an investment return. It is operated by shareowner-elected officers.

    Mutual insurance companies are formally owned by their policyholders and effectively operated by officers who are elected by its policyholders to provide insurance services for those policyholders.

17. Lloyd's is operated for a profit and insures risks outside of its syndicate members. A reciprocal is not operated for a profit but is intended to provide the best and most economical insurance for its member/policyholders.

18. Governmental insurers have come into existence when causes of loss have been considered commercially uninsurable, such as bank failure and flood. In the interest of public policy, the government can become the insurer of last resort where there is a perceived need.

19. (a) An independent agency has contracts with many insurers to generate new business and to renew and service existing accounts, and the independent agency owns the policy renewals, whereas an exclusive agency sells and services insurance policies that are limited to one insurer. This exclusive insurer holds the ownership, use, and control of policy records and expiration dates.

    (b) In the direct writing system, producers are generally employees of their companies, not independent entrepreneurs. These producers do not own the business they write—renewals belong to the insurer. Independent agents, however, "own" the business they produce in the sense that the agent has the right to change the client's insurer. The insurer in the independent agency system has no right to keep the insured—the renewal business belongs to the agent.

20. Claims, use of company draft authority to settle small losses, risk management activities, billing and premium collection, and other services on a fee basis.

21. An advantage to the nonbrokerage rule is that the producer's concentrated sales efforts in only those lines actively written by the insurer give the agent significant marketing strengths. Agents can become experts in those lines, providing better client service.

    A disadvantage is that if the exclusive agent's company does not provide a market for a prospect, the agent must pass the business up, losing good personal and commercial lines accounts to other brokerage markets. Additionally, many insureds prefer to deal with only one agent or agency. If a company does not write a line of insurance and does not allow brokerage, the client may take all of his or her business to another agency.

Assignment 1
Answers to Application Questions

1. (a) Direct property loss is damage to the property itself. Indirect loss results from the direct loss, such as loss of profits or loss of rental income.
   (b) It appears to fit four of the requirements well—those dealing with independent exposures, similar exposures, calculable loss, and accidental loss. Termite damage might not be very definite, however. Although the cause of loss and place of loss are definite, the time that the loss occurred and the amount of the loss are less definite. This is especially true of the time of the loss. Unless the premises are inspected regularly, determining exactly when the loss occurred might be difficult.
   (c) The morale hazard involves the attitude of carelessness on the part of insureds. Such an attitude could be a potential problem in this case. Workers, knowing that insurance will pay for losses that they could have prevented with more thorough work, might tend to become less careful.

2. (a) Agree. Insurance requires that a person suffer some economic loss before it will pay. If Tom and Samantha stand to lose money as a result of the claim, they are entitled to payment.
   (b) Yes. Property insurance requires insurable interest at the time of loss, while life insurance requires insurable interest at the time the policy is purchased.
   (c) The concept of indemnity is to restore the insured to the same financial position he or she held immediately before a loss: no better and no worse. In the case of Tom and Samantha's claim, if they have an insurable interest, they should be paid to the extent of their loss and under any applicable coverage. However, if they held no financial position in the property at the time of loss, there is no obligation to indemnify.

3. Because of unwanted or uninsurable circumstances, insurance companies include limitations or exclusions in their policy wording. A fundamental risk is one to which a very large number of people are subject. Insurance companies are often unwilling or unable to offer insurance for these types of risks because of the size of the total exposure. Policies will therefore be written to prevent insuring fundamental risks to avoid the insolvency of the insurer. A speculative risk is one that might economically benefit the risk taker (i.e., gambling). Insurance policies have conditions that help prevent fraud or profit from a loss. "Morale hazard" refers to the carelessness of the insured. Again, policy conditions are included to reduce this hazard, which would otherwise result in the payment of many dollars of losses that could have been prevented.

4. (a) For a recent college graduate with limited financial resources, the major advantage of both the exclusive agency system and the direct writer system is that the agent is an employee, usually salaried, and trained by the insurer without the risks of being compensated by commissions only or the expense of having to maintain his or her own office.

This is not the case with an independent agent, who must usually be an "independent," commissioned agent from the beginning. Some agencies and insurers, however, have begun more extensive training programs for their new or young independent agents. Some agencies also pay a salary for a limited initial period of employment, so some of the disadvantages of the independent system for new agents are disappearing.

    (b) For experienced producers with a substantial clientele, the independent system is usually more attractive because they know they should be able to place all their business with one of their insurers. The independent system generally pays a higher commission percentage than the other two systems and a level commission for both new and renewal policies so the potential for greater income exists.

    The exclusive agency system may be almost as attractive as the independent system if the insurer allows agents to "broker" business that the exclusive insurer is not willing to insure. If the exclusive insurer will not allow brokerage, this will be a serious restriction to the experienced agent who has renewal business.

    The direct writer system is probably the least attractive because any renewals placed with the direct writer will then be owned by the insurer. The real advantage is that the direct writing agent is often relieved of many administrative duties such as policy issuance, premium collections, and claims handling. Advertising may also be provided by the insurer.

5. (a) (1) A stock company is owned by stockholders; a mutual company is owned by its policyholders.
       (2) Management (board of directors and executive officers) is elected by the owners of the company, so stockholders elect the management of the stock company, and policyholders elect the management of the mutual company.
       (3) If a stock company needs additional capital, it can sell new shares of stock. A mutual company has no stock, so it must raise capital by improving its financial or underwriting performance.
  (b) (1) Lloyd's would be recommended to this client if it had difficult-to-insure exposures.
       (2) Large property exposure with high-quality construction and excellent loss controls (i.e., sprinklers).

Assignment 2
Answers to Review Questions

1. A tort is a civil wrong, an unjustified invasion of the legal rights of another individual, while a criminal wrong is a wrong committed against society.

2. Common law developed over time based on court decisions, with the belief that current court decisions should be based on previous decisions whenever the circumstances of the cases are similar, as opposed to developing a comprehensive body of written laws covering nearly every possible subject.

3. (1) Legal right or duty—One party (the victim) has the right not to be harmed, and the other party (the tortfeasor) has a duty to refrain from causing harm.
   (2) Breach of duty—There must be either a violation of the right to be free from harm or a breach of the duty not to harm.
   (3) Harm—Some damage or injury must come to the victim.
   (4) Proximate cause—A close causal connection must exist between the damage or injury to the victim and the breach of the duty owed to the victim by the tortfeasor.

4. (1) Awarding monetary damages—can include nominal damages, compensatory damages, and/or punitive damages.
   (2) Granting an injunction—a court order requiring an activity to be stopped or forbidding that a contemplated activity be undertaken.
   (3) Requiring restitution—the return of specific property by court order.

5. (1) Nominal damages—awarded in situations such as simple trespass when no damage to the land is involved.
   (2) Compensatory damages—those damages reasonably related to the injury.
   (3) Punitive damages—damages far in excess of the actual monetary harm involved when the court views the defendant's conduct particularly repugnant. Designed to deter and punish.

6. - Battery and assault
   - False imprisonment
   - Loss of property
   - Undue interference with an economic right or advantage
   - Damage to public esteem
   - Interference with intrafamily relationships
   - Undue psychological trauma

7. Assault is the threat of violence to another person; battery is actual intentional physical contact causing harm.

8. Some inherently dangerous activities (blasting) involve situations in which substantial benefits accrue to society when the activity is performed without problems, but substantial hardships could occur to individuals if a problem does arise. Also, the person in charge of the activity is usually in the best position to understand the potential dangers involved and, thus, is deemed strictly accountable for any harm.

9. (1) The act is that of a non-reasonable, non-prudent person
   (2) The act is one of a person who fails to live up to a standard of duty
   (3) The standard of care is relative
   (4) The act is essentially negative: the person has failed to use care
   (5) The act has no motive to cause intentional harm, which would be a criminal act

10. (1) A legal duty to use care
    (2) A failure to use that care
    (3) Injury or damage
    (4) Proximate cause—a cause that in a natural and continuous sequence, unbroken by any new and independent cause, produces an event, and without which the event would not have happened

11. (a) There is no legal duty owed by a landowner to trespassers, who are on another's property for their own purposes without the owner's permission. However, a property owner cannot deliberately set a trap, and the owner owes a duty to protect small children who might not understand they are trespassers.
    (b) A landowner owes ordinary care to licensees, who are on another's property for their own benefit and who can be assumed to have implied permission to be on the property.
    (c) An invitee is on another's property for his or her own benefit and for the property owner's benefit. An invitee is owed a greater degree of care than ordinary care, and the landowner should actively seek out hazards and remove them. If removal is not possible, signs should be posted warning of those hazards.

12. When an attractive nuisance (a swimming pool) is present, the law has found that a landowner's duty owed to the trespasser (a child) becomes similar to that of an invitee. The landowner must take active steps to prevent the child from sustaining an injury or else risk being held liable due to the attractive nuisance.

13. Comparative negligence attempts to assess the relative responsibility of the parties involved in an event, and to apply that percentage as the amount of damage owed by each party to the other. This differs from contributory negligence, which is a case of "all or nothing." The plaintiff either did not

contribute to his or her damages and therefore may collect in full if liability can be proven, or the plaintiff did significantly contribute to his or her damages and can collect nothing.

14. (a) Agency by appointment—The principal appoints the agent to act on their behalf. There is usually a written agency agreement outlining the agent's duties, responsibilities, limits of authority, and area of endeavor.

    (b) Agency by estoppel—The principal creates the appearance of a principal-agent relationship. Agency by estoppel is created by law and it acts to protect third parties from harm if the third party relied on the appearance of an agency relationship to their detriment. The principal is estopped (prevented) from denying the agency relationship.

    (c) Agency by ratification—A relationship created when the principal opts to ratify or confirm the transactions of a party who previously represented himself on behalf of the principal without the authority to do so.

15. In addition to acts of an agent committed within the boundaries of the express authority granted by the principal, the principal might be bound by the acts of an agent committed within the scope of:
    (a) Implied authority—acts not specifically cited in the agency contract, but deemed by law and custom to be included as being necessary to carry out the agent's express authority
    (b) Apparent authority—acts reasonably relied upon by third parties based on appearances created by the agent, whether or not such authority was express or implied

16. The agent owes the duty to act primarily for the benefit of the principal. An agent's duties include:
    - Loyalty
    - Obedience
    - Reasonable care
    - Accounting
    - Relaying information

17. - Lapse of time—An agency agreement is often in effect for a specific period of time only.
    - Accomplishment of purpose—If the agent's responsibility is to perform a specific task, then the relationship is finished when the task has been accomplished.
    - Revocation or renunciation—The principal can revoke the relationship at any time by any act that indicates that the agent can no longer exercise authority, and the agent can terminate the agreement through renunciation of authority.
    - Death or loss of capacity—The death of either party automatically terminates the agreement.
    - Impossibility or changed circumstances—When the subject for which the agency was formed no longer exists, then the agency no longer exists.
    - Additionally, breach of any of the duties owed by the agent to the principal—loyalty, obedience, reasonable care, accounting, and relaying of information—is a breach of the implied terms of the agreement, and can terminate the agency agreement.

18. An insurance agent is exclusively the agent of the insurer; the acts of the agent are considered the acts of the insurer. An insurance broker is an agent of the insured, except where statutes have been passed defining the broker as an agent of the company in certain aspects, such as premium collection.

19. Professionals are those whose work requires competent performance and high standards of ethical conduct, education, training, and experience. The liability exposure of an insurance producer who is viewed as a professional would increase, based upon the higher standard of care against which he or she is judged as a professional.

20. (1) Agreement—an offer and acceptance

(2) Competent parties—the parties must possess the legal capability or capacity to contract

(3) Consideration—an exchange of something of value between the parties

(4) Legal purpose—contracts must be consistent with public policy

21. The applicant is generally considered to be the party making the offer for insurance from prospective insurers or "purchasers." The completed application is considered the offer, and policy issuance by the insurer is considered acceptance. Occasionally, the applicant is considered to be soliciting an offer from the insurer if no premium or deposit payment accompanies the application. In such cases, the proffered policy is the offer, and the payment of the premium by the client is considered the acceptance.

22. (a) a promise to indemnify the insured upon the occurrence of an event insured against

    (b) the payment of the premium or the promise to pay at a later date

23. The insurance contract is called a contract of adhesion, because the insured must adhere to the agreement as written. Unlike the formation of other contracts, there is no opportunity to object to or change the terms. As a result, if there is ambiguity in the contract, the courts will largely rule against the insurer in favor of the insured.

24. A warranty is a fact regarding the subject of a contract that is guaranteed to be true. A representation is a statement by one party that is true to the best knowledge of that party; there is no guarantee.

25. Four policy provisions reinforce the principle of indemnity:

    (1) Insurable interest—To be indemnified, a policyholder must have some right, relationship, or interest in the subject covered by the insurance contract and will be hurt financially if a loss occurs.

    (2) Actual cash value—The value of the property lost or damaged must be determined in order to indemnify.

    (3) Other insurance—Different provisions apply when other insurance is involved on real and personal property, preventing multiple payments for the same loss.

    (4) Transfer of rights recovery—The typical insurance policy requires the assignment of any rights of recovery the insured may have against a third party to the insurer, to the extent of the insurer's payment to the insured. This prevents the insured from collecting twice and allows the insurer to be reimbursed for payments it made due to the negligence of the third party.

26. (1) Declarations—This section personalizes the policy by including specific information such as the name and address of the named insured, the policy inception date, the amount(s) of insurance, and the premium.

    (2) Insuring agreement—Describes the policy coverage in broad terms, including the basis of payment if coverage for an accident or loss is to be included.

    (3) Exclusions—Attaches limits to coverage described in the insuring agreement.

    (4) Conditions and Miscellaneous Provisions—Outlines the conditions with which the insured must comply if the insurer is expected to perform.

    (5) Definitions—Defines highlighted words and phrases used throughout the policy.

27. - A different form of insurance may be more appropriate
    - The premium charged may not include the exposure in question
    - To exclude coverage for exposures that are uninsurable

28. Policy analysis is the process of determining whether and to what extent a specific loss is covered under a specific policy. The process of policy analysis for a property policy includes posing questions to establish whether *any* coverage is provided under the policy, such as whether the loss is due to a covered peril or whether any exclusion applies. If coverage is provided, then the *degree* of coverage must be established, through the review of coverage limits, deductibles, and basis of valuation.

The process of policy analysis for a liability policy is similar to that of a property policy, and includes asking such questions as:

(a) Is the person against whom a claim is made an "insured"?

(b) Does the insuring agreement apply to what happened?

(c) Does an exclusion apply?

(d) Is there other insurance? If so, how does this policy interact with others?

(e) What is the limit of coverage?

Assignment 2
Answers to Application Questions

1. (a) The doctrine of contributory negligence could be applied in this situation. Both drivers appear to be negligent. If one driver sues the other, the defendant could claim the doctrine of contributory negligence as a defense. This means that if the plaintiff contributed in any way to his or her own damages, he or she is barred from recovery against the defendant.

    The doctrine of comparative negligence may also be applied, by assessing the relative responsibility John and Elizabeth each have for the accident. If John were found 60 percent at fault, he would be responsible for paying 60 percent of Elizabeth's damages. Depending on the jurisdiction, Elizabeth would be responsible for paying 0 or 40 percent of John's damages.

    (b) All essential elements of a tort action are present for both parties in this situation: there was a legal right or duty owed, a breach of that duty, harm (damage or injury) was incurred, and the proximate cause of the damage was the breach of the duty owed.

2. (a) It would have to provide coverage. Brenda, as a member of the public, believed that Frank had the authority to bind coverage because that is the custom in the insurance industry. The doctrine of apparent authority (where it appears to the insured that the agent has the authority) is especially true in this case because Frank clearly represented to Brenda that he had binding authority. Brenda had no reason to question his statement and thus relied on its truthfulness.

    (b) (1) Frank will not be personally liable to Brenda, but because of the doctrine of apparent authority, Quaking Casualty probably will be.

    (2) In turn, Frank might be liable to Quaking Casualty for this loss payment because he stepped beyond the bounds of the express authority found in his agency contract. Thus, Quaking could claim a breach of contract and attempt to recover the loss payment from Frank.

3. Because Professional Insurance Brokers, Inc., advertises its officers and producers as having "professional risk management skills," a court might determine that their conduct should be of a higher and more professional standard than someone simply holding themselves out as an agent or broker. Therefore, liability might be found against them in a case in which it would not normally be found for a basic agent or broker, and greater damages might be awarded because they failed to meet the high standard that they advertised.

4. Professionals are held to a higher standard of care than if they did not consider themselves professionals. Failure to meet that standard can result in E&O claims for unintentional torts such as negligence and breach of contract. These acts of omission and acts outside the boundaries of the contract reflect the higher standard of care to which professionals are held accountable, and standard business insurance might not offer coverage that reflects those exposures.

5. (a) The building inspector is a licensee. Bob must take reasonable care to warn the inspector of this hazard.

(b) Bob has tremendous responsibility for this young child. Even though the six-year-old is literally trespassing, Bob is responsible for any harm because of the child's age. This property might also constitute an attractive nuisance relative to children, so he must protect against injury by removing the hazard or putting a fence around it.

(c) The teenagers are trespassers, and he has no responsibility for their safety. He cannot, however, set traps or intentionally harm them.

(d) The contractor is an invitee on Bob's property for Bob's benefit. Bob must either remove the hazard or take positive action to warn and protect the contractor.

6. (a) The judge has based his decision on the fact that an insurance policy is a contract of adhesion.

(b) Because the form and wording of the insurance contract often cannot be changed or negotiated by the insured, insurance is known as a contract of adhesion. As such, any ambiguities in the policy are construed in favor of the insured.

7. (a) Probably not. The first important rule to consider is that knowledge of the agent is presumed to be knowledge of the insurer. Thus, because Bill knew of the problem with Jim, Kindling is presumed to have known it but wrote the policy anyway. Under the doctrine of estoppel, Kindling is prevented from later denying the claim based on the lack of knowledge that it is presumed to have known.

(b) Yes. A broker is legally an agent of the insurer only in the case of collecting premium on their behalf. Otherwise, a broker is not an agent, and, therefore, knowledge of the broker is not presumed to be knowledge of the insurer. Therefore, the company could be justified in later denying the claim based on concealment.

(c) Yes. The legal duties of an insurance agent to an insurance company include loyalty, reasonable care, and relaying information. All information material to the transaction must be transmitted to the insurer, all monies must be accounted for, and in every way the agent must serve the company faithfully. Bill did not meet the standard implied by these duties and could therefore be held liable for any damages that resulted.

Assignment 3
Answers to Review Questions

1. Risk management is a comprehensive process involving identifying loss exposures; developing a variety of alternatives to handling, pricing, and selecting the most efficient alternative; implementing the decision; and monitoring the results.

   Insurance management is only one potential risk management alternative and involves activities which are narrower in scope such as policy sales, policy maintenance, and the reporting of claims.

2. The goals of risk management include those to be accomplished before a loss (pre-loss goals) and those goals to be met after a loss (post-loss goals).

   Pre-loss goals include:

   (1) Social responsibility—such as being "good neighbors."

   (2) Externally imposed goals—such as complying with regulatory or contractual requirements.

   (3) Reduction of anxiety—by removing the financial uncertainty concerning loss exposures.

   (4) Economy—keeping the cost of the risk management program to a level consistent with the other goals.

   Post-loss goals include:

   (1) Social responsibility—includes community consideration. Similar to the pre-loss goal.

   (2) Financial goals—can apply to organizations, families, or individuals.

(3) Survival—continuing to exist as a going concern after a loss.

(4) Operational continuity—continuing to function at a near-normal level despite a loss.

(5) Earnings stability—maintaining earnings after a loss at the same level as prior to the loss.

(6) Sustained growth—continuing any plans for growth or business expansion that were in place at the time of the loss.

3. (a) A commercial auto is exposed to such perils as fire, theft, and collision. Resultant losses could include the loss of the auto itself, the loss of use of the auto, related increased expenses, or any claims for damages made by third parties. If the firm's driver was injured, financial consequences could include additional medical and lost wages expenses, as well as the cost to hire a replacement employee.

(b) An individual is exposed to a premature death from a variety of causes, including auto accidents, fire, or acts of violence. The financial impact of premature death can include lost wages, loss of companionship, and loss of the value of the work the individual would otherwise have produced or engaged in over the course of a natural lifetime.

4. (1) Identify and analyze the exposures

(2) Examine the risk-handling alternatives for each exposure

(3) Select the best apparent alternative

(4) Implement the plan

(5) Monitor the performance of the plan and modify as needed

5. (a) (1) Surveys

(2) Flowcharts

(3) Financial Statements

(4) Personal Inspections

(5) Loss Histories

(b) (1) Surveys—Useful as preliminary means of identifying loss exposures. However, this method alone should not be the sole tool used to identify exposures. Many surveys are checklists geared to selling insurance, and do not allow producers to identify exposures most relevant to the types of clients they serve.

(2) Flowcharts—Depending on the level of complexity, flowcharts can be very useful in identifying "bottleneck" exposures and other loss exposures. However, they should be used in conjunction with other methods of exposure identification not related to the production process.

(3) Financial statements—Of assistance in identifying exposures to loss. The entries on such statements as the balance sheet and income statement can suggest exposures to potential loss that deserve further analysis. However, they are only one example of a larger source of information: all the records and documents of an organization, not just those expressed in financial terms.

(4) Personal inspections—The personal on-site inspection, used in conjunction with other methods of identifying loss exposures, is an excellent means of developing useful information and observing first-hand an operation's exposures.

(5) Loss histories—An important indicator of an organization's future accidental losses. Losses experienced in the past often recur in the future. However, the loss history report may be incomplete or inaccurate. Also, changes in a growing organization might not be reflected in past records.

6. (a) LIFO—"last in, first out." This method assumes that inventory is sold with the newest items going first and working back to the oldest inventory item.

FIFO—"first in, first out." This method assumes that inventory is sold in the order in which it is purchased or manufactured.

NIFO—"next in, first out." Unlike LIFO and FIFO, NIFO is not a generally accepted method of accounting for inventory. It is developed by extending current costs into the future by projecting what the future cost of those items might cost be, as a way of expressing the concerns of risk management to accountants who tend to think in terms of LIFO and FIFO.

(b) Neither the LIFO nor the FIFO methods indicate what business personal property will cost to replace at current prices if it is damaged by a loss. Such a valuation could be developed, however, using the NIFO method.

7.
- The likelihood of a loss occurring (loss frequency)
- The seriousness of losses that do occur (loss severity)
- The potential dollar losses in any given period of time (frequency times severity)
- The reliability of the predictions of frequency and severity

8. (a)
- Almost nil—extremely unlikely to happen; virtually no possibility.
- Slight—it could happen, but it has not happened.
- Moderate—it happens once in a while.
- Definite—it happens regularly.

(b)
- Maximum Possible Loss—the worst that could happen.
- Maximum Probable Loss—the worst that is likely to happen.
- Annual Expected Dollar Loss—the expected average severity times the expected frequency expressed in dollars.

9. (1) Exposure avoidance—eliminates the chance of a particular loss by either disposing of an existing exposure or by not assuming a new exposure.

(2) Loss prevention—an attempt to stop losses from happening.

(3) Loss reduction—seeks to lessen the severity of those losses that do occur.

(4) Segregation of loss exposures—the reduction of concentrations of values subject to a single accident.

(5) Loss transfer—the transfer of a loss to other entities by either a business contract or an insurance contract.

(6) Loss retention—absorbing all or part of a loss.

10. (a) Loss prevention is a very effective risk management technique that is an attempt to stop losses from occurring, while loss reduction seeks to lessen the severity of those losses that do occur.

(b) Loss prevention techniques:

(1) Periodic safety inspections of mechanical equipment

(2) Implementation of driver safety training programs

Loss reduction techniques:

(1) The installation of automatic sprinklers or other fire suppression devices designed to slow or stop the spread of fire once one starts

(2) Use of "expediting expenses," which are any expenses that speed the repair of damaged property, thereby reducing the loss of income an entity might otherwise suffer

11. Loss exposures characterized by low severity and high frequency are those most commonly retained. Loss exposures characterized by high severity and low frequency are best suited to transfer.

12. Active retention is when an individual consciously decides to retain all or part of an exposure to loss. Passive retention occurs when an exposure to loss is retained because it was never clearly identified, causing serious consequence if the exposure was significant.

13.
    - Current Expensing of Losses—Losses can be paid, just like maintenance expenses, from current income. A simple way to deal with small, retained losses.
    - Unfunded Reserve—An account is set up on the balance sheet of an organization, allocating funds for retained losses. A company shows a reserve for losses in its financial statements, but no other cash or asset is specifically earmarked for retained losses.
    - Funded Reserve—With a funded reserve money is actually on hand to pay for the losses. The cash has been segregated and is available as needed by withdrawing it from the account.
    - Borrowing—Retained losses can be paid by borrowing if current income or reserves are insufficient to pay for repairs.
    - Affiliated Captive Insurer—Used only by the largest organizations because of the method's complexity and cost. The technique establishes an affiliated captive insurer to fund retained losses.

14.
    - Expected loss frequency
    - Possible loss severity
    - Probable loss severity
    - The funds available to finance a retained loss
    - The financial impact of the cost of retaining the loss exposure as opposed to using other risk management alternatives

15. (a) If losses occur as anticipated, retention can improve cash flow and reduce the overall cost associated with the risk management program. A transfer shifts responsibility for exposures to those better able to finance (an insurance company) or control (a tenant) them.

    (b) If losses exceed what were anticipated, retention can be more expensive than transfer. Additionally, retention can negatively affect cash flow, have adverse tax implications, and force the entity to forego the use of an insurer's loss control services. Because a transfer is a legal contract, the agreement is subject to a legal interpretation that may be contrary to the original intent. Additionally, if an insurance company or tenant in a hold harmless agreement is unable to comply with the terms of the transfer, the burden of responsibility reverts to the indemnitee.

16. No. Avoidance eliminates loss exposures entirely, and reduces frequency to zero. A hold harmless agreement merely shifts the financial responsibility for a loss exposure, and it does not alter the potential frequency or severity of the exposure.

17. Advantages:
    - Shifts responsibility for uninsurable exposures
    - Can be less expensive than insurance
    - Agreements are individually tailored
    - Transfer places responsibility on party best able to directly control the exposure (a tenant)

    Disadvantages:
    - Subject to adverse legal interpretation
    - Indemnitor may be unable to comply with financial terms of the agreement, forcing indemnitee to maintain insurance
    - Indemnitor may be unable to exert control over the exposure

18. (a)
    - If the insurance alternative is the best alternative developed by the risk management process, insurance sales will generate commission for the producer.
    - If other alternatives are exercised, a producer who has gained the respect and appreciation of a client will receive referrals from that client, potentially leading to sales.
    - A producer can offer stand-alone risk management services on a fee basis.

    (b) If the insurance alternative is exercised in a risk management program, the producer who developed the plan will receive the commission from the insurance sale. This issue should be fully discussed beforehand with prospective clients, but the conflict is not enough to negate the significant benefits to the prospect of a risk management approach.

19. (1) The insurance method—The producer or insurer prices all possible insurance coverages and assists the prospect in categorizing them as either essential, desirable, or available. Coverage is sold based on the prospect's available budget.

    (2) The minimum expected cost method—Compares the cost of each possible risk management technique and estimates the results of applying each technique to potential losses. The program with the lowest overall cost is the one selected if it meets the organization's pre-loss and post-loss objectives.

Assignment 3
Answers to Application Questions

Questions 1–12 (See text)

Answers will vary.

Assignment 4
Answers to Review Questions

1. (a) They are similar in that they both involve setting overall goals and outlining the strategies, objectives, procedures, and budget necessary to achieve those goals.

    (b) They are different in that a producer involved in personal sales planning must develop specific, individual objectives that will contribute to the overall achievement of the agency goal. Those objectives should be monitored throughout the year—either monthly or quarterly—and expressed in terms of the amount and kind of business to be sold. Specific sales goals should be directly linked with market analysis, segmentation, and targeting.

2. Top-down planning is when the producer's personal sales goal is set by the agency's management. On a bottom-up basis, the personal sales goal is set by the producer and approved by the agency's management.

3. A suspect is a member of an overall market class or segment towards whom the producer intends to direct a sales effort. A prospect is a member of a relatively narrow group of the market class or segment whom the producer has targeted to approach.

4. The successful producer will constantly be refining the strategy, approach, and procedures he or she uses to attain established goals and objectives. There are many different sales strategies a producer can use to improve sales performance, including:
    - Segmenting the market and targeting prospects based on product knowledge and/or industry knowledge.
    - The competitiveness of the products available.

- Client contacts.
- Referrals generated from existing accounts.

5. (a) Order processing—The producer identifies a need (automobile policy renewal is due), points out the need (sends the client a bill), and takes the order (issues renewal policy).

   (b) Missionary selling—Establishes goodwill and the competence of an agency through technical services to clients and potential clients, increasing the likelihood that the client will purchase insurance from that agency.

   (c) Creative selling—The producer brings to the client's attention his or her need for certain coverages and answers those needs with the benefits of the insurance product.

6. A joint call involving a new producer and a successful producer allows the new producer to see how a successful producer sells and allows the successful producer to guide, coach, and constructively criticize the sales technique of the new producer.

7. When the product feature can be applied to the customer's need, satisfying the customer and motivating them to buy.

8.
   - The ability to uncover prospect needs which the producer can satisfy
   - Asking leading and nonleading questions to engage the prospect in conversation
   - Learning how to handle the prospect's various reactions to the conversation, such as: agreement, disbelief, indifference, objections, and delay
   - Closing—Meeting the objective of the sales call

9. (a) A nonleading question—Allows the prospect to respond in any manner on any subject, by probing in a style where the responses are not of a limiting "yes" or "no" nature.

   (b) A leading question—Calls for a specific, limited response, typically "yes" or "no," that guides the prospect to the topic of conversation.

10. If a conversation is at an impasse and the prospect is not responding, then the producer can use leading questions. Otherwise, the producer should use nonleading questions, particularly at the outset, to encourage the prospect to speak openly and reveal his or her needs.

11.
    - Agreement—in which case the producer should go for the sale
    - Disbelief—the producer must offer proof to convince the prospect
    - Indifference—the producer should revert to asking leading questions
    - Objections—whether due to a misunderstanding or a real product or service disadvantage—the producer should immediately rephrase the question and address the objection
    - Delay—the producer should uncover the reason for the delay and then handle the reaction

12. If an objection is the result of a misunderstanding, the producer should address it immediately after rephrasing the question. If the objection is the result of a real disadvantage, it should be restated in the form of a question in which the positive overall benefits of the product or service are emphasized, outweighing any single disadvantage.

13. A closing statement should ideally summarize the features accepted by the prospect, then request a commitment. Such as: "Mr. Diaz, you have agreed that you require a higher limit of liability on your personal automobile policy, in order to better protect you and your family from damages you may be held liable for as the result of an automobile accident. Additionally, when we combine this new policy with your existing homeowners policy, we will be able to give you a combination policy discount. Would you prefer the $100,000/$300,000 liability limit or the $250,000/$500,000 limit?

14. To translate exposure identification into sales by:
    - Establishing priority accounts, including the grouping of new account and established account development priorities
    - Segregating accounts by coverage
    - Organizing client files, whether by hard copy or automated format, for ease of information extraction
    - Developing an account information sheet including the exposures, coverages, and activity of an account
15. Sales can result through upgrading the account to minimum agency standards and/or minimum account standards, and through total account selling.
16. Placing all policies on a direct bill basis.
17. Homeowners dwelling forms must be written on an HO-3 level or above.
18. Sales letters on existing basic accounts can be individually addressed and mailed before a renewal, identifying exposures that may require coverage upgrades, and suggesting coverage enhancements or additional lines of insurance.
19. The producer meets with the client already knowing that certain additional coverages are needed. The producer can use that information, together with the agency's existing positive image with that client, to generate sales.
20. Whenever state law allows it, coverage changes that bring accounts to the agency or account standards minimum can be handled as automatic add-ons at renewal, enhancing coverage and increasing sales.
21. (a) Basic accounts can be developed by automatically adding on coverage at renewal or by a personal sales contact, often made by phone.
    (b) Technical coverage accounts require a contact sale, usually in person, undertaken from a risk management perspective. It should be benefit-oriented and individually tailored for any coverage upgrades, add-ons, or new lines to be sold.
22. Benefits to both the agency and its producers include increased profits and better insurer relations via:
    - Increased commission income from account upgrading and account selling
    - Decreased expenses needed for account development sales vs. new business sales
    - Increased retention on fully developed accounts
    - Reduced E&O exposure
    - Improved producer training through working on existing accounts
    - Increased professionalism as demonstrated by the producer developing the account
    - Value-added services are made available to the insured
23. The more coverages that are offered and sold to a client, the less likely that an uncovered loss could occur where the insured then blames the agent for lack of adequate coverage.
24. A value-added service refers to the increase in the worth of a product because of an enhancement to that product. A producer adds value to an account by making suggestions to the client for coverage on uninsured exposures or to modify coverage based on underinsured exposures.
25.
    - Better service
        - Comprehensive exposure treatment—all loss exposures are identified and dealt with
        - Benefit of increased efficiencies—saving time and money by dealing with one producer

Assignment 4
Answers to Application Questions

1. (a) In segmenting the market, Joan should be very precise. If she has developed a specialty, such as serving school districts, car dealerships, or grocery stores, she could put her initial emphasis entirely on one specialty market. With market segmentation she can focus on a specific advertising campaign, specialize her presentation and product packaging, and attain maximum benefit from word-of-mouth referrals. Specializing can make the sales approach easier for Joan because the same questions, objectives, and doubts will be raised by similar types of clients.
   (b) After Joan segments the market, she should target the appropriate products for the chosen segment. For instance, if she selects car dealerships, she should promote the sale of garage policies and, if possible, work with her insurers to develop a new coverage, endorsement, or pricing structure for this market.
   (c) Joan's sales approach would also depend on her chosen market segment. For example, with car dealerships, she might attend car shows or auctions to meet prospects.

2. (a) The first selling technique is order processing, in which the client's needs are identified and pointed out and (it is hoped) the order is taken. In this case, the need is obvious to the client, and little or no persuasion is necessary. In creative selling, the second technique, the needs must be uncovered and made apparent to the client. Persuasion is often required to close the sale. The third selling technique is missionary selling, which establishes the goodwill of the organization through technical services to clients and prospects. The client in this situation buys because of this feeling of goodwill.
   (b) If the statement were 100 percent true, the property/liability agent would rely on order taking, and the life agent would use creative selling. But it is not 100 percent true. Some elements of all three selling techniques are used in both property/liability and life insurance sales.

3. (a) Tom could use market segmentation to become an expert in a narrow field of insurance. His specialty would become known and referrals would follow. His sales would increase, and his frustration level would decrease.
   (b) Most clients don't want to know the technicalities, but they do want to know how insurance will help them. Tom should show his prospects that the benefits he is presenting will prevent financial loss, but he should not get involved in long, technical explanations that might only confuse the prospect.
   (c) A joint call with Tom could help by allowing Tom to observe an experienced producer; he can then learn proven techniques. The experienced producer can observe Tom's presentations, and constructive criticism can lead to better presentations and more sales.

4. (a) When the prospect shows signs of agreement, immediately go for the close.
   (b) If disbelief is exhibited, offer some proof or examples to support what was said.
   (c) With the prospect who is indifferent, ask leading questions to uncover his or her real needs.
   (d) Objections can be overcome by restating the benefits in the form of a question or by restating all of the positive (and agreed to) benefits.
   (e) If the prospect tries to delay the sale, try to uncover the reasons for the delay and address those reasons with benefits.

5. (a) The producer's attitude seems to indicate he or she considers account acquisition more important that account development.
   (b) Renewals represent the largest portion of the book of business for most agencies. For the agency to grow and to remain profitable, the vast majority of the book must be renewed. In order to build the book of business, the producer will have to become concerned with its renewal and should be concerned about developing existing accounts.

(c) Focusing on clients and their specific initial needs tends to result in a loss of interest in the potential of the client after the client has been sold on that specific product, such as a homeowners policy. Concentrating on the account as a source of premium would allow time for determining other insurance of the client on an ongoing basis, leading to more premium from the account.

(d) (i) The idea of value-added service is a promise of future benefits to the prospect. The producer can differentiate his or her agency in the prospect's mind by offering value-added services, such as an annual risk management account review.

(ii) Failure to follow through on sales promises and provide an expected level of service or offering of products will lead to the loss of an account.

6. (a) Two sources of premium from (i) existing customers are account upgrading (selling higher limits or coverage enhancements) and account selling (selling additional lines of coverage). Two sources of business from (ii) potential customers are target marketing (selecting specific prospects to sell to) and building a temporary monopoly (selling a special product, approach, or both to a group of prospects).

(b) Minimum agency and minimum account standards set the limits and coverage that an agency desires to write or service. Standards can be set at levels that guarantee the agency a fair profit, while providing the proper amount of coverage for clients.

7. The answers to this question will vary, but there should be logical reasons for the variations.

8. (a) (1) An agency project (quickest method but potentially disruptive)

   (2) Part of the renewal process (takes longer, but least potential disruption)

   (3) Use temporary employees (reduces disruption; speedier process than the renewal method, but can be more expensive).

   The best method to use will depend on the individual circumstances of the agency.

(b) • Automatic "add-ons" of increased limits or coverage enhancements
   • Contact-type sales in which the insured will be contacted by telephone, by mail, or in person to close the sale.

(c) To support the automatic "add-ons" sale, a letter is sent advising the insured of the coverage to be automatically added at renewal, explaining why it will be added, and describing how to cancel the "add-on" if desired. To support the sale of additional insurance lines, coverage placed elsewhere is X-dated so that a quote can be prepared at renewal.

9. (a) Answers will vary, but all producers should be interested in having their insured better protected, their E&O exposure reduced, and their commission income increased—all proven outcomes of account development.

(b) Answers should include the following:

   (1) Establish account priorities
   (2) Divide accounts by coverage
   (3) Organize the file to be able to extract information from it quickly
   (4) Extract the information and placing the information in a summary or profile
   (5) Solicit the business indicated

(c) Potential producer benefits include increased premiums and commissions, decreased expenses (with resultant increased profit), increased account retention, reduced E&O exposure, better training, greater professionalism, and an opportunity to show the value added to the insurance policies.

The client will benefit by having fewer gaps or overlaps in coverage, by handling their policies and claims more easily, and by saving money through policy packaging or account billing.

10. (a) One approach would be to run a computer list of all one-policy files. Those files should be identified by the type of policy (HO, auto, and so on), and an account development program should be started immediately.

   (b) Assuming that your agency already has a minimum account standard in place, begin an automatic upgrade program to raise the liability limits to at least the minimum required.

   (c) As with (b) above, use your agency's minimum account standards as a guide to add or improve coverages.

   (d) Low premiums are the subject of minimum agency standards. Your agency should take appropriate steps to call or mail for ex-dates of policies not written for these accounts. Selling new policies to these clients will raise their premiums and, if they meet the minimum agency standards, improve the service they will receive.

Bibliography

Bach, George Leland. *Economics*. 9th ed. Englewood Cliffs, NJ: Prentice-Hall, 1977.

"How Agents Can Escape Disaster." *Best's Review*. Property/Casualty Insurance ed., vol. 93, no. 10, Februrary 1993, p. 34.

Independent Insurance Agents of America and Employers Reinsurance Corporation. *Errors and Omissions Claim Prevention Student Manual*. 1995.

Independent Insurance Agents of America and Regan & Associates. "The Best Practices of the Leading Independent Insurance Agencies in the United States." 1995.

Kotler, Philip. *Marketing Management*. 4th ed. Englewood Cliffs, NJ: Prentice-Hall, 1980.

Thompson, Seymour D. *Commentaries on the Law of Negligence*. Rev. ed. Vol. I.2. Indianapolis, IN: Bobbs-Merrill Co., 1901-1914.

Index

A

Accidental loss, 1-11–1-12
Accomplishment of purpose, termination of agency and, 2-20–2-21
Account acquisition, 4-19
Account acquisition versus account development approach, 4-19–4-20
Account development, 4-19
    benefits of, 4-39–4-46
    complete, agency procedure for, 4-34–4-39
    insurance sales and, 4-1–4-61
    sales activities supporting, 4-36–4-38
Account development priorities, established, 4-29
    new, 4-28
Account information summary sheets, 4-31–4-32
Account renewal activity, completing summaries as, 4-33
Account review, using, 4-34–4-36
Account review process, 4-28–4-33
Account review summaries, temporary employees completing, 4-33
Account review summary sheets, methods of organizing files and completing, 4-33
Account selling, 4-20
    total, 4-35–4-36
Account standards, minimum, 4-35
Account upgrading, 4-20, 4-34–4-35
Accounts, basic, 4-20–4-30
    specific sales activities for, 4-38

    priority, 4-28
        establishing, 4-28–4-29
        technical coverage, 4-29, 4-30, 4-39
Acquisition, account, 4-19
Action, direct, 2-6
Activities, liability and, 2-15
Actual cash value, 2-42–2-43
Add-ons, automatic, 4-38
Adhesion, contracts of, 2-39–2-40
Advance premium mutuals, 1-28
Advantage or right, economic, undue interference with, 2-8
Advantages and disadvantages of contractual transfer, 3-35
Advantages and disadvantages of loss retention, 3-33–3-34
Affiliated captive insurer, 3-33
Agency, 2-17–2-30
    dual, 2-18
    scope of, 2-17–2-21
    sources of business in, 4-19–4-21
    termination of, 2-20–2-21
Agency by appointment, 2-18
Agency by estoppel, 2-18
Agency formation, 2-18–2-19
Agency procedure for complete account development, 4-34–4-39
Agency and producer benefits, account development and, 4-40–4-44
Agency project, 4-33
Agency in property-liability insurance, 2-22–2-23
Agency by ratification, 2-18–2-19

Agency relationships, duties in, 2-20
Agency sales planning, 4-4
Agency standards, minimum, 4-34
Agency system, exclusive, 1-34–1-35
    independent, 1-32–1-34
Agent, 1-3, 2-17
    general, 2-22
Agents, authority of, 2-19–2-20
    insurance, duties of, 2-23
    soliciting, solicitors or, 2-22
Agreement, contract and, 2-31–2-33
    insuring, 2-45
    prospect and producer's, 4-15
Alcohol or drugs, persons under influence of, competent parties and, 2-36
Analysis, insurance policy, 2-47–2-48
    insurance policy construction and, 2-44–2-48
Analysis of loss exposures, 3-19–3-23
Anxiety, reduction of, 3-6
Apparent authority, 2-19–2-20
Appointment, agency by, 2-18
Apportionment clause, 2-43
Approaches to loss prevention and loss reduction, 3-30
Artificial entities, competent parties and, 2-36
Asking questions, 4-13–4-14
Assault, 2-7
Assessment mutuals, 1-29
Assets, human, 3-9
    physical, 3-9
        loss of use of, 3-9
Attractive nuisance, 2-14
Authority, apparent, 2-19–2-20
    express, 2-19
    implied, 2-19
Authority of agents, 2-19–2-20
Automatic add-ons, 4-38
Avoidance, 3-28

B

Balance sheet, 3-16–3-17
Basic accounts, 4-29–4-30
    specific sales activities for, 4-38
Battery, 2-7
Becoming productive, account development and, 4-43
Benefits, presentation of, 4-11–4-13
Benefits of account development, 4-39–4-46
Benefits of insurance, economic, 1-20–1-21
Better service, account development and, 4-45
Borrowing, 3-33
Breach of duty equals invasion of right, 2-9–2-12
Broker, 1-3
Brokers, 2-22–2-23
Business sources in agency, 4-19–4-21

C

Calculable loss, 1-11
Call, sales, closing of, 4-17–4-18
        concluding comment in, 4-18
Calling on prospects, 4-8–4-10
Calls, cold, 4-8, 4-9–4-10
    joint, 4-8
Capacity, loss of, death or, 2-21
Capacity to enter into insurance contracts, competent parties and, 2-36–2-37
Cash flows, statement of, 3-18
Causal forces of loss, 3-9–3-10
Cause, proximate, 2-12
Changed circumstances, impossibility or, termination of agency and, 2-21
Civil wrong, 2-4
Clause, apportionment, 2-43
    other insurance, 2-43
Client benefits, account development and, 4-44–4-46
Client files, organizing, 4-30–4-31
Closing of sales call, 4-17–4-18
Cold calls, 4-8, 4-9–4-10
Commercial account summary sheets, 4-32
Commission income, increased, account development and, 4-40–4-41
Common law, 2-5
Common law and statutes, 2-5
Comparative negligence, 2-16
Compensatory damages, 2-7
Competent parties, 2-33, 2-35–2-37

Complete account development, agency procedure for, 4-34–4-39
Completing account review summaries with temporary employees, 4-33
Completing summaries as account renewal activity, 4-33
Comprehensive exposure treatment, account development and, 4-45
Concealment, 2-40–2-41
Concluding comment in sales call, 4-18
Conditional contracts, 2-39
Conditions and miscellaneous provisions, 2-46
Conflicts among goals, 3-7–3-8
Consideration, contracts and, 2-37–2-38
Construction, policy, 2-44–2-46
Contact sales, 4-38
Continuity, operational, 3-7
Contract, elements of, 2-31–2-39
   shifting responsibility by, 2-15
Contracts of adhesion, 2-39–2-40
Contracts, conditional, 2-39
   law of, 2-30–2-44
Contracts of indemnity, 2-41–2-44
Contracts of utmost good faith, 2-40–2-41
Contractual transfer, advantages and disadvantages of, 3-35
Contractual transfers, control-type, 3-31
   financing-type, 3-34
Contributions and nature of insurance business, 1-20–1-25
Contributory negligence, 2-16
Control-type contractual transfers, 3-31
Controllable sources of additional premium, 4-19
Cooperatives, miscellaneous, 1-29–1-31
Coverage, segregating accounts by, 4-29
Coverage accounts, technical, 4-29, 4-30, 4-39
Creative selling, 4-7–4-8
Criminal wrong, 2-4
Current expensing of losses, 3-32

D

Damage to public esteem, 2-8–2-9
Damages, compensatory, 2-7
   nominal, 2-7
   punitive, 2-7
Death or loss of capacity, 2-21
Declarations, 2-44–2-45
Decreased expenses, account development and, 4-41
Defamation, 2-9
Definite loss, 1-11
Definitions, 2-46
Delay, 4-17
Development, account, 4-19
   benefits of, 4-39–4-46
     sales activities supporting, 4-36–4-38
   complete account, agency procedure for, 4-34–4-39
Direct action, 2-6
Direct writing system, 1-35–1-36
Disbelief, 4-15–4-16
Distribution systems and producer, 1-36–1-37
Distributions systems, types of, 1-32–1-37
Domino theory, 3-30
Drugs or alcohol, persons under influence of, competent parties and, 2-36
Dual agency, 2-18
Duties in agency relationships, 2-20
Duties of insurance agents, 2-23

E

Earnings stability, 3-7
Economic benefits of insurance, 1-20–1-21
Economic causes of loss, 3-9–3-10
Economic costs of insurance, 1-21–1-22
Economic right or advantage, undue interference with, 2-8
Economy, 3-6
   insurance business and, 1-22
Efficiencies, increased, account development and, 4-45–4-46
Elements of contract, 2-31–2-39
Elements of loss exposure, 3-8–3-10
Employees, temporary, completing account review summaries with, 4-33
Endorsements, 2-45
Energy release theory, 3-30
Errors and omissions exposure, lessened, account

development and, 4-42
Essential elements of a tort, 2-5–2-6
Establish priority accounts, 4-28–4-29
Established account development priorities, 4-29
Estoppel, agency by, 2-18
Exchange, reciprocal, 1-29
Exclusions, 2-45
Exclusive agency system, 1-34–1-35
Expenses, decreased, account development and, 4-41
Exposure, formulating alternatives for dealing with each, 3-28–3-35
   ideally insurable, requisites of, 1-11–1-12
Exposure avoidance, 3-28–3-29
Exposure identification, methods of, 3-10–3-19
Exposure identification and analysis, 3-10–3-23
Exposure identification methods, 3-12
Exposures, independent, 1-11
   similar, 1-11
Express authority, 2-19
Externally imposed goals, 3-5

F

False imprisonment, 2-7–2-8
Files, client, organizing, 4-30–4-31
   organizing, completing account review summary sheets and, methods of, 4-33
Financial goals, 3-7
Financial impact of loss, 3-10
Financial intermediaries, insurers as, 1-20–1-22
Financial intermediary, 1-22
Financial statements, 3-16–3-18
Financing retained losses, 3-32–3-33
Financing-type contractual transfers, 3-34
Flowcharts, 3-15
Form required by law for insurance contracts, 2-39
Formulating alternatives for dealing with each exposure, 3-28–3-35
Frequency, loss, 1-5–1-6
Fundamental or particular risk, 1-4–1-5
Fundamental risk, 1-4
Funded reserve, 3-32–3-33
Funding loss prevention and reduction measures, 3-31

G

General agent, 2-22
Goals, conflicts among, 3-7–3-8
   externally imposed, 3-5
   financial, 3-7
   post-loss, 3-5, 3-6–3-7
   pre-loss, 3-5–3-6
Goals of risk management, 3-5–3-8
Governmental insurers, 1-31–1-32
Growth, sustained, 3-7

H

Haddon's energy release theory, 3-30
Hazard, 1-7
   legal, 1-9
   moral, 1-8
   morale, 1-8–1-9
   physical, 1-7–1-8
Hazards, perils and, 1-7–1-9
Heinrich's domino theory, 3-30
Histories, loss, 3-19
Hold harmless agreements, 3-34
Human assets, 3-9
Human causes of loss, 3-9

I

Implementing chosen risk control techniques, 3-39–3-40
Implied authority, 2-19
Impossibility or changed circumstances, termination of agency and, 2-21
Imprisonment, false, 2-7–2-8
Improved producer training, account development and, 4-43
Income statement, 3-17–3-18
Incorporated proprietary insurers, 1-27
Increased commission income, account development and, 4-40–4-41

Increased efficiencies, account development and, 4-45–4-46
Increased retention, account development and, 4-41
Indemnitee, 3-34
Indemnitor, 3-34
Indemnity, 1-9–1-10
    contracts of, 2-41–2-44
Independent agency system, 1-32–1-34
Independent exposures, 1-11
Indifference, 4-16
Individual selling skills, 4-11–4-18
Injunction, 2-7
Insane persons, competent parties and, 2-35–2-36
Inspections, personal, 3-19
Insurability, 1-12
Insurable exposure, ideally, requisites of, 1-11–1-12
Insurable interest, 1-10, 2-41–2-42
Insurable interest in life insurance, 1-10
Insurable interest in property-liability insurance, 1-10
Insurance, principles of, 1-3–1-13
    risk management and, 1-12–1-13
    transfer by, 3-35
Insurance agents, competent parties and, 2-36–2-37
    duties of, 2-23
Insurance business, nature and contributions of, 1-20–1-25
    organization of, 1-25–1-37
    overview of, 1-1–1-41
Insurance business is different, 1-22–1-25
Insurance business and economy, 1-22
Insurance companies, competent parties and, 2-36–2-37
Insurance contracts, unique aspects of, 2-39–2-44
Insurance and the legal system, 2-1–2-51
Insurance management, 3-3
Insurance method, 3-37
Insurance policy construction and analysis, 2-44–2-48
Insurance professionals, 2-23
Insurance providers, types of, 1-25–1-32
Insurance sales and account development, 4-1–4-61
Insurer, affiliated captive, 3-33
Insurers, governmental, 1-31–1-32
    incorporated proprietary, 1-27
    mutual, 1-28
    nonproprietary, 1-28–1-31
    proprietary, 1-25–1-27
    unincorporated proprietary, 1-26–1-27
Insurers as financial intermediaries, 1-20–1-22
Insurers and insurance markets, 1-3
Insuring agreement, 2-45
Intentional torts, 2-9–2-10
Interest, insurable, 1-10, 2-41–2-42
Interference with economic right or advantage, undue, 2-8
Interference with intrafamily relationships, 2-9
Intermediary, financial, 1-22
Intrafamily relationships, interference with, 2-9
Invasion of privacy, 2-9
Invasion of right, breach of duty equals, 2-9–2-12
Invasions of rights protected by tort law, 2-7–2-9
Invitees, 2-15
Items subject to loss, 3-8–3-9

J

Joint calls, 4-8
Judicial remedies, 2-6–2-7

L

Lapse of time, termination of agency and, 2-20
Law, common, 2-5
      statutes and, 2-5
    statutory, 2-5
    tort, 2-4–2-17
      invasions of rights protected by, 2-7–2-9
Law of contracts, 2-30–2-44
Law of large numbers, 1-6–1-7
Leading questions, 4-13–4-14
Legal hazard, 1-9
Legal liabilities, 3-9
Legal purpose, contracts and, 2-38–2-39
Legal rights and remedies, 2-6–2-7
Legal system, insurance and, 2-1–2-51

Legal wrong, 2-4
Lessened errors and omissions exposure, account development and, 4-42
Letters, sales, 4-36–4-37
Liabilities, absolute, 2-10–2-11
    activities and, 2-15
    legal, 3-9
    sources of, 2-13–2-15
    strict, 2-10–2-11
    strict and absolute, 2-10–2-11
    vicarious, 2-17
Licensees, 2-14–2-15
Life insurance, insurable interest in, 1-10
Loss, 1-4
    accidental, 1-11–1-12
    calculable, 1-11
    causal forces of, 3-9–3-10
    definite, 1-11
    economic causes of, 3-9–3-10
    financial impact of, 3-10
    human causes of, 3-9
    items subject to, 3-8–3-9
    natural causes of, 3-10
Loss of capacity, death or, 2-21
Loss exposure, elements of, 3-8–3-10
Loss exposures, analysis of, 3-19–3-23
    segregation of, 3-31
Loss frequency, 1-5–1-6
Loss histories, 3-19
Loss prevention, 3-29
Loss prevention and reduction, approaches to, 3-30
Loss prevention and reduction activities, 3-30–3-31
Loss prevention and reduction measures, funding, 3-31
    timing of, 3-31
Loss of property, 2-8
Loss reduction, 3-29
Loss retention, 3-32–3-34
    advantages and disadvantages of, 3-33–3-34
Loss severity, 1-5–1-6
Loss of use of physical assets, 3-9
Losses, current expensing of, 3-32

M

Mail order system, 1-36
Management, insurance, 3-3
Management, risk. *See* Risk management
    sales, 4-3–4-6
Market, 4-5
Market segment, 4-5
Market segmentation, 4-5
Marketing, 1-3
    target, 4-20
Markets, 1-3
    insurance, insurers and, 1-3
Matrix, product-customer marketing, 4-20–4-21
Method, insurance, 3-37
    minimum expected cost, 3-37–3-38
        department store case and, 3-37–3-38
Methods of exposure identification, 3-10–3-19
Methods of organizing files and completing account review summary sheets, 4-33
Minimum account standards, 4-35
Minimum agency standards, 4-34
Minimum expected cost method, 3-37
    department store case and, 3-37–3-38
Minors, competent parties and, 2-33, 2-35
Miscellaneous cooperatives, 1-29–1-31
Miscellaneous provisions, conditions and, 2-46
Misrepresentation, 2-41
Missionary selling, 4-7
Mixed systems, 1-36
Monitoring and modifying risk management program, 3-40–3-41
Monopoly, temporary, 4-21
Moral hazard, 1-8
Morale hazard, 1-8–1-9
Mutual insurers, 1-28
Mutuals, 1-28–1-29
    advance premium, 1-28
    assessment, 1-29
    perpetual, 1-29
    pure assessment, 1-28

N

Natural causes of loss, 3-10
Nature and contributions of insurance business, 1-20–1-25
Need, prospect does not mention, 4-12–4-13
    prospect mentions, 4-11–4-12
Needs-based selling, 4-10
Negligence, 2-11–2-13
    comparative, 2-16
    contributory, 2-16
    determination of, statutes affecting, 2-15–2-17
New account development priorities, 4-28
Nominal damages, 2-7
Nonleading questions, 4-13
Nonproprietary insurers, 1-28–1-31
Nuisance, attractive, 2-14

O

Objections, 4-16–4-17
Operational continuity, 3-7
Order processing, 4-7
Organization of insurance business, 1-25–1-37
Organize client files, 4-30–4-31
Organizing files, completing account review summary sheets and, methods of, 4-33
Other insurance clause, 2-43
Ownership, property, 2-13–2-15

P

Particular risk, 1-4–1-5
Perils and hazards, 1-7–1-9
Perpetual mutuals, 1-29
Personal account review sheets, 4-31–4-32
Personal inspections, 3-19
Personal sales planning, 4-4–4-6
Persons under influence of drugs or alcohol, competent parties and, 2-36

Physical assets, 3-9
    loss of use of, 3-9
Physical hazard, 1-7–1-8
Planning, agency sales, 4-4
Policy analysis, 2-47–2-48
Policy construction, 2-44–2-46
Post-loss goals, 3-5, 3-6–3-7
Pre-loss goals, 3-5–3-6
Premium, controllable sources of additional, 4-19
Presentation of benefits, 4-11–4-13
Principal, 2-17
Principles of insurance, 1-3–1-13
Priorities, established account development, 4-29
    new account development, 4-29
Priority accounts, 4-28
Privacy, invasion of, 2-9
Probability, 3-20–3-21
Producer, 1-3
    distribution systems and, 1-36–1-37
    risk management and, 3-1–3-49
    selling and, 4-7–4-10
Producer and agency benefits, account development and, 4-40–4-44
Producer training, improved, account development and, 4-43
Product benefit, 4-10
Product feature, 4-10
Product targeting, 4-5
Product-customer marketing matrix, 4-20–4-21
Productive, becoming, account development and, 4-43
Professionalism, account development and, 4-43
Professionals, insurance, 2-23
Project, agency, 4-33
Property, loss of, 2-8
Property-liability insurance, agency in, 2-22–2-23
    insurable interest in, 1-10
Property ownership, 2-13–2-15
Proprietary insurers, 1-26–1-27
    incorporated, 1-27
    unincorporated, 1-26–1-27
Prospect does not mention need, 4-12–4-13
Prospect mentions need, 4-11–4-12
Prospect's reactions, 4-14–4-17
Prospects, 4-5
    calling on, 4-8–4-10
Prouty measures, 3-19–3-20

Provisions, miscellaneous, conditions and, 2-46
Proximate cause, 2-12
Psychological trauma, undue, 2-9
Public esteem, damage to, 2-8–2-9
Punitive damages, 2-7
Pure assessment mutuals, 1-28
Pure risk, 1-5
Purpose, accomplishment of, termination of agency and, 2-20–2-21
Putting account review to use, 4-34–4-36

Q

Questions, asking, 4-13–4-14
    leading, 4-13–4-14
    nonleading, 4-13

R

Ratification, agency by, 2-18–2-19
Reactions, prospect's, 4-14–4-17
Reciprocal exchange, 1-29
Recovery, transfer of rights of, 2-44
Reduction of anxiety, 3-6
Relationships, intrafamily, interference with, 2-9
Representation, 2-41
Requisites of an ideally insurable exposure, 1-11–1-12
Reserve, funded, 3-32–3-33
    unfunded, 3-32
Responsibility, social, 3-5, 3-6
Restitution, 2-7
Retention, increased, account development and, 4-41
Retention of loss, 3-32–3-34
Review, account, using, 4-34–4-36
Review process, account, 4-28–4-33
Review sheets, personal account, 4-31–4-32
Revocation and renunciation, termination of agency and, 2-21
Right, invasion of, breach of duty equals, 2-9–2-12

Right or advantage, economic, undue interference with, 2-8
Rights and remedies, legal, 2-6–2-7
Risk, fundamental, 1-4
    fundamental or particular, 1-4–1-5
    particular, 1-4–1-5
    pure, 1-5
    related terms of, 1-4–1-5
    speculative, 1-5
Risk control technique(s), selecting the apparently best, 3-36–3-38
Risk control techniques, 3-28–3-31
    implementing chosen, 3-39–3-40
Risk financing techniques, 3-32–3-35
Risk management, 3-1
    goals of, 3-5–3-8
    selling and shift to, 3-3–3-10
Risk management and insurance, 1-12–1-13
Risk management process, 3-10–3-23
Risk management and producer, 3-1–3-49
Risk management program, monitoring and modifying, 3-40–3-41
Risk manager's role, 3-3–3-4
Risk transfers, 3-34–3-35

S

Sales, contact, 4-38
Sales activities for basic accounts, specific, 4-38
Sales activities supporting account development, 4-36–4-38
Sales call, closing of, 4-17–4-18
    concluding comment in, 4-18
Sales letters, 4-36–4-37
Sales management, 4-3–4-6
Sales strategy, 4-5
Scope of agency, 2-17–2-21
Segregate accounts by coverage, 4-29
Segregation of loss exposures, 3-31
Selecting the apparently best risk control technique or techniques, 3-36–3-38
Selling, 4-6–4-18
    account, 4-20
    creative, 4-7–4-8
    missionary, 4-7

needs-based, 4-10
    total account, 4-35–4-36
Selling and producer, 4-7–4-10
Selling and shift to risk management, 3-3–3-10
Selling skills, individual, 4-11–4-18
Selling techniques, 4-7–4-8
Service, value-added, 4-43
    account development and, 4-43–4-44
Severity, loss, 1-5–1-6
Sheets, account information summary, 4-31–4-32
    commercial account summary, 4-32
    personal account review, 4-31–4-32
Shifting responsibility by contract, 2-15
Similar exposures, 1-11
Social responsibility, 3-5, 3-6
Solicitors or soliciting agents, 2-22
Sources of additional premium, controllable, 4-19
Sources of business in agency, 4-19–4-21
Sources of liability, 2-13–2-15
Specific sales activities for basic accounts, 4-38
Speculative risk, 1-5
Stability, earnings, 3-7
Standards, account minimum, 4-35
    minimum agency, 4-34
Statement of cash flows, 3-18
Statistical probability, 3-20–3-23
Statutes, common law and, 2-5
Statutes affecting determination of negligence, 2-15–2-17
Statutory law, 2-5
Stock insurance company, 1-27
Strategy, sales, 4-5
Strict and absolute liability, 2-10–2-11
Strict liability, 2-10–2-11
Summaries, account review, temporary employees completing, 4-33
Summary sheets, account information, 4-31–4-32
    account review, methods of organizing files and competing, 4-33
    commercial account, 4-32
Surveys, 3-12
Survival, 3-7
Suspect, 4-5
Sustained growth, 3-7

T

Target marketing, 4-20
Targeting, product, 4-5
Technical coverage accounts, 4-29, 4-30, 4-39
Techniques, risk control, 3-28–3-31
    implementing chosen, 3-39–3-40
    selling, 4-7–4-8
Temporary employees, completing account review summaries with, 4-33
Temporary monopoly, 4-21
Termination of agency, 2-20–2-21
Time, lapse of, termination of agency and, 2-20
Timing of loss prevention and reduction measures, 3-31
Tort, 2-5
    essential elements of, 2-5–2-6
Tort law, 2-4–2-17
    invasions of rights protected by, 2-7–2-9
Torts, intentional, 2-9–2-10
Total account selling, 4-35–4-36
Training track, account development and, 4-43
Transfer, contractual, advantages and disadvantages of, 3-35
Transfer by insurance, 3-35
Transfer of rights of recovery, 2-44
Transfers, contractual, financing-type, 3-34
    control-type, 3-31
    risk, 3-34–3-35
Trauma, undue psychological, 2-9
Trespass, 2-8
Trespassers, 2-13–2-14
Types of distribution systems, 1-32–1-37
Types of insurance providers, 1-25–1-32

U

Underage persons (minors), competent parties and, 2-33, 2-35
Undue interference with economic right or advantage, 2-8

Undue psychological trauma, 2-9
Unfunded reserve, 3-32
Unincorporated proprietary insurers, 1-26–1-27
Unique aspects of insurance contracts, 2-39–2-44
Upgrading, account, 4-20, 4-34–4-35
Utmost good faith, 2-40

Value, actual cash, 2-42–2-43
Value-added service, 4-43
　account development and, 4-43–4-44
Vicarious liability, 2-17

Warranty, 2-41
Wrong, civil, 2-4
　criminal, 2-4
　legal, 2-4

X-dating, 4-37–4-38